LION IN THE SKY

LION IN THE SKY

US 8th Air Force Fighter Operations 1942-45

JERRY SCUTTS

Patrick Stephens
Wellingborough, Northamptonshire

© Jerry Scutts 1987

First published in 1987

British Library Cataloguing in Publication Data

Scutts, Jerry
    Lion in the sky.
    1. United States. *Army Air Force*
    2. World War, 1939-1945—Aerial operations,
    American 3. Lightning (Fighter planes)
    4. Thunderbolt (Fighter planes) 5. Mustang
    (Fighter planes)
    I. Title
    940.54'4973   D790

    ISBN 0-80859-788-9

*Patrick Stephens is part of the
Thorsons Publishing Group.*

Printed and bound in Great Britain

Contents

1 Legacy of Eagles

England's weather was certainly not unseasonal that Tuesday, 29 September 1942. An autumnal drizzle soon soaked the parade ground at Royal Air Force station Debden, Essex, where officers and men of Nos 71,121 and 133 Squadrons were drawn up on parade. By late afternoon the ceremony of hand-over was completed and those same men marched off the parade ground as the cadre of three new units of a new command in an air force that was still young; the famed RAF Eagle Squadrons had become respectively the 334th, 335th and 336th Fighter Squadrons, 4th Fighter Group, VIII Fighter Command, 8th United States Army Air Force. The leaders of the Eagles attending the parade as RAF squadron leaders, left it as USAAF majors, Gus Daymond leading the 334th, Jim Daley the 335th and 'Mac' McColpin the 336th.

Among the dignitaries at Debden that day were Major General Carl A. Spaatz, in overall command of the 8th Air Force, and Brigadier General Frank O'D. Hunter, head of VIII Fighter Command. Representing the RAF was Air Chief Marshal Sir Sholto Douglas, C-in-C Fighter Command, who in his address to the transferring Eagles, included these words:

'We of Fighter Command deeply regret this parting. In the course of the past eighteen months we have seen the stuff of which you are made. We could not ask for better companions with whom to see this fight through to the finish.'

Reiterating the reason the Eagle Squadrons had been formed he continued: 'You joined us readily and of your own free will when our need was greatest and before your country was actually at war with our common enemy. You were the vanguard of that great host of your compatriots who are now helping us to make these islands a base from which to launch that great offensive which we all desire. You have proved yourselves great fighters and good companions. We shall watch your future with confidence.'

Although the move to American control was generally welcomed by the Eagles, some of those who exchanged their RAF uniforms for those of the AAF had reservations; the RAF had nurtured them,

Exemplifying the fighting spirit of many young Americans who sought action before their country entered World War 2 were the volunteer pilots who flew with the RAF. Their numbers grew sufficiently for three Eagle squadrons to be formed, composed almost entirely of US personnel. Pilot Officer Wendell Pendleton was a member of the first unit, No 71 Squadron. The 'fighting cock' later became the badge of the 334th FS, 4th Fighter Group (via Bruce Robertson).

passed on the benefit of its experience, and equipped them with its finest fighters. Their traditions were those of the British service, and they had flown in what was recognized as the toughest school of air combat experience there was. They had come to trust their leaders, rely on their nimble Hurricanes and Spitfires, and had generally acquitted themselves well in battle. What would this Army Air Force offer them?

While the Eagle Squadrons had been front-line fighter units engaged on bomber support and offensive sweeps across the Channel in line with RAF policy, rumour had it that the primary task of the 8th AF fighter force was bomber escort. To some minds this duty was only marginally less irksome than trying to protect ships, the universally hated convoy patrols. No 133 Squadron particularly had reason to rue its

Indulging in a little 'hand flying' to show Intelligence Officer Mike Duff Smith (left) how No 121 Squadron fared in a recent combat is Jim Daley. Other pilots comparing his version of events with their own are (1 to r) Wing Commander Peter Powell, Richard Patterson (on wing) Squadron Leader Hugh Kennard, Leroy Skinner and Clarence 'Whitey' Martin (Fox Photos).

first escort to American B-17s. On 4 September it had despatched twelve pilots in brand-new Spitfire IXs to cover Fortresses attacking Morlaix. They took off from Great Stamford at 16:00hr, met the heavies in mid-Channel and proceeded to the target area. A navigational error, compounded by bad weather and enemy fighter attacks, resulted in only one of the Spitfires making it home. Lack of fuel increased the problems faced by the rest of the pilots, all of whom were obliged to crash-land their aircraft on the Brest Peninsula. Four were killed and the rest made prisoner.

Not the least casualty was No 133's pride; it and the other Eagles had notched up 73½ kills during their time in England and the squadron was elated to receive a quantity of the then-scarce Spitfire IX. The 4 September débâcle meant that the unit had once again to fly the older, far less able Mk V in the relatively uneventful transitional period after it officially took its USAAF title on 28 September 1942.

For all three squadrons of the 4th Group the winter months were a period of limbo, with American pilots flying British fighters marked with US stars,

occasionally escorting American bombers while getting used to addressing each other by unfamiliar Army ranks. It was a little ironic that the Spitfire, the very aircraft on which the Eagles had honed their skills, the bedrock on which the 4th based its reputation and cut its combat teeth, was indirectly the cause of an VIII Fighter Command being established in Britain. Superb point defence fighter though the Spitfire was, it had one major drawback which prevented it figuring very highly in 8th Air Force planning. That drawback was range—or rather, lack of it.

It came as something of a shock to AAF planners to learn that the RAF's principal fighter type not only had barely enough internal fuel capacity to enable it to reach the outskirts of Paris — but that it was, at that stage of the war, official British policy not to develop a single-seater fighter with a radius of action anywhere near what VIII Bomber Command felt it would need. Further, it was believed that such an aircraft could not even *be* developed. Sir Charles Portal, British Chief of the Air Staff, was of the firm conviction that such an aircraft could only be operated at extreme range at the expense of performance and manoeuvrability and, therefore, had little practical value. Irrespective of whether range was achieved by carrying extra fuel tanks or by being built specifically for the purpose, the CAS believed that a long-range fighter would be at a distinct disadvantage over the short-range, defensive fighter.

Admittedly, when replying in this vein to questions put by Churchill in mid-1941, Portal could have had little inkling of what North American Aviation and Rolls-Royce would eventually achieve with the Mustang — or indeed what pilots of the Imperial Japanese Navy were even then training to do with their Mitsubishi Zero-Sen fighters in the Pacific — but it is fairly clear that he had not sought a cross-section of industry views on the subject, either at home or abroad.

Portal's view prevailed and inevitably led to some heated discussions with the Americans. Army Air Forces chief General 'Hap' Arnold's opposing view was somewhat enforced in 1943 by experimental flights across the Atlantic by Spitfires fitted with long-range tanks, but the CAS did not modify his views. In fact it is fair to state that the potential development of single-seat fighters was given very low priority in Britain both before and during World War 2. Certainly the incredible faith pinned on the bomber in pre-war pronouncements by the Air Staff contained little about fighters, which were seen almost totally in a defensive role.

While Portal was keen to see American fighter units in Britain re-equip with Spitfires until these could be replaced by suitable types of American

Although as stated in the original caption to this photograph 'Convoy protection is a vital part of Fighter Command's work', the Eagles were all too aware that the work was tedious in the extreme. Jim Daley nevertheless puts on a happy face for the cameraman at Kirton-in-Lindsey on 27 November 1941 (Fox Photos).

origin, it is certain that had the Supermarine fighter been blessed with only half as much more range than it possessed in Mk V form, the early history of VIII FC would have taken a different turn. As it was, the 8th Air Force was faced with a problem of considerable proportions which, as subsequent events proved, was to worsen even further.

Notwithstanding the British views on long-range fighters, the 8th arrived in the UK convinced that its B-17s and B-24s could give a good account of themselves on precision bombing raids in daylight. As regards fighters, the policy was not quite so clear-cut — indeed the 8th had no yardstick with which to measure its intended performance because nothing like it had been tried before, certainly not with the type of aircraft it intended to use. Naturally their British hosts provided details of their own forays over enemy territory in daylight in heavy bombers, and did not minimize the disastrous results. They had to admit that none of their aircraft had the firepower of

the US heavies, and that the size of formation the USAAF planned to use had rarely been possible with Stirlings or Halifaxes — but few realized that even with very tight formations and massed defensive fire *any* bombers were vulnerable to determined fighter attack. All the 8th AF really knew was that the RAF had doubts, based on 2½ years of wartime operations, that the idea would work at all.

The VIII Fighter Command had been in existence for as long as VIII BC, both having been constituted on 19 January 1942. Activated on 1 February, the fighter element of the 8th was originally Interceptor Command and was redesignated Fighter Command on 23 May 1942. It was assigned the 6th Wing with 'organizational components' in the form of the 1st Pursuit Group, the 31st PG, the 36th Fighter and the 52nd PG. These groups were activated and equipped with the P-38, P-39 and P-40 and all but the 36th were scheduled to move to England. In the event, developments in the Pacific delayed overseas rotation and the 1st Group did not arrive in the UK until 27 July 1942. It was, however, equipped with the P-38 Lightning, potentially the best long-range fighter in the world at that time.

British scepticism of US air war plans for the European Theatre of Operations extended to aircraft as well as policies. Both the P-39 and P-40 had previously been tested by the RAF under lend-lease arrangements and while the Warhawk was cleared for duty in the Middle East (with some second-line service in Britain) the Airacobra had been rejected as

unsuitable. The Americans noted the views of their allies and did not consider either type for escort duty over Europe.

Unsupercharged examples of the P-38 had also been tested in England and found to be lacking in capability, although as with the B-17, the Americans had developed the basic design and brought much-improved versions of both types to England.

The lack of suitable fighters to equip US groups in the UK led to some change of emphasis, particularly in view of the widespread belief that the Fortress and Liberator could protect themselves; General Arnold didn't feel that all five fighter groups that had been designated for service in Britain need be used on escort duty but that two of them should be tasked with the defence of US installations in Northern Ireland. And given that part of the 'Germany first' priority decided among the Allies was an early as possible invasion of the continent of Europe, Arnold saw the other three as providing the basis for a ground-attack/fighter striking force against the German air force.

When it rapidly became clear that this invasion would not be possible for some time, these tentative plans were modified. When the nucleus of the 8th Air Force was established in the UK, fighters would be required to furnish escort 'to the limit of their endurance', with the heavies taking care of their own defence thereafter. With the P-40 and P-39 rejected, Portal was questioned on the subject of a suitable replacement. Spitfires were the natural — and in fact

Left *Wearing the full RAF life assurance kit at Kirton in November 1941, No 121's Sergeant Pilot John Mooney of Long Island (left) talks with Pilot Officer Donald McLeod of Blackstone, Mass.* (Fox Photos).

Right *Engine change for a Spitfire V of the 336th Squadron in April 1943, a month or so before switching to the P-47. The 336th was the last 4th Group squadron to make the change — a highly traumatic one for some of the pilots* (USAF).

A sight to gladden the hearts of bomber crews was the early indication that they would be escorted by the P-38. This was to come, but some time after this photograph was taken early in 1943. It shows a P-38F-15, 43-2082 of the 78th FG which made a practice of applying plane-in-squadron numbers as shown. The B-17 in the background indicates that this aircraft, which also has drop tanks, was conducting fighter affiliation duties at the time (RAF Museum).

only — choice for short-range work, with the P-38 undertaking any longer missions when these became necessary.

Allied war plans for the Mediterranean Theatre of Operations were, however, to change these plans again. The invasion of North Africa in November 1942 required massive air support and as the only source of trained groups within practical distance of the new battle front, the 8th Air Force had little choice but to give up a major part of its striking power to support the newly created 12th Air Force.

The 14th Fighter Group had also arrived in the UK under the aegis of VIII FC and like the 1st Group, was equipped with the P-38. But the Lightning was seen as a type particularly useful to operations in the MTO and by the end of 1942 virtually every example had left England to support the Operation 'Torch' landings and make good combat attrition in the theatre.

The effects of 'Torch' were far-reaching: even if personnel were not required, a group newly assigned to the 8th would very likely lose all its aircraft with no guarantee that it would be re-equipped with the same type. This was the experience of the 78th Group, which retained its P-38's for a mere few weeks. Based at Goxhill, Lincolnshire, from 1 December 1942, the 78th managed to organize itself quickly and had progressed as far as practising fighter escort tech-

niques with the 305th Bomb Group at Chelveston before all its aircraft and all but fifteen of its pilots were spirited away to desert climes.

While the USAAF built up its strength in the UK to support 'Torch', General Arnold fretted over replenishing the strength of the 8th Air Force and getting more heavy bombers into action. 'Germany first' may well have been the affirmed policy — and 'Torch' was a positive step to fulfilling that pledge — but it did not prevent suggestions, primarily from America's allies, that the heavies the 8th was bringing to England could well be employed against the Germans on tasks other than daylight precision bombing.

With even his bomber force slimmed down for the North African invasion, General Carl Spaatz knew that only by flying combat missions of the kind that the USAAF had planned for would change the minds of the sceptics. For him and Arnold 17 August 1942 had not come around quickly enough, and the first few missions had appeared to vindicate the plan. But these were early days.

With the 4th Fighter Group left as the only unit of VIII Fighter Command able to fly combat, and there being little point in equipping more groups with Spitfires, a new build-up would have to be achieved with American aircraft. Due to its ability to fly as far as the German capital, the P-38 was preferred, but at that time every theatre commander wanted a fighter with this kind of range. Lockheed was simply not geared up to meet the demand and in the meantime another type would have to be used — Republic's P-47 Thunderbolt.

While not possessing the 520-mile range of the P-38, the P-47 could — according to reports — reach

*With four P-38 groups in the ETO, early bomber escort was a distinct possi-
bility, but the demands of the MTO were voracious and by the spring of 1943
they had all left England. This aircraft, P-38F-1 41-7571, demonstrates a
one-point touchdown at an English base in the autumn of 1942 (IWM).*

areas of the continent 230 miles from UK bases, and
was being produced in substantial numbers. More to
the point as far as 8th AF planners were concerned,
Thunderbolts were not required for service in the
MTO. The first example of the P-47 for the 8th Air
Force was shipped to Britain as deck cargo on 20
December 1942.

Plans now called for the 4th FG to be operational
on the P-47 by 1 March 1943, news that was not
exactly welcomed by pilots at Debden. Used to the
sleek Spitfire, the ex-Eagles looked upon the massive
Thunderbolt with considerable trepidation. The
British, having always flown fighters with the
smallest possible airframe, concurred — would a
thing that size really be able to 'mix it' with German
fighters which had even more compact dimensions
than their own? While the fact may have been lost on
the military personnel who first caught sight of it in
Europe, there was a sound technical reason why the
Thunderbolt was so big.

Designer Alexander Kartveli's efforts to produce a
reliable high-altitude interceptor fighter meant that
room had to be found in the airframe for a turbosupercharger. In order not to compromise the basic
layout of the P-47 (the design parameters of which
had been proven in the Republic P-43 Lancer) it was
decided that this could be only positioned in the rear
fuselage. This meant that carburettor air, collected
via an intake below the engine, had to be fed back
some twenty feet to the turbocharger. This air needed

to reach the second-stage turbocharger at the rear of
the engine and finally a turbine before being
exhausted through gates in the fuselage side. The size
and length of all that vulnerable ducting dictated the
overall dimensions of the P-47 airframe, and as well
as being huge by contemporary standards, it was also
extremely strong. Kartveli had to accommodate
some sixty feet of air ducting in the fuselage space
below the cockpit and the turbocharger had to be set
far enough back to balance the weight of the Pratt &
Whitney R-2800 radial engine. Adding all military
equipment, particularly the battery of eight .50-in
machine-guns and ammunition, raised the total
weight of the P-47C to 13,500 lb gross — very close to
that of a twin-engined P-38 at basic (empty) weight.

The initial reaction, without benefit of a test flight
in the beast, was bound to be sceptical; no other air
arm in the world had brought such a large single-
engined fighter into service at that time. The
Thunderbolt seemed to reverse everything that
designers of the classic lightweight pre-war 'pursuit'
type aircraft had striven for and it is small wonder that
doubts were expressed as to its ability to overcome
such types in combat. Among the comments were
those who said Republic had really designed a dive
bomber, not a fighter...

Supporting the build-up of the 8th Air Force in
Britain was a massive logistical undertaking, aided
immeasurably by the British Government and the
RAF. The AAF required numerous buildings, a far-
reaching airfield programme was started, although
initially some bases previously occupied by RAF
squadrons were turned over to their allies 'for the
duration', and equipment of all kinds was loaned.
But the engineering work on US aircraft would be

The first production P-47C-5-RE represents the second C model sub-type of the Thunderbolt to see action with the 8th Air Force, seen here prior to any identification markings being applied (RAF Museum).

handled primarily by 8th AF technical sections, assisted by company representatives who were stationed in the UK throughout hostilities. Based in Britain from the earliest days of the US sojourn was Lieutenant Colonel Cass S. Hough, head of VIII FC's Office of Flight Research and Engineering at Bushey Hall, Hertfordshire. A small unit, this embarked on an extensive programme of trouble-shooting using the airfield at nearby Bovingdon, with Hough doing the flying and Technical Sergeant Robert H. Shafer undertaking crew chief duties on the ground. The unit became the Air Technical Section in late 1942, and its contribution to the 8th's war effort became vital and out of all proportion to its size.

The first version of the Thunderbolt shipped to England was the P-47C. Little data on performance was then available and Cass Hough set about compiling a file of facts on the new fighter before the trickle of machines from the US became a flood. He embarked on a comprehensive series of test flights from Bovingdon. One area which Hough needed to be sure about was the behaviour of the P-47 in a high-speed dive. At that time there was much discussion on the effects of compressibility on airframes which were pushing towards the limits of piston-engined power-plants. Some effects on structures in terminal velocity dives had been startlingly revealed and the last thing air commanders wanted was rumours circulating that their new aircraft was a pilot-killer due to massive stress by forces little understood. Such rumours spread fast and if not checked or the reasons behind them explained, a serious morale problem could result.

Tests by AAF and Wright Field test pilots had

determined that the P-47C had a terminal velocity of about 600 mph in a dive and speed restrictions were initially posted in the cockpit, warning the pilot not to exceed 250 mph above 30,000 ft. As altitude decreased, the speed could be raised progressively to a maximum of 500 mph at 10,000 ft. A continuing programme of flight testing gradually came to terms with the bogey of compressibility, the pilot's manual maintaining that the aircraft should not exceed 250 mph IAS above 30,000 ft; 300 mph at 25,000 ft and 350 mph below 25,000 ft. The book further advised that diving a P-47 should be initiated from level flight rather than a split-S. The procedure was to trim until it was slightly tail heavy, whereupon only slight pressure was necessary to hold it in a dive. The cowl flaps were closed and manifold pressure decreased to avoid engine over-boosting. Rapid throttle retardation was warned against, as such action steepened the dive. Gradual recovery was recommended, avoiding a sharp pull-out which placed undue loads on control surfaces.

The early revelation of the effects terminal velocity dives had on fabric control surfaces helped the parent Republic plant at Farmingdale to initiate timely improvements and metal-covered elevators and rudder surfaces were introduced on the P-47C-2 model. This version incorporated other changes made to the P-47C-1, the first deemed to be combat-ready. One important modification was the fitting of bob weights to the elevator control system to give more 'bite' during dives. Other changes included linkages for the cockpit throttle, engine revolutions and turbosupercharger control, so that co-ordinated operation was but a single movement. Designed to ease pilot workload during cruise flight, this feature was incorporated on subsequent production models.

Operational requirements led to the fitting of two-point belly shackles for a bomb or drop tank, and a revised radio mast — although this proved to be a primary source of trouble to VIII FC, as did radio interference in general. All US fighters operating from the UK required substitution of the American HF system for British VHF equipment, but the radio problem was not immediately overcome.

Cass Hough traced the radio trouble to the ignition system for the engine, the harness of which was not adequately insulated. Effective sealing of the harness to prevent 'leakage' was an interim fix, although a new harness was designed and fitted on production lines for subsequent Thunderbolt models. The propensity of radio mast failure during high speed flight was overcome by installing stronger masts which would not break, but solving the radio problem took some forty man-hours per aircraft.

One of the chief criticisms of the P-47 was its poor rate of climb; there was little that could be done to improve this, as the aircraft needed time to get to a useful operating altitude due to its weight. If fully loaded to 13,500 lb the P-47 broke ground in about 2,500 ft. Up to twenty seconds was needed for the landing gear to retract fully while the pilot waited for the speed to build up to a climb speed of 170 mph. Once the machine had accelerated to this speed and attained some 300 ft, power was reduced to close to maximum continuous and the initial climb rate maintained at between 500 and 800 ft per minute.

The P-47 had extremely sensitive trim which could give the pilot difficulty in holding altitude. Even when trimmed carefully, a few moments' inattention on his part would result in the loss of a few hundred feet of altitude. Normally there was no change in engine note to warn him of this occurrence — a common characteristic of the P-47 in general and the D model in particular. This tendency was not so manifest when the aircraft was flown on instruments or when making ground attack runs, however. Flying

in formation with numerous reference points would also reduce the penchant to wander, but an experienced pilot's sixth sense did not aid him in a P-47 cruising at altitude. The smooth P&W R-2800 purred along whereas other fighters, particularly those powered by liquid-cooled engines, would run quite normally with numerous changes of note.

The early P-47s were also plagued by engine problems. Among the trouble-shooting the VIII FC was obliged to undertake was oil starvation. This often occurred during inverted flight and was found to be caused by a counterbalance in the feed line from the tank. The remedy was a redesigned counter-balance and the fitting of pendulum-type oil tank feeds to prevent the supply being cut off during violent manoeuvres. Pratt & Whitney worked on this problem and came up with a series of interim remedies which proved to be so complex and time-consuming that the command decided to fit new engines incorporating all the modifications rather than be faced with a backlog of aircraft awaiting attention at depots. New engines were shipped in time for them to be fitted prior to the P-47 entering combat.

During the spring of 1943 the supply of aircraft spare parts became acute, and numerous items including propeller blades, tailwheel tyres, oxygen regulators and gun cameras were the subject of urgent cables. Alternatively some items could be obtained locally, and as the number of Thunderbolt groups in the UK rose, so too did their technical staff, who undertook an increasing amount of modification and repair work at operational base level. And although shortages and delays in delivery continued, the expertise and efficiency of AAF technicians ensured that Thunderbolts were not grounded for extended periods.

Only combat operations would highlight further deficiencies and by the end of 1942 the training period was all but complete for the group destined to become the 8th Air Force's leading exponent of the P-47 Thunderbolt, the 56th Fighter Group. By the early part of 1943 supplies of P-47s would reach England so that the 78th and 4th Groups could be equipped; it was hoped that the work that was necessary before-hand would not delay all three groups' entry to combat for too long.

2 'Thunderbolts kommen'

During the spring months of 1943 the hard work undertaken to ready the P-47 for ETO operational conditions began to bear fruit. With the 4th Group declared operational in March, the 56th and 78th needed a few more weeks before they too would fly their first missions. While the Thunderbolt had its share of technical difficulties, the configuration of the aircraft also caused some concern; from certain angles it could be confused with the Fw 190 and steps were taken to make it more recognizable. The easiest and quickest way to achieve this was in paint and on 20 February VIII FC signalled Debden, Goxhill and Wittering with instructions to apply white bands to the horizontal and vertical tail surfaces, and add a white ring around the nose cowling. These markings were duly applied and proved highly effective, the white bands contrasting sharply with olive drab camouflage.

On 16 March the 4th Group officially withdrew the Spitfire from operations, by which time three squadrons had received enough P-47s to replace the British fighter on a one-to-one basis. The Spit did not disappear from Debden overnight, however, and the squadrons flew sorties in it until 1 April, the date the Eagles thankfully flew their last convoy patrol.

On 3 April the 78th Group — equally thankfully — packed its bags and moved south from Goxhill, its theatre training over. The new base was Duxford in Cambridgeshire, affectionately nicknamed the 'Duckpond'. A further move on the 5th saw the 56th move into Horsham St Faith, four miles north of Norwich. The 78th would remain at Duxford for the rest of the war, but Horsham was only a temporary home for the 56th, which would be off to Halesworth within a few weeks. Both groups were, however, now nearer their operational area and located so that their aircraft would not waste precious fuel overflying the UK en route to joining up with the bombers they were to shepherd over Europe.

As related previously, a good deal of radio interference was caused by the P-47's own engine, and among the 'fixes' initiated in the ETO was the fitting of brass rings in the distributors. These gave a perfect bonding between distributor and the metal casing of the spark plug leads. Other sources of trouble were found to be magnetos and generators. Gradually these interim fixes reduced the deafening crackle of static the pilots heard through their headphones every time they attempted to talk to one another in the air, but as the 1 March deadline passed, VIII FC decided that the 4th should be declared operational on the P-47 even though more work was required on the aircraft. Consequently on 10 March Lieutenant Colonel Chesley Peterson, with Colonel Edward Anderson as his wingman, took off from Debden for a sweep in the vicinity of Walcheren. The radio problem became so acute, however, that everyone was glad when the formation turned for home, all fourteen aircraft involved landing safely. It was not an auspicious start, but the enemy did not put in an appearance, fortunately.

While the 4th Group's experience on Spitfires stood it in good stead, by the time it went operational on the Thunderbolt it had absorbed a high number of new pilots fresh from flying schools in the USA. Many of the Eagles had dispersed to add their experience to that of other groups, while others, tour-expired, had returned home. At this time the 4th's pilot roster contained the name of L.W. 'Bill' Chick Jr, who managed to fly a few Spitfire sorties before transitioning to the Thunderbolt. Chick is believed to be the first US-trained pilot to fly operations in fighters from the UK, and he was subsequently attached to 8th AF HQ for a stint in fighter operations; he returned to combat with the 355th FG for a period before transferring to North Africa in December 1943.

While its operational equipment left something to be desired, the P-47 took some getting used to in other ways. The 4th Group, inevitably comparing its performance with the Spitfire, found little to enthuse over. Major Don Blakeslee, the man who led and inspired the group through its early operations, summed up many of the pilots' feelings by commenting succinctly on what he felt was the aircraft's only saving grace — its ability to dive. Blakeslee added a rider — 'It ought to dive, because it certainly can't climb'. The 4th would fly the P-47 in combat well enough, but the general view was that nobody said they had to like it as well.

Accidents claimed a number of lives during the working-up period although the sturdy airframe of the P-47 saved many a serious injury or incapacitation, particularly during belly landings when the supercharger ducting under the pilot's legs absorbed most of the impact.

★   ★   ★

As the AAF bomber offensive settled into a pattern of operations, limited in scope by the small number of aircraft available, and VIII FC flexed its muscles for the forthcoming deployment of its P-47 groups, the Luftwaffe fighter arm was obliged to maintain forces in France and the Low Countries to meet the threat. Like the 8th Air Force, the *Jagdverbände* had been slimmed down when units were transferred to counter the Allied invasion of North Africa, and fighters were required for continuing 'hit and run' raids on English coastal targets and anti-shipping patrols, as well as interception duties.

Occupying bases in four geographical areas: western France: north-western France and Belgium; northern Germany and Holland; and Norway, elements of *Jagdgeschwaderen* 1, 2, 5 and 26 were joined by *Gruppen* of JG3, 37 and 54 from other fronts during 1943, although rotations to more critical battle areas were continuous as German fortunes on other fronts gradually waned.

A pilot's attitude to a particular aircraft type was influenced in various ways, not least of which was his own personal experience of flying it in combat, where its qualities would be revealed fully. He may also compare it with other types he has flown, and the general view for or against might have its origins in such comparisons, or stem from the early days, when a mishap resulted because he had had little time to master its idiosyncracies. It depended very much on the individual.

One man who did not let a bad early experience with the P-47 colour his judgement of the aircraft was the 56th Group's Robert S. Johnson. Taking up a P-47B for the first time in July 1942, he experienced a loss of hydraulic power pressure which meant he could only lower the flaps to about the halfway point. Luckily Johnson managed to land the aircraft without any problem.

The 56th was at that time in the process of 'wringing out' the P-47 in the USA. As the first group to be equipped with it, the three squadrons had a demanding few months to come to terms with what was a radically different aircraft to others in inventory at that time. Johnson's 61st Squadron and the 63rd shared Bridgeport Municipal Airport, while the 62nd was ensconced at Bradley Field, Windsor Locks. Shortly after Johnson was assigned, the 61st moved to Bradley and was introduced to the big Republic fighter. Checked out by First Lieutenant Gerald W. Johnson, his namesake was grateful for the superior facilities at the unit's temporary home. Had he had his hydraulic problem at Bridgeport, Johnson reckons that the results could have been far more dramatic, to say the least. The runway there was only 3,000 ft long and the P-47 needed at least 2,500 ft to get down without mishap — and that meant with full flap travel available.

Johnson makes no secret of the group's early losses prior to being alerted for overseas movement: eighteen men were killed. He put at least some of the fatalities down to the inadequacies of the base — but stresses that the number might well have been higher had the 56th not been flying an aircraft as durable as the Thunderbolt. On more than one occasion pilots could only stand in awe at the degree of sheer strength its designer had built into this remarkable fighter. Men who would have been killed instantly in a flimsier aircraft walked away from write-off crashes with cuts and bruises. Countless P-47 pilots would

Detail view of the starboard wing battery of four .50-in machine-guns of the P-47. The usual complement of eight guns proved more than enough to knock down enemy aircraft despite the latter's widespread use of cannon. Each wing held up to 1,700 rounds of ammunition. (Flight).

add their endorsement to the 56th's faith in the ruggedness of the machine in operational theatres across the world.

★   ★   ★

On 16 September 1942, the redoubtable Hubert Zemke took over the 56th shortly before the group was ordered overseas. Ordered, but not actually sent — it was to be 6 January 1943 before the group personnel finally found themselves shuffling up the gangplanks to board the *Queen Elizabeth* at New York's Pier 90. The dubious pleasure of an ocean crossing, even on such a prestigious vessel as one of the 'Queens', was put behind them as the group personnel greeted Gourock, Scotland on 12 January and King's Cliffe, Northants on the 13th. The delights of the ETO awaited.

Bob Johnson did not mince words about his new home: 'We were made to feel at home through the necessity of standing impatiently for hours in the cold mist until our train arrived. By ten in the evening we had managed to achieve normal confusion, and the group had jammed its way into the mechanical disaster the English identify as a railroad train.

'At our new station in England we discovered that the dire warnings of older veterans were all too well founded. Breakfast, if I may be flexible with the term, consisted of Brussels sprouts, powdered eggs and an eerie liquid which with unbounded imagination the English called coffee.'

Johnson and his comrades in arms faced other horrors in wartime England with equilibrium — the London fogs, the blackout and the bombing — but

their hosts' views on the Thunderbolt struck a raw nerve. It did not bolster anyone's confidence to be told bluntly that as a fighting machine, their aircraft was a non-starter. As yet untried in combat, the 56th could only sit there and take it from men in a position to know — men who had met the enemy in combat flying one of the world's finest fighters. It was a sobering time. Equally, the RAF pilots did not gloss over the fact that even their Spitfires were having a hard time of it with the Focke-Wulf 190. The Americans were warned to play it very safe indeed and let discretion be the better part of valour if it came to mixing it with what was widely acknowledged as the Luftwaffe's finest.

Awed they may have been but the men of the 56th brought with them an inherent faith in the quality of their aircraft, which helped sustain them through this difficult pre-combat period. Above all they wanted to put the first few operational missions behind them, to perhaps lay a few ghosts and find out for themselves what air combat in Europe was all about . But first, it was back to school: gunnery, navigation, radio procedures, interception and bomber affiliation practice. There were many low-level passes on King's Cliffe during those short winter days before

Below and below right *Port and starboard views of* 41-6209, *a P-47C-5 of the 62nd FS, 56th Group, showing the early form of 'plane-in-group fuselage numbers used prior to the application of code letters. The aircraft shows four stages in evolution of P-47 identification markings: yellow-outlined fuselage insignia (ordered 1 October 1942); enlarged underwing insignia (5 January 1943); white bands (20 February 1943); and the 56th's short-lived fuselage numbers used only between mid-February and mid-March 1943 (Flight).*

the 56th was allowed to seek out the enemy across the Channel. In the meantime friendly aircraft doubled as the enemy and the airfield and its surrounding area became mock targets for ground strafing work-outs, adjacent dwellings reverberating to the roar of Pratt & Whitney engines. All this activity and noise became too much for the locals, who protested with almost equal volume. Group HQ responded with a not-too-strictly enforced ban on buzzing and fines for pilots who persisted in the sport. Everyone paid up willingly in English funny money, but there was some surprise to learn that those strange 'bedsheet' size five pound notes were actually worth around twenty dollars!

If King's Cliffe did not overly impress the 56th, the 78th Group had even less to say in praise of Goxhill — 'Goat's Hill' was the derisive nickname the place soon acquired. Established as the 8th's fighter training base, Goxhill was the most northerly of all UK airfields used by the AAF and is remembered chiefly for its isolation and unpleasant habit of depositing coal dust from industrial Humberside on the unfortunate inhabitants.

The 78th received its first Thunderbolts in January and slowly began to master the entirely different technique required to hit towed targets with wing-mounted guns. The P-38 concentrated all its fire-power from nose-mounted guns without any 'gap in the middle' created by wing guns, a fact the 78th's pilots had fully appreciated. But with their Light-nings gone, training settled down on the P-47. As following freshman groups were to realize, a smooth work-up to operational proficiency meant a move to an operational station. For most, there was little sadness in bidding farewell to Goat's Hill.

As in-theatre training proceeded for its two new fighter groups, VIII Bomber Command looked forward to the day when P-47s would be available for longer range cover for its heavies than had been possible with Spitfires. By 30 December 1942 the command had despatched 27 missions with the B-17 and B-24, and lost 31 aircraft. There had as yet been little to shake faith in the concept of daylight bombing, but the ability of the Luftwaffe fighters to knock down bombers had been demonstrated. The RAF had provided able withdrawal support and the 4th's Spitfires had flown escort missions, primarily to RAF medium bombers rather than AAF heavies. Weather had played its part and bomb aimers had on occasion been hard put to find, let alone hit, their designated targets. By the turn of the year the 8th had four B-17 and two B-24 groups, although repeated diversions of the Liberator force meant that it was the Fortress groups which undertook the majority of the sorties.

On 16 January 1943 the 4th Group recorded the arrival of its first P-47s for training purposes and all three groups continued the trouble-shooting pro-gramme begun by Cass Hough, pooling their experi-ence to achieve operational status by March. Unfor-tunately, the various troubles of the P-47 were not all cured; the aircraft was the subject of 190 unsatis-factory reports during the early months of the year, the most serious of which was still ship-to-ship com-munications.

RAF stations were host to numerous 'brass visits' during the war and the Americans found that their presence was the focus of considerable interest. On 7 April Debden recorded a visit by none other than

'father' of the RAF Lord Trenchard, accompanied by Ira C. Eaker, 8th AAF Bomber Command chief, General Hunter and a delegation of Russian officers. The Russians took a keen interest in Allied war planning and there was a very great deal of support for their own war effort from the people of Britain. The Americans were later to have direct contact with their eastern allies when the 8th's bombers undertook shuttle missions, using bases in the USSR.

On 8 April all three groups provided aircraft for *Circus 280,* the 56th and 78th despatching four and twelve aircraft respectively. A sweep to St Omer, the operational debut of part of two groups, and the 4th's second mission, it otherwise proved uneventful. No enemy aircraft were sighted and all aircraft returned safely without damage.

The 4th mounted a patrol by a single P-47 on the 10th and six aircraft flew a *Rodeo* to Calais on the 11th, but it was 13 April that went down in the records with a little more emphasis. Both the 56th and 78th mark this day as their entry to combat, two missions, of thirty six and forty Thunderbolts each, being despatched. As a precaution the inexperienced Americans were supported by RAF Spitfires on these early missions, which were primarily intended to provide experience for group and squadron leaders.

The 78th Group's contribution was made by pilots from both its 82nd and 83rd Squadrons led by Lieutenant-Colonel Arman Peterson, these aircraft joining two squadrons of the 4th for a sweep to St Omer lasting an hour and three-quarters. From 30,000 ft the pilots watched for any signs of enemy activity and the 335th FS chased a couple of Fw 190s without any tangible result. On the way home the 78th Group's Executive Officer, Lieutenant Colonel Joseph E. Dickman, was forced to bale out when he suffered engine failure. RAF Air-Sea Rescue plucked him from 'the drink'.

The afternoon mission got underway at 18:05 hr. The 56th despatched four aircraft from Debden and eight from Horsham, and twelve 78th FG aircraft flew from Duxford. The formation swept the Berck/Mardyck area at 29,000 ft but neither the Luftwaffe nor the flak showed much interest. All aircraft returned by 19:30 hr. Again the P-47's engine was the cause of an aircraft being forced down, but this time the pilot made a safe landfall, putting his aircraft into a field near Deal. It was, however, determined to have suffered Category E damage and therefore beyond repair.

Only 48 hours later the P-47 was in action in the ETO for the first time. Again all three groups participated but it was only the Debden fighters which got into a fight. The Thunderbolts were over Cassel, France when Don Blakeslee spotted three Fw 190s 6,000 ft below his formation. Blakeslee bounced the enemy formation and stayed with one '190 down to 500 ft, his fire hitting the enemy machine repeatedly. Although attempting to bale out, the German pilot crashed with his aircraft.

Blakeslee's formation was composed of the 335th and two squadrons of the 56th, and in the meantime the rest of the 4th was over Ostend. Four miles from the coast, five Fw 190s intercepted and a dogfight ensued. Two 190s fell but two Thunderbolts were also lost during the combat. On the way out of the target area, Arman Peterson's ship developed engine trouble and he had to bale out into the Channel. In some 45 minutes, an RAF Walrus alighted and took him aboard.

The fighters continued to fly sweeps which, on the occasions when the Luftwaffe put in an appearance, helped the American pilots get the measure of the enemy, gain an insight into his tactics and develop their own techniques. Not that the Luftwaffe always obliged; by the time the American fighters came on the scene, it had been combatting short-range penetrations of its airspace for well over two years, and while it gave as good as it got from the RAF, German air commanders were well aware that *Rodeos, Ramrods* and *Circuses* were designed primarily to whittle down its effectiveness, by killing or incapacitating its best pilots. The regular incursions of USAAF bombers, bent on destroying targets vital to the war effort, had to be countered — and that meant conserving the fighter force. Equally, the Luftwaffe could not ignore the US fighters — their qualities had to be measured against the capabilities of its own fighters. However good the American fighters were, the Germans could make a fair estimate of the numbers they were up against — indeed, their intelligence appeared to be remarkably good in this respect. Groups new to the ETO were startled to be 'welcomed' to England by Axis radio broadcasts, which not only knew the group number, but also the bases from which it intended to operate and even the name of its commanding officer. It was, therefore, a basically sound move to increase the number of fighters in the areas where they could intercept incoming raids with the minimum delay and in 1943 Luftwaffe fighter units in the west grew from 350 in January to nearly 600 by June.

In general, the early 1943 sorties were more successful for the 56th Group than for the 4th, with the 78th making the best of an aircraft radically different from the P-38. A comparison with a twin-engined fighter was not really very realistic and the Duxford group settled down with the P-47 well enough. The 56th, with most experience on the type, weathered the technical troubles with equilibrium and appreciated its undoubted qualities, building further a loyalty to the Republic heavyweight that did

Briefing: Duxford's fighter pilots listen attentively to the details of another mission (IWM).

not wane. It was the 4th that had most doubts. Having flown a well-proven aircraft in action, it was especially irksome to the group to experience the technical difficulties that became a hallmark of the early career of the P-47 in Europe. Not all pilots agreed with Blakeslee's judgement, but as the oldest group in VIII FC the 4th felt it had some say in the way things were being run and its officers did not shrink from telling headquarters how they felt. For the time being there was little choice for the 4th but to 'press on regardless' with the P-47 — a British phrase well known in Debden circles. The 4th was renowned for its perpetuation of RAF terminology and jargon, which only faded when the 'old hands' had for one reason or another left the group.

Since 27 January when the target had for the first time been situated on German soil, VIII Bomber Command had extended its reach, although efforts had still been very much at the mercy of the weather. Results varied considerably; more losses had been sustained but with the 'kindergarten' period behind

them the crews at least knew what they were up against. The future held the promise of new groups to enable larger formations to be used, thereby increasing the weight of bombs on target, although there was no sign of the Luftwaffe decreasing its efforts to inflict maximum casualties and reduce the effectiveness of the American formations — quite the reverse. It came to be seen that only fighter protection would make the difference, and a lengthy period of tests began in order to boost the range of the P-47.

Although drop tanks had been carried on some of the earliest AAF fighter flights into Britain, the main problem in developing a suitable tank for high-altitude escort was pressurization. Producing enough tanks of the right type was also something of a headache for VIII FC; local sources were obviously preferable to shorten delivery time, although the scarcity of sheet steel mitigated against this and caused delays.

A seemingly simple device with moving parts confined to its pump, a drop tank had to be efficient in use: it had to hold fuel at high air pressures, be plumbed for release, and to drop cleanly away from the aircraft without fouling control surfaces. While those rules applied to any aircraft configured for the carriage of external tanks, the P-47 was not initially equipped with wing pick-up points and had to accommodate a tank under the belly. With precious little ground clearance, the design of the tank was important, as was the surface of the runway. Numerous early P-47 sorties were made from grass and AAF fighter bases in the UK were usually planned so that drainage was adequate. But rain could still cause the heavy fighters to sink into soft earth, and the problem became acute on those occasions when missions were flown from advance or temporary bases not intended for regular fighter operations. Also, the P-47 was not fitted with gauges for external tanks, pilots having to estimate the amount of gasoline used by timing consumption against known figures.

It was therefore realized that unreliable drop tanks could be more of a hindrance than a help and VIII FC had to ensure a high degree of reliability from the tanks before planning missions which would rely solely on fighters being able to reach a certain point carrrying the fuel required. All these factors surrounding drop tanks took time to overcome.

The Thunderbolt model that all three 8th AF fighter groups had entered combat with began to be replaced in April 1943 by the principal wartime production version, the P-47D. Externally little different from the C model apart from two extra sections to the cowl flaps on each side and redesigned vents for the engine accessories, the P-47D was built both by the parent firm at Farmingdale and a new plant at Evansville, suffix letters denoting origin. The 8th received examples from most subsequent production batches, each of which incorporated changes in equipment, engine power and so forth, but Air Service Command continued to refine the aircraft and introduce adaptations to fit its particular needs. Early production D models, for example, used a constant speed booster pump to draw fuel from external tanks into the main system, but in May ASC successfully tested a 100-gal tank for pressurization by utilizing air pressure supplied by the exhaust of the vacuum pump. This system was introduced as standard on the P-47D-15, and it meant that the 8th's aircraft could operate as high as 35,000 ft without fear of tank malfunction. Control vanes were fitted to ensure constant pressure was maintained and glass connectors in the tank-to-fuselage plumbing solved the problem of release.

3 Longer legs

Delays in delivery of enough suitable drop tanks for the P-47 dictated a continuing series of fighter sweeps rather than direct escort to the heavies into the summer of 1943. Such missions were in the nature of bomber support, as they occasionally stirred up a hornet's nest of enemy fighters which were drawn into combat. This undoubtedly gave the bombers some respite. Also, the fighters ventured across the Channel on days that otherwise saw little 8th AF activity due mainly to the weather.

Occasionally the fighters ranged ahead of bomber strikes on joint targets, such as airfields, timing their arrival so that they were safely away before the rain of high explosive began. Alternatively VIII FC planned diversionary penetrations to areas away from the bombers's targets, such operations by both fighters and bombers being an integral part of 8th AF planning. Fighters were also kept busy on ASR patrols, looking out for their own pilots and bomber crews down in the North Sea or English Channel. A clampdown on regular bomber operations invariably brought some work for small numbers of fighters, the AAF P-47s also flying with RAF squadrons and escorting Allied medium bombers.

By early May there was a new type in the 8th AF inventory — not a heavy but the B-26 Marauder medium. Part of the 3rd BW, the Marauders were tried in Europe chiefly as an operational experiment, and after some disappointing missions, the type settled down to an excellent pattern of reliability, ruggedness and bombing accuracy. But while the B-26 groups would pass from 8th AF direction to that of the 9th AF in due course, the B-17 and B-24 were very much in England to stay. The arrival of the Marauder groups also coincided with a doubling of 8th AF striking power with five more groups of Fortresses. These were soon organized into a fourth wing, one of the component group's squadrons being equipped with the YB-40 'escort Fortress'. This was the 92nd Group's 327th at Alconbury, with thirteen of the special up-gunned B-17Fs.

Although an interesting idea, it was soon found that B-17s weighed down by more than 12,000 rounds of .50-cal ammunition for their fourteen guns were too heavy to keep up with the formations they were intended to protect. The concept had further flaws in that, to be effective, the YB-40, rather than standard bombers, had somehow to attract the enemy fighters which it was hoped would promptly be destroyed by withering defensive fire. After a few combat sorties in which they achieved little, the YB-40s were withdrawn from service.

The new muscle of the 8th was flexed quickly; 159 B-17s, 39 Liberators and eleven B-26s set out on 17 May to attack respectively Lorient, Bordeaux and Ijmuiden, 113 P-47s flying a sweep to the Brest/Cherbourg area. While the heavy bombardment groups recorded seven MIA, the 322nd Group lost ten of its B-26s to the murderous flak surrounding the Dutch power station complex. It was a disastrous start to 8th AF medium bomber operations but one which the 322nd put behind it. The fighters reported no contact with the enemy.

With an average of 75 to 100 B-17s to protect, the fighter force was, due to its limited numbers, hard put to offer very effective cover for all groups in each wing despatched for a 'maximum effort'. During June 1943, however, the P-47s began escorting individual wings of bombers all or part of the way, depending on where the target was. Short-range support was usually provided by the RAF on missions where the AAF fighters were 'spread thin'.

Bomber losses during the early summer months were relatively light, as were those from the fighter groups. Many missions resulted in no contact with the Luftwaffe, which could afford to operate beyond US fighter range and select those raids which constituted the biggest threat — or found conditions where the odds were in its favour. Such an occasion was 28 July when the Luftwaffe's success against the bombers overshadowed a significant date in the 8th Air Force calender — not only was it the first time that P-47s had penetrated German airspace, but the 4th Group flew the 'first belly tank show in the ETO', to use the unit's own way of describing the mission.

Fitted with 200-gal 'bathtub' belly tanks, the

Thunderbolts surprised the Germans over Holland. Failing to find the B-17 formation they were expecting to meet, the Debden pilots instead pounced on Fw 190s and Bf 109s harrassing another group of Forts. It was estimated that there were up to sixty enemy fighters in the vicinity as the P-47s went into action. The battle raged for 25 minutes over Dutch and German territory, resulting in an American victory totalling 9(destroyed)-1(probable)-6(damaged). One Thunderbolt went down, the pilot

Above *On 3 June 1943 the 56th Group laid on some formation flying for the press, this view showing the 62nd Squadron nicely framed against the clouds In the lead is a P-47D-1 named* Happy *with three C models following* (Fox Photos).

Below *Due to the speed at which air actions took place, it was important for bomber crews to recognize 'ours' from 'theirs'. Visits like this helped reduce mistakes in identity. It took place on 10 July 1943 when the 4th Group flew over to Ridgewell, home of the B-17s of the 381st BG* (USAF).

becoming a prisoner. Colonel Anderson's score was two 109s.

The thirty extra miles the partially filled unpressurized tanks had given the P-47s had proved to be more than enough — a boost to the Republic fighter's radius of action that was far more significant than it might have seemed to the Germans at the time.

The target for a force of 182 1st Wing B-17s was the Fieseler Works at Kassel, while 120 aircraft of the 3rd Wing drew Oschersleben. The raid on the latter location turned into a disaster for some elements of the force, while the leading 94th and 388th Groups hit it hard on what was the deepest penetration the 8th AF had achieved up to then. But the cost of that endeavour, which interrupted Fw 190 production for a time, was high. Three Forts collided under the first recorded attack by fighters equipped with underwing tubes to launch air burst rockets, and altogether fifteen were lost.

Heavy cloud ruined the strike on Kassel, well over 100 crews deciding that their trip was not really necessary and returning early. The difficult low visibility conditions dispersed formations and the Luftwaffe exploited the situation. The 96th Group suffered the most, with seven aircraft missing.

As the whole object of carrying long-range fuel tanks was not to bring them back, the supply had to keep up with demand when most of the Thunderbolt

force was tasked with heavy bomber escort, and by no means every succeeding bomber mission after 28 July was able to be escorted. There was another sweep on the 29th, together with support to a diversionary raid by B-26s, but the penultimate day of the month saw some very promising action.

On the second occasion when Thunderbolts used belly tanks, it was the Duxford group which came out on top. Returning to Kassel were 186 heavies aiming to complete some unfinished business with the Fieseler concern. This time their lethal calling cards were more definitely deposited on both Bettenhausen and Waldau branches of the company. Cloud again shielded the targets to some degree and only 131 B-17s were recorded as having released their load as briefed. The fighters had their best day for months, scoring 25(destroyed)-4(probable)-8(damaged).

The youngest of the three P-47 Groups downed sixteen for the loss of four of its own aircraft, one pilot being rescued by ASR. Detailed to pick up returning bombers near Haldern, the 78th met a fixed formation of Focke-Wulfs and Messerschmitts. The victories of Major Eugene Roberts (two Fw 190s and a Bf 109) brought the 84th Fighter Squadron's CO the accolade of the first US pilot to shoot down three aircraft in a single mission in the ETO. But 8th AF public relations had something even better to celebrate; when the combat claims were assessed, it was announced that Captain Charles P. London was the first ace. His two victories that day had clinched the title and the pilots and ground crew hardly needed a better excuse to celebrate.

Charley London recounted his combats for the pressmen in graphic terms:

'We ran into about a hundred of the Jerries all over the damn sky. You know, they were sort of surprised

Below and below right *About the same time Ridgewell also hosted the 78th Group for a similar purpose. One of the P-47s sharing a hardstand with the 'Big Friends' was Captain Charles London's El Jeepo, 41-6335, mount of VIII FC's first ace. London got his fifth on 31 July shortly after these photographs were taken. Four swastikas adorn the aircraft as well as 34 mission markers, and the badge appeared on both sides (via George Porter).*

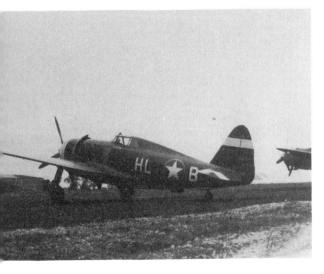 

Major Eugene Roberts in his Spokane Chief, 41-6630, with Captain Charles London posing for a 'double ace' publicity shot at Duxford. Roberts was the first 8th AF pilot to score a triple, and the second ETO ace. His score reached nine and he commanded the 364th Group in 1945. London's score remained at five as he returned home in the summer of 1943 and saw no further combat (IWM).

Another P-47C from the 84th FS pictured at Ridgewell during the July 1943 visit was 41-6246 (via George Porter).

Colonel James J. Stone (in cockpit) was an early scorer for the Duxford Group. He commanded the 83rd Squadron and went on to lead the Group. Newspaper correspondent Bill Hearst is the man 'signing off' (IWM).

to see us there. Didn't think we could go so deep, I reckon. I got lined up on an Fw 190, slick as a whistle, and doggone if an Me 109 wasn't flying right alongside of me, not bothering about what I was doing at all. He must have thought I was another Fw. I was scared he would get on my tail when I climbed up on the '190, but I scrunched my shoulders, looked straight ahead, prayed and gave the '190 a squirt in the tail. He broke up and went down.'

The elation of the 78th was tempered by the loss of a single P-47 — that flown by Lieutenant Colonel Melvin F. McNickle. Flying his third mission that day, McNickle was last seen following a '190 down through a formation of Forts. Both fighters apparently crashed but the American at least survived to become a PoW.

Charley London meanwhile went after his second victim. The results were spectacular:

'I climbed back up after the first kill and got my sights on a '109 coming out of a dive below. I went down on him quick before he even saw me. Must have hit the cannon ammunition in his wings or something, because that Jerry didn't just burn, he flat ol' blew up. Both wings tore all to pieces and the fuselage went up too, like he was carrying bombs in it.'

Ever hungry for a good story and having covered the dramatic exploits of the 8th's bombers for some time, the publicity men gave London's achievement a good airing. Fighter pilots became the new stars in a country no stranger to massive coverage of the famous. On radio and newsreels throughout the land America's fighting airmen told their stories and bases in the ETO regularly played host to get the message across to the 'folks back home'.

Many fine words were penned on the experiences of the men of the 8th, the details being constrained only by the need to cloak UK locations and unit numbers in anonymity. Occasionally, this applied to individuals who had relatives in the occupied countries but otherwise the wartime narratives of the 8th are remarkably candid, with few punches being pulled by officialdom in publicizing the job the AAF had been sent to England to do.

Although the men themselves were in a combat zone with the danger — however slight it actually was — of their bases being identified and bombed, their homes in America were under no such threat. Home towns and states were freely quoted, this being particularly welcome at local level where small town USA was hungry for news of events abroad, and keen to read what happened to the 'boy next door' who had gone such a long way to fight.

British fighter stations hosting American groups became the focus of unprecedented attention by civilian and service PROs and the flow of words both written and spoken continued almost without interruption until the invasion of Europe. Human nature being what it is, it was inevitable that the better equipped, longer established bases tended to get the lion's share of the publicity. For a fighter story, few newsmen would turn down a visit to Debden, 'Pearl of the ETO' with its permanent quarters, American food and, indeed, a continuing fund of stories emanating from the oldest American group in the theatre. Other groups equally deserving of attention might actually get less coverage simply because their station was not so well appointed. Debden's nearness to London also had a bearing on the amount of column inches the 4th Group got during hostilities, other bases not perhaps boasting the same resources to entertain visitors, or there being not so open an attitude to publicity by the group commanders.

If it was Charley London's day on 30 July, the records contained another less noticeable first for the 78th. En route home Lieutenant Quince L. Brown shot up a locomotive and a flak position west of Rotterdam. This unofficial ground strafing was a pointer to things to come...

Tactically, the 30 July air battle had gone the Americans' way primarily because they exploited the element of surprise. They were up against *Jagdgeschwaderen* 1, 11 and 26, all combat experienced and on the face of it, well able to recover from any initial disadvantage. But the Americans found that while the Thunderbolt's qualities must have been well realised by that time, German pilots were still trying to out-dive it. Few aircraft anywhere could do so, but the Luftwaffe seemed slow to learn; evasion was often the half-roll and dive — which on occasions, proved fatal. And this was by no means the last time that the enemy would make the mistake.

The early days of August saw a lull in the heavy bomber offensive and the fighter force continued to fly support missions to mediums. All three P-47 groups participated until 9 August when a new number appeared on the duty rosters — that of the 353rd Group. Having arrived in England in early June the 353rd spent the arbitrary two months at Goxhill awaiting enough P-47s to equip it. The pilots moved down to Metfield, Suffolk, on 3 August. The base was near the 56th's home at Halesworth and, as was to become standard procedure, the freshman 353rd joined the more experienced unit for its first few operational forays. On the first day it fielded sixteen P-47s for a sweep into Holland and Belgium.

Delivery of pressurized belly tanks had speeded up and by the 12th there were enough to outfit 131 Thunderbolts of the three established groups for an escort to B-17s attacking various targets in Germany. The 353rd meanwhile put up 27 aircraft for a high altitude sweep over Belgium, the group's first

The classic 'finger four' formation worked out by the Luftwaffe over Spain, was copied by most air forces in World War 2. This four-four P-47 formation was flown by the 78th Group from Duxford (IWM).

mission of the war, but on that occasion involving only two squadrons, the 350th and 352nd.

The 353rd crammed three missions into the next two days, a reflection on the importance VIII FC attached to having more groups operational. These missions were led by the group CO, Lieutenant Colonel Joseph A. Morris, and were uneventful, the only loss on the 15th being a P-47 from the 78th which crash-landed at Duxford killing its pilot. Two days of little action were followed by a complete contrast on the 16th when the four groups contributed to a large force of 180 aircraft. Assuming all eight guns in every Thunderbolt worked, such a formation packed 720 heavy machine-guns — that only a small proportion of them could prove decisive in combat was ably demonstrated. Sufficient belly tanks were available for all participating aircraft to escort B-17s attacking air depots in France. Keeping enemy interceptors away from the Forts proved highly rewarding for the 4th Group which, under the able direction of Don Blakeslee, shot down 18. Only one P-47 was lost, and all the bombers returned safely from the 4th Wing although the 1st Wing groups had four missing and again, both brought home damaged aircraft. The air action represented the most serious defeat the Luftwaffe had yet sustained in combat with American fighters.

The Americans lost three, one Thunderbolt being that piloted by the 353rd's CO. Joe Morris was last seen diving on an Fw 190 which he may have destroyed before his aircraft crashed. His loss was a bitter blow to the group as Morris had built it up in the US, gave it cohesion and guided it through training, preparing it well for the rigours of the ETO. VIII FC transferred Colonel Loren McCollom from the 56th to take the reins of the Metfield group for the time being.

The 56th's single kill on 16 August was followed by an outstanding display of tactics and gunnery a day later — one of the blackest days in the 8th Air Force's history. The 17 August anniversary raid on Schweinfurt and Regensburg is remembered mainly for the terrible bomber losses as the 1st and 4th Wings of B-17s ran the gauntlet of aggressive defences, the latter wing making the first shuttle mission of the war as it flew on from Germany to land in North Africa. But the day also marked a change in the fortunes of the Wolfpack which had up to then little to show for its efforts.

It was in the afternoon of 'Black Wednesday' that the 56th met with success, the morning mission to support the bomber forces heading for Regensburg's Messerschmitt production plant yielding little in the way of action. The second outing was to meet the survivors of the Schweinfurt force and the group stretched its range by using belly tank fuel for ten minutes more than usual, enabling it to pick up its charges some fifteen miles from Eupen, at 16:21.

As high cover for the Fortress boxes, the Wolfpack clashed with elements of JG26 attempting head-on passes on the B-17s. Hub Zemke chose his targets carefully, reading the battle. Ensuring that enough Thunderbolts were detached from his interceptors to cover exhausted crews and a number of bombers already damaged from the murderous slog into the ball-bearing production centre, Zemke's men shot down seventeen of the enemy without loss to themselves. In fact there were no casualties from a total of 240 P-47s despatched that day, the 56th being joined by the 4th, 78th and 353rd. The last-mentioned group recorded its first ETO aerial victory in the afternoon combat, only it and the 56th flying the withdrawal support operation. Among the German casualties was Wilhelm-Ferdinand Galland of JG26, brother of the famous Adolf Galland with 55 victories to his credit. He went down in the vicinity of Liége.

The Wolfpack continued its run of good fortune over the Luftwaffe on the 19th when the bombers, badly depleted after the double strike two days before, drew a short-range mission to various enemy airfields in the Low Countries. The 56th got nine, the 78th one and the only loss of the day was a Halesworth

P-47 that went down due to mechanical failure. Captain Gerry Johnson shot down a Bf 109 to become the first ace in the 56th.

September 1943 was a significant month for VIII Fighter Command, although for the 8th Air Force it was a period of low-key activity. Reluctant to lay on another deep penetration raid and risk a repetition of the 17 August casualties, VIII BC awaited the outcome of tests of new larger-capacity fuel tanks for the P-47s. Although operational experiments had been made with Thunderbolt tanks of up to 200 gals capacity, fitted on racks carried between the inboard undercarriage doors and the fuselage, these had not been very reliable. Unpressurized, they were prone to leakage and the 8th's fighter force had standardized on the bulky radome-like belly tanks. These had also had their share of problems but they had proved their worth. Behind the scenes the 8th's technical teams had by the summer of 1943 developed a four-point shackle to enable the P-47D to carry a 75-gal US teardrop tank, used primarily on the P-39 and P-40.

Of metal construction and far less cumbersome, these tanks did not actually reduce capacity significantly, as it had rarely been practicable to put more than 100 gals in the 200-gal tanks. Fitting B-7 shackle conversion sets to the belly of the P-47 enabled teardrop tanks to be carried without any detriment to performance; aircraft could also attain a higher altitude without the pilot having to worry that his tank would burst or leak under pressure, as was often the case before.

Teardrop tank conversion sets were issued to the 4th and 56th Groups during August and by the following month production of metal 108-gal tanks

was underway in the UK. Based on the cigar-shaped impregnated paper tank used by RAF fighters, this would become the standard type for wing hardpoints in the months to come, although the P-47s were to use the 75-gal teardrop type as standard equipment until availability improved.

By August/September VIII FC had five more groups in the process of preparing for their first operational sorties and two, the 352nd at Bodney and the 355th at Steeple Morden, were ready. Both these had P-47s as did the 356th then in training at Goxhill while the 55th and 20th at Nuthampstead and King's Cliffe were equipped with the P-38.

For its first ETO mission the 352nd supported operations against French airfields involving bombers from all three divisions. The group's aircraft covered the P-47s of the 56th and 353rd Groups landing after their escort duty was completed. The 355th took the opportunity to fly a practice fighter sweep on a day when the experienced groups lost two of their own and shot down one. Both casualties were from the 4th, one pilot being picked out of the Channel two days later. The single kill of the mission went to the Wolfpack.

Nicknames of pilots, groups and squadrons became common in the ETO, some perpetuating since the origins of the unit, others bearing an association with service in Europe. 'Eagles' was a natural for the Debden-based 4th while 'Wolfpack' for the 56th reflected a desire to get among the enemy with disastrous results to him. Other titles would suggest themselves in the fullness of time, when units began to specialize in a particular line of work as the command's war role developed and diversified. An

Newly applied 'star and bar' national insignia on a P-47D of the 352nd FS, 353rd Group (via George Porter).

Spitfires will always have a place in the history of US fighter presence in the UK. This example, Mk II (as built) serialled P8048 is believed to have been retained as a station hack long after its operational days were over. (US Air Force Museum).

example was the 355th, the 'Steeple Morden Strafers'.

On 23 September, the 4th staged into Warmwell to lessen the range needed to fly target support to bombers attacking Nantes, Vannes and Kerlin. Three other fighter groups, the 56th, 78th and 353rd, used Thorney Island as their forward base on the first occasion that VIII BC sent out two escort missions in one day.

The Eagles found that operating away from home base produced its problems if facilities were limited. At Warmwell it took seven hours to top up the tanks of all the Thunderbolts earmarked for the morning escort, only then it being realized that the group could not take off from the grass airfield carrying the weight of external tanks! They all had to come off and be left behind and en route to France, to add potential injury to insult, the P-47s were fired on by German flak located on Guernsey in the Channel Islands. Better facilities existed at Exeter from whence the 4th operated for the second mission of the day, target support in the vicinity of Dinan-Nantes. Airfields and port areas were bombed with patchy results due to bad weather. The 4th returned to Debden the following day.

On 25 September an auspicious event for the future of VIII FC occurred at the 4th's base when the first P-51B arrived for evaluation. Don Blakeslee was foremost among the pilots who quickly saw the potential of the aircraft and the possibility of the group getting back on an aircraft not unlike the Spitfire, now little more than a fond memory. Test-flying the P-51 made Blakeslee realise that this was the aircraft the 4th must have.

Two days later the P-47 force flew a milestone mission — for the first time they would penetrate the German border and escort the bombers right into the target area. The target for a force of 308 B-17s was Emden's industrial area, supported by virtually the entire Thunderbolt force — 262 aircraft drawn from five groups. Those based furthest from the bombers' intended route out over the North Sea — the 4th and 78th — used the B-24 airfields at Hardwick and Hethel as forward bases. For the first time, 108-gal drop tanks were used by the 4th Group for the 200-mile flight into France, the fighters splitting up to shepherd two task forces of B-17s. Other groups retained the 75-gal tanks although the freshmen 352nd and 355th were then without their own supplies of drop tanks. These units flew sweeps over Holland while the 2nd Bomb Division sent 24 B-24s as a diversionary force in support of the main operation. Other activity included raids by 36 3rd Wing B-26 Marauders on airfields at Beauvais and Conches and flights by three F-5 Lightnings of the 7th Photographic Group to locations in France and

Colonel Bill Cummings led the 355th Group for a week short of two years, from November 1942 to November 1944, helping to forge it into one of the most effective fighter outfits in the ETO. He is pictured here with an early 357th FS P-47 (355th FG Association).

north-west Germany to assess target strike effectiveness — another important 8th AF fighter task.

Bad weather intervened but did not prevent the 4th and 353rd Groups meeting their charges off the Frisian Islands and taking them to the target on schedule. An ensuing combat with Luftwaffe interceptors netted a total of eight victories for the 353rd and one for the 4th. German fighter pilots were mightily surprised to be met by Thunderbolts as well as the usual massed guns of the B-17 force, and suffered accordingly. Before the day was out JG11, one of the opposing units, would record the loss of twenty Bf 109s to all causes.

Covering the second task force, the 56th and 78th could not rendezvous at the stipulated time but combat produced another fifteen kills, five falling to the 56th and the rest to the boys from the Duckpond. It was a resounding confirmation of what the

American fighters could do to protect the bombers provided they had fuel enough to be present during the most critical phase of a raid; the day's final score was 21(destroyed)-2(probable)-6(damaged) for the loss of one 61st FS Thunderbolt.

There was a repeat mission to Emden on 2 October, the Thunderbolt force again providing heavy escort. This time the Luftwaffe was conspicuous by its relative absence — only five fighters were shot down. Of the three that fell to the 56th, one was Hub Zemke's fifth, making him the group's second ace. Few could claim the magic five more deservedly than Zemke, who had weathered the early misfortunes and seeming lack of confirmed victories for his group to see it posed on the verge of much improved success — and over the enemy homeland. A healthy rivalry with the 4th meant that the Wolfpack could afford to crow a little — it led the Debden flyers 2-0 in 'acedom'.

The 56th's run of success in air combat continued on 4 October when the P-47s surprised a group of Bf 110s attempting to attack a rear box of B-17s. Weighed down with rocket tubes, the *Zerstörers* were decimated by the swift Thunderbolts and sixteen went down without loss to the Americans. Walker Mahurin accounted for three of them to reach ace status. The day's total reached nineteen, both the 355th and 353rd being credited with kills, and the 56th had notched up another first with a distance flown of 750 miles. Judicious use of engine power, plus the 108-gal tanks, had made it possible to attain this record range.

The victories of 4 October were confirmation for the Luftwaffe high command that the use of twin-engined fighters for bomber interception was becoming an increasingly risky business; useful though the heavier aircraft were for carrying cannon, rockets and occasionally bombs and theoretically able to bring down US heavies with ease, the speed penalty imposed on the carrier aircraft was suicidal if American fighters were present. The Germans had no reason to suppose that the events of the autumn of 1943 would change radically in their favour — but just how much worse things were to become in only a few months was probably very much outside their planning or, indeed, their power to prevent.

Elated as it was with its autumn victories over the *Viermots* (four-engined bombers), the Luftwaffe fighter force must have seen that the longer range of the American escorts was leading to a turning point; on the one hand it realized correctly that the USAAF could not sustain the percentage loss of numerous Schweinfurt-type missions. On the other, the 17 August attacks had been carried through. Not on this or any other occasion did the Luftwaffe ever turn back an American heavy bomber strike and if recent losses had been grievous there was a certainty that the innovative Americans would do something to ensure that they would never be so heavy again.

The Thunderbolt had come to be seen as a dangerous adversary, even though its flight performance could in some respects be bettered by both the Bf 109 and Fw 190. Individual pilots of the *Jagdverbände* noted in their diaries the deceiving characteristics of the P-47. One said, comparing it with other US fighters he met in combat:

'The P-47 wasn't so bad because we could out-turn and out-climb it, initially. But that big American fighter could roll with deceiving speed and when it came down on you in a long dive, there was no way you could get away from it. It must have had a huge brick built into it, somewhere.'

4 Finding the form

Few in VIII Fighter Command expected the 56th's leadership in fighter aces to last very long, and on 8 October the 4th's determination that it should not came a step nearer to reality. Both B-17s and B-24s were despatched, the targets lying in the cities of Bremen and Vegesack. Again the Thunderbolts were out in force and the more modest total of twelve victories nevertheless resulted in the mantle of ace falling on Ralph 'Kidd' Hofer and Roy Evans. These two Debden pilots were fêted as the first of the Eagles' aces but another five kills were added to the already impressive total achieved by the 56th.

When the P-47s went to Bremen part of the defending force was JG1. In combat with the 56th near Nordholm, one of the Fw 190s that fell was the aircraft flown by the wing's Kommodore, Hans Philipp. But the German fighters struck back to the tune of fourteen bombers missing to VIII BC, plus 110 damaged and two damaged beyond repair as Category E write-offs. Bomber losses were reaching the point of being prohibitive despite the increasing protection afforded by fighters and October was something of a watershed — before the month was out the 8th AF would have to count 126 heavy bombers missing in action.

As a counter-balance to such figures the death or incapacitation of the most experienced Luftwaffe fighter pilots, many of whom had become *Experten* in the demanding art of knocking down the well-defended American heavies, was working through to the detriment of the Germans' effectiveness. Flak, always a factor to contend with, was proven not to be half as adept in defending targets as were well flown and armed interceptor fighters. This fact was recognized by 8th AF planners who knew that if the intended invasion of Europe were to go ahead, Allied bombers had to succeed not only in destroying the flow of replacement aircraft to Luftwaffe units, but also in cutting off the fuel and oil necessary for them to operate and in rendering their airfields untenable. With the defenders' ability to destroy bombers greatly reduced, if not eliminated, then, and only then, could those same bombers be expected to achieve the degree of destruction of strategic targets that would materially contribute to final Allied victory. The German air force therefore became the primary target; rendering it impotent would help not only the 8th Air Force but the Allied air offensive in general. Equally, given that it was impossible to locate every dispersed factory, to prevent the production and delivery of every gallon of fuel and oil, or to be sure that every airfield available to the enemy be rendered permanently unserviceable, this left only one way to ensure that the Allied cause would prevail — to overwhelm his fighters in aerial combat.

The history of the 8th Air Force includes a number of days where the calendar qualifies for a black ring. Schweinfurt and Regensberg on 17 August 1943 is one. Münster on 10 October is another. This operation, marked by one of the bitterest air battles of the war, did not result in bomber losses as high as 17 August, with thirty B-17s MIA — but mere statistics mask the drama played out by those on the receiving end. At Münster, a member of the 100th Bomb Group counted himself lucky to return home at all — only one B-17 did so out of fourteen despatched. Twelve Thorpe Abbotts' Fortresses were MIA from the operation while a thirteenth machine crashed in England on return.

On a less realistic note, VIII BC allowed claims for 183 enemy aircraft shot down by bomber gunners, plus 21 probables and 51 damaged. Unlikely though this figure seems in retrospect (it was an all-time high for the 8th on one bomber operation) the intensity of the air battle is reflected in it. More credence can be attached to the fighters' score of nineteen down for one P-47 lost in action.

Watching out for the B-17s that day was Major Eugene Roberts leading the 78th Group at the controls of his P-47D *Spokane Chief*. On withdrawal support the 78th and 353rd clashed with enemy fighters and were welcome reinforcements to the 56th which had already had a hectic time. Roberts saw: 'Dense smoke coming up from Enschede (a suburb of Münster) and a group of B-17s flying through fairly accurate and heavy flak. From our position at 28,000 ft, I saw some straggling Fortresses being attacked far below the main boxes, so I commenced a long, steep dive. Earlier, I had seen a Fortress on fire, breaking up and spilling parachutes, heading down towards Haaksbergen.

'I lined up on an Me 110 which was itself firing on a B-17. The damaged Fortress went into a steep diving turn to the left, pouring white smoke. I rapidly closed on the Me 110, swinging in behind him, and opened fire at about 350 yd. I was now closing at a terrific rate and at about 100 yd range I completely smothered the enemy aircraft in strikes. I was practically jamming my guns into him. The left engine belched smoke, and at about 30 yd I broke sharply to avoid a collision. The last I saw of him he was in a vertical dive with both engines on fire from 15,000 ft.

'I pulled up to about 18,000 ft and then spotted an Me 410 positioning himself on a B-17 below and to my left. I dived down and closed from the rear, again opening fire at about 350 yd. I closed to point-blank range and saw dozens of strikes all over the aircraft. Pieces of fuselage flew off and whipped past me, and again I almost rammed my target. Pulling up sharply to avoid him, and to cover my rear, I climbed back to 24,000 ft to rejoin the bombers on their route out. From their observations, other pilots in my group later confirmed these two aircraft as destroyed.'

The 353rd met the Münster bombers at 15:29 hr and was immediately in action, the pilots pushing their seven-ton fighters into screaming dives to clear the path for the battered survivors of the raid. Captain Walter 'Turk' Beckham's *Little Demon* was seen to plunge below a B-17 of the 384th Group and single-handedly shoot down three. The gunners picked out the white recognition stripes on the American fighter split seconds before they were about to open fire on it. Two German fighters were down and Beckham prepared the coup de grâce for number three:

Top right *The 355th also boasted one of the most able artists in the ETO in the person of Arthur DeCosta, who brought his talents to 'bare' on convenient walls and doors as well as Republic products. This is one of his best on the aircraft (coded WR-U) flown by Henry Kucheman who perpetuated Lil Lo on his Mustangs — a later era which saw the general disappearance of the accompanying ladies (355th FG Association).*

Above right *Paul Ellington's P-47C (41-6214 of the 335th FS apparently) forced to land at Ridgewell en route to enemy territory, judging by the in-place 108-gal belly tank. The reason as nearly always was weather — the Germans' finest weapon against the 8th! (USAF).*

Right *Thunderbolts proved well able to 'take it' and bring the pilot home, despite initial doubts about their fighting ability. This not atypical example of air combat was recorded by the 353rd Group on 3 October 1943. Note open wing ammunition bay and gun breeches (USAF).*

'Tracer bullets appeared while I was shooting down the third German fighter, indicating that I was running out of ammunition. I closed to very short range and emptied my guns from dead astern. A fourth Me 110 banked round to attack me, so I instinctively turned sharply towards him. He then broke off the engagement, diving violently downwards, evading a P-47 with empty guns.

'I turned towards home and looked around to clear my tail. Eight or ten single-engined enemy aircraft were behind, but a bit too far away to fire at me. I used full throttle and nosed down at about 1,000 ft a minute, and turned slightly off my homeward course to the left so as to be flying directly into the sun. I must have begun to widen the gap, because after about five minutes, I was about one third of the way across the Zuider Zee heading directly towards Amsterdam when the enemy fighters gave up the chase and turned away.'

Also on the lookout for American bombers were the personnel of Flak Regiment 3/989 situated north of Münster. Their battery was equipped with 20 mm guns and one of the crew was Hans Hessling who remembers the 10 October raid; at that time he and four other schoolboys were acting as *Luftwaffenhelfern* getting down to their lessons during the morning and undertaking flak duty in the afternoons:

'On the afternoon of the raid, an Fw 190 shot down a P-47 coded *UN-D* near the Dortmund Ems Canal. The P-47 flew into a tree trunk and came over the canal with only its right wing. It crashed on the other side. The pilot was killed and laid to rest 10 cm from his aircraft.

'In 1943 the enemy air raids increased and my class (Gymnasium-Becknum) was ordered to help the flak batteries around Münster for a period which for me lasted from 1 September to February 1944.

'Every week a Dornier Do 17 or Bloch 152 flew *Zieldarstellung* or training flights for the flak, and we used models to identify the various British and American types we could expect to see. We had both 20 mm and 8.8 cm fixed flak guns and there were respectively five and eight men in the crew composed of a *Geschützführer* (Gun-leader) plus the appropriate number of *Kanoniers,* identified as K1, K2, K3 and K4. In the smaller crew K5 was responsible for operating the range-finder equipment as the *Entfernüngsmesser.*

'In my area there were two three-gun 20 mm installations and one Flak Zug with three guns; three kilometres south of us there were four 8.8 cm sites with four guns each. Every day late in the afternoon all flak and Luftwaffe units irrespective of where they were located received a top secret new identification to be used for a 24-hour period. These 'colours of the day' were designed to prevent any accidental incidents involving friendly aircraft and were known as the *Erkennungssignale* (ES), a system of flares. In a typical week, these would be: ES 2 — one red, three white; ES 3 — four white; ES 4 — four red; ES 5 — six white; ES 6 — six red and ES 7 — three white and three red. These flares would be used by German aircraft to warn flak of their approach.'

After Münster there came the return to Schweinfurt. Costlier in terms of human life even than the first mission to the centre of ball-bearing production, although the number of B-17s missing was the same, VIII BC's Raid 115 finally proved that unescorted daylight bombing was simply too costly beyond fighter range. While the bomber force licked its wounds the fighter force was able to add another thirteen to its 'box' score.

The second Schweinfurt operation, like the first, did not go entirely according to plan. Bad weather hampered the fighters considerably and the 4th, one of four P-47 groups involved, failed to rendezvous with its designated bomber boxes and was recalled. The 352nd Group tagged along with the only bombers it found, these being 29 B-24s flying a diversionary operation. That left the 56th and 353rd

to give penetration support and these two groups scored the victories — an impressive ten for the latter and three to the 56th. These victories changed the leading runners in the 'ace race' again, the 353rd's Walter Beckham joining that select band with his three on the Münster raid, the day that had made Dave Schilling and Robert Johnson new aces in the 56th. The highest scoring individual pilot was Eugene Roberts, who had eight, one more than Gerald Johnson of the 56th. The 56th's aces were by chance all grouped in one squadron at this time, the 61st. Robert Johnson said of the squadron's prowess:

'The 56th was well on the way to acquiring a galaxy of aces; indeed, the very presence in the sky of our group forbode ill tiding for the enemy. This is no empty phrase. In the early days of fighting, when more often than not the Germans ended the day by cuffing us about, our squadron adopted the name of "Avengers". Under McCollom's and later Gabreski's skilful air leadership, the Avengers slowly but surely began to cut a swath through the Abbeville Boys and their compatriots. We had Gabreski, myself, Joe Powers, Bob Lamb, Jimmy Stewart, Gerry Johnson, Frank McCauley and Don Smith, among others. All of us became aces.'

The 14 October mission marked a highpoint in terms of fighter victories for the month, the only other escort missions taking place on the 20th when bombers were sent to Duren. This was the first time that the 55th FG flew escort in the P-38, although the group had given its new aircraft an airing previously in four separate sweeps of the Dutch islands and Northern France. The group was tasked for its first escort sorties on 18 October, but inclement weather prevented rendezvous. The abortive day's operations also resulted in the 55th's first loss.

The 15 October mission had also introduced a second new group to ETO conditions when the 356th put up 34 Thunderbolts from Martlesham Heath in support of the 36 Lightnings of the 55th. The 356th's second mission was to escort 9th AF B-26s on 22 October.

November 1943 began with a 566 bomber effort against one of the 8th AF's original targets at Wilhelmshaven on the 3rd. The bombers used H2X radar carried by Pathfinder aircraft for the first time and the fighters were drawn from the seven Thunderbolt groups, plus the 55th with P-38s. These latter aircraft, 45 in number, claimed 3(destroyed)-5(probable)-5(damaged) enemy aircraft to enter the Group's ETO scoring record. Other groups claimed eleven for the loss of two P-47s. Two days later the 56th was part of the fighter force that escorted 1st and 3rd Bomb Division B-17s to Gelsenkirchen, while the 2nd BD despatched its unescorted B-24s to Münster. Again the Thunderbolts proved their superiority, with thirteen German aircraft downed for the loss of four of their own. When the 56th landed the group was able, by recording George Hall's victory that day, to announce 100 enemy aircraft shot down in air combat. This feat, celebrated in time-honoured tradition with a party, was a credit not only to tenacity but to leadership. Top dog was a position the 56th delighted in holding and it was not in fact to concede it to any other group for the duration of the war in terms of air-to-air kills, although its closest rivals at Debden led overall by combining air and ground victories.

There was no single fundamental quality that made one pilot into a top scorer while his squadron colleagues soldiered on, maybe getting one or two victories during the course of a tour — or maybe not being credited with any enemy aircraft at all. That did not mean that such pilots made no worthwhile contribution to the success of the group — quite the reverse was true. War, like many other human endeavours, invariably relies on quantity as well as quality making the difference between victory or defeat — it was certainly so in World War 2. Each successful pilot had his own particular technique in combat, just as his flying skill could not be exactly copied by anyone else. Many factors combined to give a man the right aptitude to score victories, and each swore by methods he would use whenever the circumstances were right for him to do so. A very great deal depended on the position, numbers and degree of skill of the opposing forces.

Most fighter pilots liked their work and while they had sympathy for the bomber crews, rarely did they envy them. It did happen though that a bomber pilot with a few missions under his belt applied for and was granted a transfer to fighters. The chance to fly a nimble Thunderbolt or Mustang was a privilege attained by the few in the early days of the offensive but when VIII Fighter Command formed group scouting forces in late 1943 to provide more immediate information on conditions likely to be encountered on missions, bomber pilot skills were very much in demand. It was realized that only a man who had sweated out raids on *Festung Europa* from the cockpit of a Fortress or Liberator could really appreciate the particular problems the heavies faced in doing their job efficiently. There was no shortage of volunteers.

People could look at the record of a good fighter pilot and, if they knew the details, point to such and such a factor that made the difference between him and the others. Personal qualities such as extremely good eyesight, a good physique and an almost instinctive judgement of height and distance were basics, added to which could be quick reflexes, an understanding of the capabilities and limitations of his own machine and those of the enemy, and the most indefinable quality of all, the 'hunter/killer' instinct. In practical terms, pilots indulged in unofficial modifications to their regular aircraft which they believed gave that slight edge. Speed was important to some — Hub Zemke particularly. He, like other pilots, took an interest in his aircraft and thought up ways to improve it. In order to cut down the weight Zemke even went to the extent of having the bullet-proof windshield taken out of his P-47. Even when the unprotected plexiglass was pierced on a subsequent mission, the heavy armoured glass was not put back.

Francis Gabreski's belief concerned guns. He refused to have tracer bullets included in his P-47's ammunition load because, he said, 'Sometimes you miss with the first bullets and the tracers give you away'. Gabby also went into battle with less than the full number of rounds in his fighter's guns, as he felt that full ammo tanks (holding up to 3,400 rounds) for eight guns made the wings too heavy to turn tightly enough.

It was also not uncommon for individual pilots to reduce the P-47's gun battery to six. This reduced weight even further and it was well known that if a pilot was capable of destroying a target with eight guns, six would do just as well — and the slight saving in performance and manoeuvreability might one day make the difference between catching or losing the quarry. Most aces believed that the only way to make sure of a kill was to get in close and do the job with economical bursts. Gabreski's view was: 'Wait until you get 'em right in the sights then short bursts. There's no use melting your guns.'

Zemke's comment on tactics ran like this: 'A fighter pilot must possess an inner urge to do combat. The will at all times to be offensive will develop into his own tactics. I stay with an enemy until either he's destroyed, I'm out of ammunition, he evades into the clouds, I'm driven off, or I'm too low on gasoline to continue the combat.'

Bob Johnson's advice to new pilots was: 'Never let a Jerry get his sights on you. No matter whether he is 100 yd or 1,000 yd away, a 20 mm will carry easily that far and will knock down a plane at 1,000 yd. It is better to stay at 20,000 ft with a good speed with a Jerry at 25,000 ft than it is to pull up in his vicinity at a stalling speed. If he comes down on you, pull up into him and nine times out of ten, if you are nearly head-on with him he'll roll away to his right. Then you have him. Roll on to his tail and go get him.'

Don Blakeslee put over similar advice to new boys. At one briefing he was expounding the theory of killing without being killed in combat, and stressing that if attacked his pilots should immediately turn into the enemy and meet him head on. Under no circumstances should they break from this course. This worried a young Lieutenant who raised his hand with a question: 'But Colonel, what if the German doesn't break either?'

'Then, young man', said Blakeslee, 'you'll have just earned your hazardous duty pay.'

The key to survival in air-to-air combat often relied on not one pair of eyes but two. The wingman system, whereby one pilot would cover the other and stick with him throughout the mission, was well developed by the 8th Air Force for its fighter force. Often it happened that a wingman covered his leader so well that he himself had few chances to run up his own score, although there were 'double acts' in which each man made a name for himself. Don Gentile and John Godfrey of the 4th developed mutual co-operation to a remarkable degree during the Mustang period and among the Thunderbolt teams were George Preddy and Bill 'Whizz' Whisner of the 352nd, both of whom became aces. They were together when Preddy scored his first kill during an escort to Solingen on 1 December 1943. His encounter report emphasizes the 'close in' tactics invariably employed by the aces.

'I was leading Crown Prince Red Flight in a section of twelve ships. We came in over the bomber formation at 30,000 ft and went into a left orbit. I saw one Me 109 behind the rear box of bombers about 3,000 ft below me. I started a quarter stern attack and when about 1,000 yd from the enemy aircraft, it started a steep spiral dive to the left. I followed closing to 400 yd. As I closed from 400 to 200 yd, I fired and saw strikes on the wing roots and cockpit. The airplane began smoking and fell out of control at about 7,000 ft. I fired another burst closing to about 100 yd. After I broke off the attack, the enemy aircraft disintegrated. The Me 109 was carrying a belly tank which did not drop.'

Bill Whisner's outstanding combat record spanned two tours with the 352nd during which he had that other indefinable factor with him — luck. There were those who said that luck didn't come into it at all but there must have been some guardian angel riding in Whisner's cockpit because: 'The interesting thing was the fact that for the first time in 100 missions a German fighter shot me up. Within one minute after take-off this '190 put seven twenties into me. An HE just forward of the windshield and three AP through

A Malcolm hood providing better all-round visibility to the pilot of 42-106942, a P-51B-15 of the 374th FS, 361st FG.

each wing. The only effective damage, however, was a broken aileron cable. Since the field was alive with '190s and '109s, it was impossible to land, so I stayed around and got three more of them before the air cleared. This was my final air-to-air contact with the Jerry in World War 2.'

The mission Whisner described was on 1 January 1945 — but the point is that by that time his score stood at 'lucky' thirteen. There again, perhaps the number momentarily worked against him. A superstitious person might well have thought so. In any event Bill Whisner pushed his luck for another 37 missions, the three kills he had made that day bringing his final score to sixteen.

If talismen and mascots were more for bomber crews than fighter pilots the single-seater men were occasionally prey to the luck syndrome. With his score at nil, Walter Beckham once shaved off his moustache, believing it to be a jinx. Bare-faced, Beckham subsequently got eight in seven missions.

Behind the scenes, great strides were being made to get aircraft to the 8th Air Force in adequate number for operations to be maintained on the one hand and with the necessary reliability to withstand the demanding type of operation they were flying on the other. And not always was it major items of equipment which made a difference. Debden's historians record that on 16 October 1943, a shipment of 600 Spitfire rear-view mirrors arrived for the group's P-47Ds. Fitting these made life a little easier for the pilots as they improved considerably the fatiguing requirement to keep a continuous watch in the fighters' vulnerable rear quarter. The high 'razor-back' fuselage of the Thunderbolt was always a problem in this regard, and individual pilots tried out various ways to improve all-round vision. Mirrors were one way, but more preferable was a clear-vision canopy. In this respect the 8th looked, as so many times before, for help from the RAF.

Rear visibility from single-seat fighters was a problem that had been experienced by the RAF since the earliest days with modern fighters, particularly the Hurricane. The Spitfire, far better than its counterpart in this respect did at least have a clear-vision sliding hood. Wing Commander Malcolm was among those who worked on ways to improve the P-47 and later the early versions of the P-51. Prior to 1944 adaptations on Republic and North American production lines, both of which required major engineering changes to give their single-seaters all round 'bubble' canopy vision, Malcolm's ingenuity resulted in limited supplies of the hood section he designed reaching Thunderbolt units. These were duly fitted at 'field level' as well as at service depots but the bulk of production from UK sources was reserved for the P-51B/C model when this type was slated to largely replace the Thunderbolt in VIII FC service.

Having an American fighter group at full strength in the ETO in late 1943 meant that it had over 100 aircraft on charge, a basic unit establishment of 25-30 aircraft per squadron with the rest as 'spares'. Calls for equipment on all war fronts meant that this kind of number could only be achieved over a period of time. Luckily fighter losses were such that maintenance echelons could usually maintain unit establishment: in November the 78th at Duxford had enough P-47s (108) to operate with its force divided into two separate (A and B) groups. Under this system VIII FC could despatch experienced groups on both escort and support-ground attack missions without reducing its bomber protection. With adequate numbers of aircraft arriving from the US, the command was also able to raise group establishments in both aircraft and personnel, the increased availability also resurrecting the idea of employing the 8th AF fighters in a ground attack role.

P-47D-2, 42-8400/WR-E, of the 354th FS, 355th Group outward-bound (RAF Museum).

5 Fork-tailed friend

When Frank Hunter handed over VIII Fighter Command to Major General William Kepner in August 1943, some eight months had elapsed since the 78th Group had passed its P-38s into other hands. It was believed that only the Lightning could immediately escort bombers another fifty miles — about 400 miles from England — and thereby alleviate the losses being suffered after the P-47s were forced to turn for home. On the face of it, the P-38 certainly could do the job but precious few were assigned to the 8th Air Force as the outstanding success of the type in other theatres meant that long before bomber escort was seen to be so important in Europe, commanders of groups in the Mediterranean and Pacific theatres had staked their claims to it. But in the latter half of 1943 the re-assignment of Lightnings to the ETO became possible, if only in limited numbers.

Consequently, it was with much relief that the command recorded the arrival of the 20th Group in August. But although this group had flown the Lightning in the States, theatre indoctrination and work-up to operational efficiency took time. Arriving without aircraft, the 20th was initially ensconced on two airfields, the 77th, 79th and headquarters establishments going to King's Cliffe, Northants, and the 55th to Wittering, Northants, sharing the living quarters with No 141 Squadron RAF. This temporary arrangement ended within weeks, however, and the entire 20th Group was established at King's Cliffe by 26 August. A number of P-38Hs had in the meantime arrived.

Perhaps fortuitously — although it hardly seemed that way to the pilots, eager as they were to put the first operational missions behind them — the 20th was not destined to fly this model of Lightning in combat. Instead, most of its aircraft were passed to another group new to the ETO, the 55th based at Nuthampstead, Herts, and before the 20th flew its first mission it received new P-38Js. Only a handful of the earlier models remained at King's Cliffe for training purposes.

Even though the 20th's pilots were familiar with the P-38H, the 55th had had more experience of the aircraft in general, having received some early production P-322s in the spring of 1942. Improved Lightning versions had followed and it was therefore deemed preferable to have the 55th make the P-38's 'second debut' in the ETO.

Only gradually did the three squadrons of the 55th, the 38th, 338th and 343rd receive enough Lightnings to bring them up to full strength, and with the weather very much dictating the level of operations, late 1943 was a dismal period. Unable to make much headway, the pilots and ground crews of the 55th found the reality of war very different to what they had imagined. Their aircraft revealed numerous drawbacks which were not envisaged and line chiefs and mechanics needed all their skills to prepare enough aircraft for mission requirements, often working round the clock to cure engine and hydraulic troubles — and far more frequently than anyone liked — only to find on the morning of the mission that it had been 'scrubbed' once again. But the short range missions that did take place were preludes to greater action in the future. And although the 55th had a disappointing start, it at least made the kill ratio to aircraft lost on operations the same. In 28 missions between its debut and 31 December, it destroyed 27 aircraft in combat and lost 27 P-38s.

The group had flown 26 missions by 24 December and had been accompanied by squadrons of the 20th Group since early November, the latter unit flying its full ETO P-38 effort on 28 December. Fighter operations were only possible on eleven days in December 1943, although the month was a significant period for VIII Fighter Command. As well as a second P-38 group being declared operational, an eighth P-47 group took its bow on the 13th, this being the 359th at East Wretham, and on the first day of the month the 354th Group of IX Fighter Command operating under 8th AF control went on its first sweep with P-51Bs. At that time the 8th also had a ninth Thunderbolt group, the 358th having been established at Leiston on 29 November. While useful, increased Thunderbolt strength did little to solve the

When P-38s returned to the UK in the autumn of 1943 for operations with the 8th they carried only national insignia and serials. This H-5 model has red-bordered star and bar (RAF Museum).

Within a short time Lightnings were given codes to conform to standard 8th AF practice. This view shows H models of the 20th Group taxying out for another long, cold escort mission (RAF Museum).

range problem; the Merlin-engined P-51 looked promising but the P-38 had the most immediate potential — or so it was thought.

The story of the Mustang in AAF service is well enough known not to be retold at length here, but it is worth highlighting the background to what appeared at the time to be an extraordinary decision on the part of the war planners to assign the new aircraft to the IX rather than VIII Fighter Command. The answer was that the Army Air Forces had long considered the P-51 to have been a supplementary type to the P-47 and P-38; it had been designed expressly at the behest of the British Purchasing Commission and had entered service with the RAF first. While AAF units around the world subsequently used the P-51, P-51A and A-36 models, these were primarily employed in the ground support role — and this continued to be the aircraft's forté until installation of the Rolls-Royce Merlin engine changed its capability into a long-range escort fighter par excellence.

AAF planners still thought of the Mustang as a tactical, ground-attack aircraft, however, and with its new-found performance and range untried it seemed logical to allocate it to the new 9th AF which had been moved from North Africa and reconstituted in England in preparation to support the invasion of the continent of Europe. Among those who saw that the Merlin-engined Mustang could be better employed by the beleaguered 8th Air Force was the US ambassador in London, J. G. Winant, and Lieutenant

Colonel Tommy Hitchock of the embassy staff. By the spring of 1943 Merlin-engined examples of the P-51 were available for testing at Bovingdon by Cass Hough. His enthusiastic report confirmed that the P-51B was both easy to handle and fast but that directional stability was rather poor.

In the meantime the first production P-51Bs were allocated to the 9th AF's 354th Group, which sailed for the UK on 20 October 1943. The group received its first P-51Bs at Greenham Common on 11 November and two days later left its temporary home for Boxted, Essex. On 1 December the new Mustangs flew the 354th's first operational sorties, to Belgium and the Pas-de-Calais area. Having trained on P-39s, few of the group's pilots had much experience with the Mustang and the first missions were led by a man who was delighted to be at the controls of a fighter which was far more like the Spitfires he had been forced to relinquish same eight months previously. Don Blakeslee, never completely at home with the P-47, had been loaned by the 4th Group to initiate the new 9th AF group and in company with the 354th's CO, Colonel K. R. Martin, led 23 aircraft on the first sweep. Blakeslee again led the group on 5 December, its first escort mission.

Early 354th operations were relatively uneventful until the mission to escort bombers to Bremen on 16 December. Mixing it with a number of single- and twin-engined German fighters, Lieutenant Charles F. Gumm of the 355th FS brought down a Bf 110 to record the first kill for the 'Pioneer Mustang Group'. Three other enemy aircraft kills had been notched up before the group took its Mustangs to Kiel on the 20th, a flight of 490 miles each way, the furthest yet for a single-engined fighter on escort duty.

Although the Kiel operation was a pointer to great things to come, these early P-51B operations were not without incident; numerous technical difficulties were experienced with the aircraft, not the least of which was gun jamming. Windscreen defrosting was found to be insufficient at high altitude; coolant leaks occurred and spark plugs failed due to retarded engine settings.

Of a different but equally dangerous nature was the outline shape of the new Mustang. Even at short distances it bore a very close resemblance to the Messerschmitt Bf 109 — a fact highlighted by an incident on 20 December when the 354th was nearly attacked by Thunderbolts. As a precaution, VIII FC ordered that Mustangs in the ETO should bear white recognition bands around the nose, wings and tail unit, similar to those that had been designed for the P-47 to avoid confusion with the Fw 190. Problems with the guns persisted until a remedy was introduced in the form of modifications to the ammunition belts.

At the end of 1943, the Mustang was available but not in significant numbers; much work was being done to hone it for reliable long-range escort work, including fitting the necessary feed system for the extra wing tanks. The 354th Group, although

credited with eight kills by the end of the year, had lost eight pilots. In contrast, the 'old stagers' in their Thunderbolts continued to hog the headlines.

The Wolfpack had a field day on 11 December when the victory tally reached seventeen. Led by Gabreski, the 61st Squadron tore into a pack of Bf 110 *Zerstörers* before they could open fire on the rear of a box of bombers heading for Emden. As had happened before, the heavily-laden Bf 110s suffered grievously at the hands of the Thunderbolts, and fourteen of their number were brought down. Other enemy aircraft clashed with the 56th, which crossed the enemy coast in the vicinity of Texel Island at 11:51 hr.

In battle formation at 30,000 ft, the group's three squadrons were in line abreast with the 61st on the left flank, the 63rd in the centre and the 62nd on the right flank. Both flanking squadrons had Yellow Flights acting as scouts. In the Zuider Zee area up to twelve Bf 109s were seen approaching the group at 35,000 ft, up-sun from the 62nd. These aircraft launched attacks on the squadron in elements of two-three machines and all but Blue Flight engaged them, en route to their rendevouz with the bombers.

While Blue Flight continued to the R/V, the 62nd's other three Flights were forced to patrol Leeuwarden to the limit of their endurance, the earlier combat having made them short of fuel. The 61st and 63rd Squadrons picked up the B-17s north of Wangerooge Island and Essen-Hugh area respectively, flying at

Early morning mist clears at Bassingbourn, Cambs, to reveal P-38Hs of the 338th FS, 55th FG preparing to leave the 91st BGs base on 12 December 1943. Note the groundcrewman with the chequered flag waiting to wave the Lightnings away (USAF).

30,000 ft. Thus 31 Thunderbolts — sixteen from the 61st, four from the 62nd and eleven from the 63rd — shepherded the Fortresses to Emden. The 61st lost two aircraft when Lieutenants Strand and Kruer collided during combat which took the fighters down from 27,000 ft. Varying sizes of enemy formation were seen — one of up to 100 aircraft. The Luftwaffe tactics were to send two or three aircraft down to attack under a top cover, the interceptors then zoom-climbing to change places with the top cover, aided by ground jamming of US radio transmissions.

Such occurrences were reported as fully as possible by bomber crews and fighter pilots at mission debriefings and the details analysed by qualified personnel in order for comprehensive dossiers on the enemy to be made up for distribution to 8th Air Force units. One of these appeared in late 1943. Entitled *German Fighter Tactics against Flying Fortresses*, the document was the result of over 2,500 separate encounters over a period of six months. Illustrated by diagrams, it contained details of thirteen different attack approaches to typical six-ship elements of B-17s, although it stressed that the Luftwaffe was likely not to conform directly to what was in the manual — these were the most consistent interception paths witnessed by bomber crews and confirmed by escorting fighter pilots. For their part, German fighter pilots studied their own notes and devised the kind of tactics all too many bomber crews could confirm as extremely effective.

As the year 1943 drew to a close, however, the picture was about to change; reports on the Mustang were encouraging, the 8th was about to receive more Thunderbolt groups, and the P-38 was continuing to build up combat hours — only time would tell how useful a twin-engined fighter would actually be. Nobody doubted that the aircraft could get to Germany but the pro-Lightning lobby was offset by an equally vociferous group of doubters. There were few things more likely to shake up an inexperienced pilot than a group commander who made no secret of the fact that he would far rather be flying missions in an aircraft other than a P-38. Personnel of some of the squadrons flying the aircraft were undoubtedly less than correct in this respect, as reflected in notes individual pilots made at the time. One confided to his diary that 'leadership is definitely lacking'.

In mid-1943, Lockheed production was modest in comparison to what it would be eight months hence: the AAF accepted 1,111 P-38s in the five months August to December 1943 and by no means were all these fighters, as photographic reconnaissance F-5s were equally in demand. This figure compares with 2,634 P-47s, the majority of which were earmarked for the 8th. In fact AAF P-38 acceptances were approximately half those for the P-47 for the full year 1943 (2,213 as against 4,426) and only a little over

half in 1944 (4,186 and 7,036).

It can therefore be seen that the relatively few P-38s which saw service in the UK were at some disadvantage, particularly as Lockheed was then planning a more efficient method of 'breaking down' the Lightning into more manageable sub-assemblies and was gearing up to build only P-38s rather than diversify its efforts into other types, as had previously been the case. The P-38 itself was also undergoing a significant degree of modification and the assembly lines were changing over from the H to J model. More powerful Allison F-15 and F-17 engines were fitted — which necessitated an entirely new system of cooling if the old bugbear of detonation/pre-ignition was to be eliminated. The Lightning improvement programme also required completely redesigned Prestone coolant scoops on the tail booms to give improved flow characteristics and resulted in a fatter, more egg-shaped scoop. These, together with the P-40-type 'chin' intercoolers incorporating core-type radiators and numerous less-obvious changes, turned the P-38 into an excellent aircraft.

Lockheed pushed through these changes with all speed, but any interruption in production results in delays in deliveries to operational units even for a limited time, and the 8th AF groups were obliged to fly their first Lightning missions with the P-38H. Consequently a successful escort mission was very much in the hands of the individual pilot acting in accordance with his understanding of the complexities and characteristics of his aircraft, particularly its engines, and at least a basic knowledge of not only what could go wrong, but why. A significant degree of 'retraining' was necessary to fit a man for combat in the ETO and it is a fact that flying training in the USA during World War 2 often left a lot to be desired. A man who could competently handle a PT-19 or T-6 trainer and make a fair showing at the controls of a clapped-out P-39 in glorious weather with unlimited visibility could hardly be expected to master a highly temperamental machine in weather conditions which would have daunted even the most reckless flyer in peacetime — and with people trying to kill him while he was trying to do so. Small wonder that the Lightning was the subject of so many incidents and accidents attributable to technical failure, but in many cases this was aggravated by pilot inexperience.

Lockheed monitored the reports from the ETO and tried its best to re-educate the young Army flyers, many of whom were abusing the product to a degree that almost guaranteed failure. One reason was that training had taught them to use high rpm and low manifold pressure. They thought that if jumped they would be in a better position if already at high revs. With the P-38, the opposite was true — low rpm and high boost gave a higher turbocharger speed. With the turbo running, an increase in rpm gave the desired power.

Lockheed issued instructions to pilots to stop cruising at 2,600, 2,800 and even 3,000 rpm and devised a 'tender loving care for your Allisons' guide: 'Use 2,300 rpm and 36 in as the maximum for auto lean and cruise conditions. In reducing power from this setting, reduce ½ in to 1 in for each 100 rpm; for going above this setting, put your mixture in auto rich and increase the manifold pressure 2 in for each 100 rpm.' Even with these precautions, the notorious European weather could, and all too often did, foul things up. Cold and damp air would congeal lubricants in turbocharger regulators and force the waste gates closed; if that happened the manifold pressure rose and could eventually lead to a blown engine. Another problem was that the intercoolers separated the lead from the gasoline, causing detonations in the engine which could cause the

generators to fail. This in turn led to loss of propeller control or complete engine failure.

Experienced crew chiefs did their bit to back up the Lockheed advisory notes and it was said, rightly, that a good ground crew could almost perform miracles of repair and maintenance on sick airframes or engines — but it was not, of course, the ground crew who took the aircraft into action. A thoughtless action on the part of a pilot in the heat of battle could undo all the good work done on the base. Equally, nobody would deny that the exact circumstances of air action could never be preplanned — the pilots alone were in the front line.

In the early days before European combat had highlighted the drawbacks in it, the P-38 was *the* hot ship. There was often fierce pride in being able to fly what was widely regarded as one of the Army's best aircraft — there was no reason to believe otherwise in the autumn of 1943. And quite a number of pilots in the 55th and 20th Groups had previously seen action in the Pacific theatres, some of them from the cockpit of a P-38 — they especially were the ones whose pride was in danger of taking the biggest knock.

Even Thunderbolt men could appreciate the big Lockheed's undeniable advantages — two engines were good for starters. If one failed the Lightning

With the earlier models proving less than capable of handling escort from England, VIII FC eagerly awaited the improved P-38J. This scene, on 15 February 1944, shows AAF technicians checking partially dismantled J models after unloading from ships (Fox Photos).

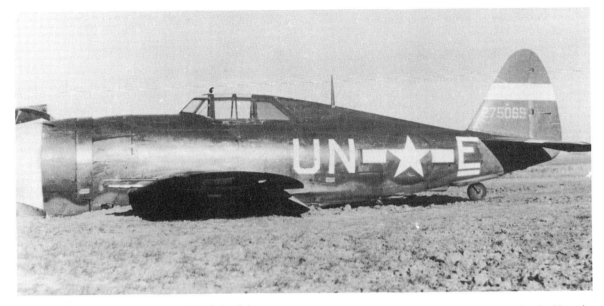

pilot could make it home, couldn't he? And the guns. No other 8th AF fighter had such heavy armament and it was the first (and only) one to provide the destructive power of cannon for US fighters in the ETO. Subsequently the cannon was not always installed in operational P-38s, the reliability of the .50 cal machine-gun being found to be effective enough, and considerably lighter.

One man who boldly ventured an opinion of the P-38 vis-a-vis other fighters in the ETO was the 20th Group's first boss, Colonel Barton M. Russell: 'I'll take the Lightning any day. The Spitfire? Not enough airplane!' Bold indeed! Major David McGovern, CO of the group's 55th Squadron, endorsed this with a comment on the P-38's ease of handling in the air — 'A Link trainer between two P-40s'.

Irrespective of the level of experience of individual fighter pilots posted to the USAAF in England, there was a general feeling that they were in the front line and up against the world's best in the Luftwaffe. Those who had previously seen combat against the Japanese were scathing about America's enemy from the other side of the Pacific. This attitude had a lot to do with Japan's action at Pearl Harbor — but those who had seen how the Japanese waged war were sickened. It was, to quote one fighter pilot, 'more personal'.

The debacle in the Pacific in the early months of 1942 had bred a burning desire to strike back at the Japanese — after the Germans were beaten. Pilots also felt the Oriental enemy to be a far easier

As the 8th AF offensive built up bellied-in American aircraft with varying degrees of damage became a familiar sight in England. This P-47D, 42-75069, was one, it being the second UN-E in the 63rd FS at the time of the crash, as indicated by the underlined individual code letter.

adversary than his Luftwaffe counterpart. The war in the ETO was more detached, more a job to be done; rarely was there any smouldering desire for revenge. Also, the British trait of playing down the cool, professional job the RAF had and was doing, helped put the American attitude to the European war in perspective, in a less emotional light. Charley London summed it up in eleven words: 'Whipping Germany is business; whipping Japan is going to be fun'.

Not that emotion did not play its part. Few fighter pilots were left unmoved if they saw German aircraft hacking down a crippled heavy bomber, as frequently occurred, and the loss of comrades was a bitter blow, whatever the circumstances. But in essence the 8th Air Force's fighter pilots went into action with innate confidence, faith in their ability and their equipment and any feeling of gross over-confidence was soon dispelled once the quality of the enemy was a known factor. Pilots knew that an ETO kill was invariably hard-won, particularly during 1943, when the enemy reached a zenith in numbers of skilled pilots available for fighter combat. Americans quickly realized that to beat the Germans was to beat the best. And they all knew that beating the Germans was the priority job.

6　No quarter

Under the agreed goals of the Combined Bomber Offensive, the plan which blueprinted the future course of Allied strategic air attacks on Germany, a primary requirement was for the RAF and USAAF to ensure that the invasion of Europe could go ahead without prohibitive casualties. The origins of the CBO were laid early in the war, given substance at the Casablanca Conference of January 1943 and became policy following a directive from the Combined Chiefs of Staff on 10 June 1943.

The CBO did little more than put an official stamp on the strategic bombing campaigns then being conducted by the RAF at night and the 8th and 12th Air Forces by day. But what it *did* do was shift the list of priority targets, which had to be all but neutralized for D-Day to succeed; consequently the reduction of the Luftwaffe to the point where it could not constitute a threat became the most important immediate objective. This was the crux of the directive, codenamed Pointblank. Fortunately for the timescale laid down for the invasion, the 8th Air Force was ready to renew the offensive against targets in Germany with much more confidence and strength than it had had in the autumn of 1943. Early in the new year General Kepner deliberated on the air combat situation; to meet the criteria of the CBO, some fundamental changes were necessary. Hap Arnold's new year message to his field commanders was to the point — they should make every effort to 'Destroy the enemy air force wherever you find them, in the air, on the ground and in the factories.'

Kepner's compliance with the message was only possible if the Luftwaffe was sought out — never mind the air victories when it chose to put in an appearance; never mind fighting on the enemy's terms when *he* called the tune; it was too late for that now. The 8th Air Force, together with a new strategic air force in the Mediterranean, had to become a bludgeon not a rapier if the Allied cause was to prevail on 6 June.

By November 1943 the peak inventory of the P-47s was reached with 1,200 examples on charge both with operational squadrons and at depots. Thereafter the number gradually declined as VIII FC converted all but one group to the P-51. But first the P-47 development programme bore fruit in terms of even longer range capability. Underwing racks developed for the D model were capable of accommodating the 108-gal cigar-shaped tank which would not fit under the belly due to lack of ground clearance at the point where the shackles were located. Wing racks solved the P-47's range problem almost overnight — but in operation it was found that a 'flat' 150-gal capacity tank was adequate. This could be attached to the belly shackles and, as Thunderbolts went increasingly over to ground attack, the wing racks were utilized mainly for a range of fragmentation, GP or HE bombs.

At the turn of the year the Thunderbolt was also given a boost in engine power through the availability of water-injection, and the paddle blade propeller. Despite some initial teething troubles the latter improved the rate of climb significantly and the P-47 was no longer at some disadvantage at heights below 15,000 ft; water injection provided up to 300 more horsepower.

Escort duty underwent some changes at this time with the introduction of a relay system. It was decided in January 1944 that fighters would no longer fly to a predetermined rendezvous and cover particular elements of the bomber force, but patrol areas along the whole of the bombers' route. Each group's position in the relay was determined by the aircraft it flew — the P-38s and (eventually) P-51s went up to the actual targets while the shorter range Thunderbolts were strung out along the route, providing penetration support, with all three supporting the bombers' withdrawal routes.

Throughout January the weather stayed so bad that only eleven missions were flown, one to Frankfurt on the 29th nevertheless bringing American fighters more victories. It was a day particularly pleasing to Captain Lindol F. Graham of the 20th Group, who shot down one Fw 190 attacking bombers on the way into the target. On return Graham's P-38 despatched two more to make him an ace. Closing in from 800 yd, he opened fire at 75 yd, the withering cone of fire being sufficient to explode both the German fighters.

The duo of George Preddy and Bill Whisner was still working well out of Bodney, although for them the 29 January mission was to bring its share of drama. Preddy's encounter report tells the story of that mission as seen from his cockpit:

'I was leading Crown Prince Yellow Flight and we were escorting two boxes of bombers. The Group leader called for everybody out and I started to join him when my number two man, Whisner, called back that the bombers were being attacked. I turned back coming in behind the bombers and saw an Fw 190 below and behind them. Whisner had started a bounce on another enemy aircraft so I went down on this '190.

'He went into a steep dive and I closed to about 400 yd and started firing. I was closing rapidly and saw a few hits and a little smoke before I broke off. I lost the enemy aircraft momentarily but picked him up again on my left at about 4,000 ft. I started after him and he made a steep turn to the left. I turned with him and started firing at 300 yd and 60 degrees deflection. He straightened out and started down at about 45 degrees. I got a good long burst at 300 yd and saw hits all over the ship. The engine was evidently knocked out as I closed very rapidly after that. The last I saw of him he was at 1,500 ft going down at an increasing angle to the left.'

Heading home with the fuel in their tanks a little too low for comfort, Preddy and Whisner crossed the coast in the vicinity of Calais. Flak opened up and hit Preddy's Thunderbolt, which began to smoke. Calling a Mayday, Preddy hit the silk as his engine quit at 2,000 ft. The emergency call had been picked up by air-sea rescue, however, and an RAF Walrus came puttering in to pluck him from the Channel, the waters of which are not the warmest place to be on a late January afternoon. Back home, Preddy filed his claim for one Fw 190 destroyed.

As mentioned, the early Mustangs were prone to gun stoppages which, for a time, gave pilots and armourers alike considerable headaches. But malfunctioning .50s did not prevent a superb display of flying skill and determination on the part of Major James Howard, CO of the 354th group, on the Oschersleben/Halberstadt mission of 11 January. Howard, separated from his group, came upon a gaggle of Bf 110s positioning to attack the bombers. Wading into the *Zerstörers* he shot down six while his unreliable guns gradually stopped until only one would fire. Howard's courageous act earned him the Medal of Honor, the only such award made to a US fighter pilot in Europe. Overall, the 354th had a good day's hunting, and received credit for a total of sixteen, while the 56th bagged ten.

January saw the 20th and 55th continuing their 'war on two fronts' battling the weather and the Luftwaffe, definitely in that order, in their P-38s. Colonel Jack S. Jenkins, CO of the 55th at the time, submitted a comprehensive report on the P-38 to 67th Fighter Wing. In part it stated: '. . . it is the opinion of the experienced pilots in the Lightning groups that with favourable — or at least not unfavourable — winds, we can successfully execute a target cover mission to coastal targets, such as Kiel, or Bordeaux, each some 400 miles from the English coast. However, we take a dim view of doing target support at a greater distance than our maximum calculated range if the target is well inland and enemy superiority is certain'.

There was indeed widespread criticism when Lightnings were expected to remain in the target area

A P-38J-10, 42-67757, on the strength of the 55th Group's 38th Squadron early in 1944. Although the J model offered some improvements, the modification programme did not go far enough for prevailing ETO conditions.

for twenty minutes, during which fuel was drawn from that remaining in the external tanks, each of 165-gal capacity. It was seen that out of a total of up to 630 gal carried, the allowance of 107 gal burned in twenty minutes of combat was unrealistic — this figure represented fifteen percent of the P-38H's total tankage. By comparison a P-47 would burn 80 gal during twenty minutes' combat. Commanders allowed 40 gal for take off and landing using internal tanks, leaving only 260 gal for the flight to and from the target area including orbiting and combat. But with just 153 gal left the returning P-38 pilot could not afford to have to fight en route home — a situation he could hardly control. Also, had he been jumped earlier than the 'ideal' time for him to release his external tanks, the whole fuel consumption chart became fictitious. Other factors eroded fuel faster than anticipated, including extra drag induced by damage; leaking tanks; high power settings especially in a climb, and, as indicated by Colonel Jenkins, headwinds.

Despite its critics, its thirsty Allison 'time bomb' engines and its inability to stay aloft on a single engine long enough for many a damaged aircraft to get back to base (as some of the pilots had believed), the P-38 could never be accused of being a basically unsound design. Probably more than a great many other fighters, each P-38 varied in individual characteristics, as did its engines. There were plenty of examples of untroubled combat sorties, but they tended perhaps to rely heavily on the pilot's deep understanding of the machine he was flying and at the same time treating it with respect. This requirement to 'take it easy' was not in all the pilots — it was probably unrealistic to expect it to be.

It came to be seen then that the P-38 possessed serious drawbacks in the task it was assigned to do. Even without a sign of the enemy, pilots became increasingly frustrated trying at the same time to shepherd their charges, watch for any threat — and more often than they liked attempt unsuccessfully to forget that a change in engine note could herald a long glide to the ground and at best, incarceration in a prison camp for the rest of the war. Single-engined P-38s were not renowned for their ability to stay aloft for long, as the remaining healthy engine would often prove unable to take the added strain. Such manifestations soon drained away enthusiasm for the Lockheed fighter in the minds of 8th AF planners, although Lightning pilots themselves did their best in very trying circumstances. Not the least of these was the freezing, debilitating cold, it not being uncommon for air temperatures above 25,000 ft to drop to − 30°C. So bad did the damp, all pervading low temperatures become that they brought a dangerous side effect. Cold put a mental straitjacket on the pilot

which could sap his awareness to the point where he became a potentially easy victim for a prowling German fighter. And unlike his American adversary, the Luftwaffe pilot had absolutely no doubt about the nationality of his quarry, for the P-38 was one of the most universally recognisable aircraft of the war.

This fact worked for as well as against the P-38 pilot; while aircraft recognition was not the strongest point of all bomber crews' training, there were few who mistook the Lightning for anything else. *Any* single-engined fighter could be the enemy before it closed enough for the bomber gunners to make positive identification, but the twin-boomed Lightning was definitely 'friendly'.

Lightning pilots who had occasion to put down at bomber bases found themselves held in high regard, irrespective of any shortcomings in their aircraft. Almost to the point of embarrassment, they were fêted by the bomber boys. One factor that brought about this regard was to a certain extent due to the P-38's troublesome performance. It was far safer for a fighter with a malfunction to seek the protection of the massed guns of a bomber formation than risk a lone foray across enemy territory at half power or less. While close escort had sometimes to be interpreted too literally for their liking by some P-38 pilots, the bomber crews' enthusiasm for the aircraft never waned.

Colonel Russell of the 20th emphasized the B-17 crews' affection for the close escort his pilots provided when he said, 'I've talked a lot to these Fortress fellas, and they sure are glad to see us over here with the Lightnings. Guess its about the first time I ever did see a bomber outfit glad to see fighters.'

★   ★   ★

In order to comply with Arnold's directive, VIII Fighter Command ordered that the strafing of Luftwaffe aerodromes be intensified and become not only an integral part of escort missions but be broadened under a programme of tailor-made ground attack operations. Providing that the primary escort requirement was met Kepner knew that he could step up the war of attrition against the Luftwaffe. Fighter and fighter-bomber attacks would invariably catch aircraft at their most vulnerable while refuelling, rearming and under maintenance. And not only would more enemy fighters be crippled on the ground, but necessary support facilities, personnel and installations be put out of action. With more groups promised for his command the 8th AF fighter chief estimated that he could spare a proportion of the Thunderbolt and Lightning squadrons for ground attack work in the six months or so before the 'second front' in Europe was opened.

Continual improvements were made to both the P-38 and P-47 to fit them better to the operational requirements of the ETO.

By January 1944 8th AF squadrons had received P-38Js which, with their additional 110-gal wing leading edge tanks (achieved by the relocation of the intercooler intakes to 'chin' intakes below the spinners) were far more useful for escort work than earlier models. But the problems of their Allison engines persisted, and cockpit heating had not improved. Pilots subsequently obtained supplies of RAF electrically-heated flight suits which alleviated the latter problem to some extent, although little it seemed could be done to overcome the engine malfunctions which were directly attributable to extreme cold at altitude.

The lengthy Thunderbolt improvement programme extended to many minor items which were incorporated during 100 hr inspections, although it was rare for any one machine to have them all. Base engineering units could only handle so much work on a busy fighter station and the longer it took to modify all the older aircraft in inventory the more likely it became that not only would the group receive newer aircraft incorporating the latest series of modifications, but that the whole programme would be overtaken by re-equipment with the P-51.

Base personnel also had cause to resort frequently to the spray gun; coloured group markings replaced the existing nose and tail recognition bands; there were directives such as that in late 1943 to the effect that Thunderbolt interiors were to be finished in dull black and, from January, P-38s were to be identified by geometric symbols on each outer vertical tail surface, these corresponding with an individual aircraft letter on each inner surface. Overall paintwork was equally subject to revision: on 13 February 1944 overseas AAF units were notified that from that date, camouflage finish would no longer be applied at the factories.

Natural metal finish, while generally unembellished in 8th AF bomber units, was not accepted so readily by the fighter groups. It was widely felt with some justification that the expanding tactical role demanded a degree of camouflage, at least on the upper surfaces so that strafing fighters might hide their presence from enemy aircraft which happened to be flying above them. If only seconds were thus gained from the use of such paintwork, certain group commanders wanted that advantage — it seemed throughout the lifetime of the 8th, that whatever was done at home under the heading of 'improvements', ETO requirements were at variance in some respects, leading inevitably to more work for the long-suffering ground crews.

Looking to its future requirements, VIII Fighter Command was well aware of the merit of standardization of the aircraft it operated. General Kepner was among those who realized that his maintenance echelons — not to mention his operational efficiency — would benefit from re-equipment with just one type, namely the P-51. The immediate need was for the 8th to get the 354th under its permanent control and as soon as possible reverse the decision to have new Mustangs issued to 9th AF squadrons. In the meantime, the 354th built on its early experience by remaining under the control of the 8th.

In many respects, the Mustang was well named; pilots new to the type were warned that undue care could lead them into a potentially dangerous situation with an aircraft that did not take kindly to being flown at anything less than maximum speed — like the wiry wild horse of the north American prairies after which it was named, the aircraft took some taming. The result of the marriage of the Rolls-Royce Merlin engine to the P-51 airframe was aptly described in Robert Gruenhagen's book *Mustang*: comparing the characteristics of the new powerplant in relation to the Allison V-1710, Gruenhagen said:

'The Allison was a smooth running engine over all ranges of power settings and when properly tuned the V-1710 was a reliable, worthy engine. The Merlin, in contrast, gasped for air at any power setting below barometric and lurched in the mounts whenever a deceleration or power increase was called for. The cooler outside air provided a firecracker noise when drawn across the exhaust valves and into the combustion chamber during deceleration. The noise was accompanied by a galloping rhythm as the carburettor idle system strove for the right mixture settings at lower power. When idle speed was finally stabilized, the engine would smooth out and snort vigorously from each exhaust stack as the cylinders fired in protest at the reduced speed.

'The Merlin was a high performance powerplant and when unleashed to full throttle it rounded out the Mustang namesake to provide the ultimate in response and performance to the fighter. The sound of the Merlin was an unforgettable event.

'The location of the exhaust stacks provided the pilot with an ear-shattering noise at full power and an individual report from each cylinder during cruise power settings. During deceleration on landing pitch out, the Merlin would provide a series of reports and a corresponding shudder throughout the airplane in a cadence comparable to a flaming string of firecrackers.'

In the light of such skittish behaviour, new pilots were thoroughly schooled in the P-51B's power response and capabilities of its Merlin engine — which with 200 more horsepower for take off and resultant increase in torque, created a degree of

A great many British and American aircraft supported the three fighter and two bomber types that constituted the 8th's striking force. Although not used on operations they performed a variety of useful tasks. The 8th had but one P-40E in 1943 after one other crashed in 1942, this being 41-35934 used by VIII BC for high speed liaison by the HQ Flight. This photo is believed to show that aircraft, although the serial is not apparent (via George Porter).

directional instability that could be hard to control. The problem was that North American had not modified the airframe to soak up the additional torque; the four-bladed propeller helped but it was seen to be insufficient — indeed the new propeller itself caused a sidewash and later instability during accelerated manoeuvres that was never completely overcome. These were characteristics that pilots nevertheless learned to allow for, and there was no question that the P-51B was superior to most other Allied fighters. More importantly, it was equal to if not better than every enemy fighter type it was likely to encounter at the time of its combat debut.

The need to build up pilot experience on the Mustang was the main reason the 9th Air Force was reluctant to part with the 354th — if this was the machine which the new tactical air force was being asked to fly on ground support operations, it had to be thoroughly mastered first. But at that time it cannot have been a totally unknown fact that a liquid-cooled engine was more prone to lasting damage from ground fire than one which was air-cooled, and this was undoubtedly stressed when the 8th AF further pressed for priority in supplies of early production

Merlin Mustangs. This and other relevant observations were ultimately to bear fruit.

By far the most serious of the P-51B's teething troubles was the incidence of gun jamming. Jim Howard's epic air battle with the Bf 110s was perhaps an extreme example of gradually dwindling firepower, but it was by no means unique. As the pioneer Mustang group, the 354th was also cast in the role of pioneer trouble shooter and to its ground crews go credit for tracing the root cause of the problem, which was misalignment of rounds in relation to the breech bore of the side-angled M-2 machine-guns as they were fed from the ammunition storage tanks. The 354th's armourers found that locating a Martin electric ammunition booster on the gun feed chute prevented 'pulling' of the traced rounds when the load on the trace exceeded 17 lb. The booster cut in when the load reached 15 lb and all but eliminated the problem.

Gun troubles were also aggravated by a common 8th AF bugbear — cold. Freezing breech assemblies were traced to instructions to pilots not to switch on gun heaters until entering the combat area. Although the Mustang's guns were charged in flight, they could not be recharged once a jam had occurred. This problem was solved more or less by simultaneously switching on the heaters when the guns were charged but no in-flight gun recharging or clearance system was introduced during the P-51's lifetime.

Pilots, labouring as they were under technical deficiencies of their aircraft, nevertheless appreciated the qualities of the P-51B, particularly its ability to fly to

the most distant of targets with adequate fuel reserves for combat. Negotiations for the 8th to get its own Mustangs finally turned into reality at the end of January 1944 when the second group assigned to the 9th Air Force was transferred to the 8th. This was the 357th, which had arrived at Raydon, Suffolk on 4 December. A new airfield (AAF Station 157), Raydon was formally opened on the 7th by which time it was only partially finished. It could at least operate aircraft and a training programme was initiated without delay. The same day the group was assigned to the 70th Fighter Wing of the 9th AF. This news had not exactly been welcomed in Kepner's headquarters and after a few more weeks agreement was reached whereby the new Mustang group would be exchanged for the 358th, the P-47 outfit which had already flown a number of missions with the 8th. Apparently though, nobody thought to inform the personnel of the respective groups about this arrangement and it took a day or so to get clarification from

The turning point. North American's superlative P-51B gave VIII FC a new edge over the Germans — but it took some time to convince AAF high command that this was not just another ground-attack refinement of the A-36 and earlier P-51s. Low over the water in this view is Cisco of the 354th Group — which had the right aircraft in the wrong air force!

headquarters. It was then to take a few more days to reorganize the 357th and instigate a move of base, to Leiston. Also in Suffolk, this was the former base of the 358th, although the facilities were not exactly superior — 'from one mudhole to another' was the comment made at the time.

By 22 January, however, the 357th had fifteen P-51Bs and on 30 January it was officially the first Mustang group in the 8th. Inventory had risen to 74 aircraft by 5 February. This did not go down very well with the pilots of the 4th Group who belonged to what they viewed as the premier fighter outfit in the 8th. Don Blakeslee cajoled, pleaded and argued with those in authority to get the Eagles the P-51s they desired. Having flown this 'second generation Spit-fire' on a number of missions, Blakeslee impatiently awaited the arrival of the first Mustangs at Debden when it was confirmed that the 4th would indeed be the next group to get them. The great day was 14th February. Three P-51Bs were provided, one for each squadron to use for conversion training.

Not wishing to have any stand-down period while the pilots became familiar with their new mounts, Blakeslee asked that everyone should put in Mustang conversion time between Thunderbolt missions to speed the process. So keen was the 4th's CO to be declared operational with the P-51 that he made it clear that any man who felt this was asking too much could put in for a transfer to another group. There were few takers. Fortunately there was a period of inactivity coming up. The weather was still bad and the 4th did not fly operationally for four days between 15 and 20 February. It proved nonetheless to be an exciting period, all told. The group had drawn a dive bombing mission combined with a fighter sweep on the day after the Mustangs arrived and, although this was abortive due to weather, the 20 February mission proved more fruitful when Jim Goodson's with-drawal support aircraft got among rocket-carrying Fw 190s and shot down four for the loss of the P-47 flown by Richard Reed, who was killed.

The day previously the Luftwaffe had put in one of its rare appearances over England, an estimated thirty to forty enemy aircraft seeking Debden as their target. Fortunately the raiders missed the airfield and dumped their incendiaries into woods a good half mile away.

The 357th became operational and on 11 February flew its camouflaged P-51Bs on a short penetration sweep to Rouen, led by Jim Howard of the 354th. Some pilots had previously joined the pioneer group

for a single mission and the 357th had opened its account with the Luftwaffe with a damaged claim. On the 12th and 13th Don Blakeslee led the 357th, both missions being uneventful apart from a number of early returns and some inaccurate light flak. One pilot again tested the reactions of the British air-sea rescue service by baling out into the North Sea.

Along with the changes at fighter group level, 8th AF headquarters itself underwent revision in the early months of 1944. General Ira Eaker transferred to the Mediterranean theatre and Lieutenant General Jimmy Doolittle took over 8th Air Force direction on the same day, 6 January. In mid-February 8th AF headquarters was transferred to High Wycombe, Buckinghamshire, the remaining HQ at Bushey Park becoming US Strategic Air Forces in Europe (USSTAF) under General Carl Spaatz.

As of 1 January the 8th boasted 37 operational groups to undertake the offensive outlined in the Pointblank directive, and this figure would gradually increase as new fighter and bomber groups arrived in England. The American force was then opposed by 38 full *Gruppen* of German fighters, plus eleven *Stabsstaffeln*, a single *Stürmstaffel* and the *Jagdgruppe zbV,* a special unit tasked with bomber attack.

On 21 January the eleventh fighter group assigned to the 8th was declared operational, one day after initiating the so-called 'Big Week'. Flying from Bottisham, Cambridgeshire, the 361st was the last Thunderbolt-equipped group to arrive in the ETO, under the command of Colonel Thomas J.J. Christian, Jr. The group was part of a 628-fighter force which supported bomber operations in the Cherbourg and Pas de Calais areas; there was little time for the 361st to fly shakedown missions as the pace of operations was quickening.

Appropriately named P-51 pictured at Leiston (via Paul Coggan).

7 Ace race

As the winter of 1943/44 gradually waned, the 8th AF fighter force went increasingly over to the offensive, seeking out the enemy on the ground. By February, there had already been a number of individual strafing attacks and some small-scale squadron-strength forays against Luftwaffe airfields, all of which had brought results — positive and negative. On the latter side was the loss of experienced pilots whose leadership and inspiration were missed by the groups to which they belonged. But by early 1944 the AAF training programmes had been strengthened by the return of veterans of all war theatres able to pass on their practical tips to instructors, and in the ETO particularly there were then enough seasoned fighter pilots to rapidly fill the ranks of those who went down.

One of the first to be shot down in 1944 was Walter Beckham of the 353rd, the second highest scoring ace in the theatre. Having achieved his sixteenth victory on 3 February, Beckham was neck and neck with Walker Mahurin of the 56th. Then Mahurin jumped ahead by scoring two more kills on 8 February. On 22 February the 353rd was en route home from bomber support when Colonel Glenn Duncan initiated attacks on Ostheim airfield, then home to a Luftwaffe unit equipped with the Ju 88. A number of these had been spotted. Beckham led another formation down after Duncan's flight which had made its strafing run by the time the second group of Thunderbolts came screaming in. This was the most dangerous slot to have, as the defending gunners were often surprised by the first pass — but they were rarely caught napping by the second. There was usually enough time to sight the guns, judge the range and be ready for the next intrusion. This is exactly how the gunners got Beckham. His P-47D *Little Demon* took a burst under the engine, which promptly lost power. Managing to pull up to sufficient height, Beckham took to the silk.

The loss of Beckham was a sad blow particularly to Glenn Duncan, the two men having worked and flown together since before coming to England and both had been instrumental in evolving dive bombing techniques for the P-47. Using the standard gunsight Duncan and Beckham found that it was possible — despite considerable scepticism on the part of others — to dive the P-47 at near vertical angles without the bomb falling into the propeller arc.

Beckham subsequently related details of his bale-out with more than a touch of theatre: 'I may have been one of the first pilots to eject from a P-47. After sprinkling some parked planes with .50 calibres and departing the air base, smoke continued to pour from the engine cowling. I undid the seat belt and shoulder straps, ran back the canopy and hoped. When fire appeared under the rudder pedals, there was nothing to do but bale out. On trying to do so from a standing position, I couldn't budge. Perhaps a strap in the 'chute caught? The fire was growing. I sat back down in the seat and kicked the stick as hard as I could. It worked. The plane dived away, leaving me happily free. So, a kind of ejection. On to German prison camp for fourteen months.'

That same day the 353rd's Gordon B. Compton scored his first kill. There was nothing unusual about it — except that he had flown 130 operational hours before an enemy aircraft was trapped in his gunsight. Six days later Compton took up a P-47 for a test hop. On approach the aircraft caught fire and exploded. Compton managed to walk away from the ensuing crash but was hospitalized for two months. He returned to active duty and ended the war as an ace with 5½ kills to his credit and with 420 operational hours in his log book.

The first mission for the 357th Group was preceded by the moving in of the 8th's third Lightning group 24 hours before. This, the 364th, occupied Honington, Suffolk, for the duration of its stay in the ETO. Under the command of Lieutenant Colonel Frederick C. Grambo, the group put up its first mission on 2 March, being a component of the force of 589 fighters despatched in support of 481 B-17s and B-24s attacking various targets, mainly in the Frankfurt area. Although the freshman P-38 group made no claims, the 8th AF box score was 17(destroyed)-2(probable)-4(damaged) for the loss of four US fighters. The first mission was tempered with sadness as once again Fate singled out a group commanding officer before he had a chance to prove his unit in action. Flying with the 20th Group to gain combat experience, Lieutenant Colonel Grambo lost both engines of his P-38 and crashed to his death near Zwolle.

It came as little surprise to the other P-38 groups that the 364th had a hard time during its first weeks on operations. The Lightning's problems, combined with pilot inexperience, the weather and the enemy resulted in the loss of sixteen aircraft before March was out. A new CO, Colonel Roy W. Osborn, took over the group and was to steer it through the P-38 period and on to better things in the form of the P-51.

★   ★   ★

All through nearly two long and hard-fought years of war the 8th AF had planned for the day when it could announce that its bombers had successfully punched through the defences to hit the German capital. The first Berlin mission had been scheduled for the previous November but had not taken place. Inclement weather was foremost among the factors that prevented another try in 1943, but 3 March '44 appeared to offer another chance, with improved weather and a bomber force which was better protected. But once again the weather held things up. The mission did get underway and the force of 748 bombers had reached Schleswig-Holstein before responding to the recall order. Unusually heavy cloud and conspicuous contrail conditions, plus the fact that many bombers had consumed more than the usual amount of fuel during assembly, forced the mission to be abandoned. Most of the fighters heard the recall, but among those who did not were P-38s of the 55th Group led by Lieutenant Colonel Jack Jenkins in his *Texas Ranger IV*. Elsewhere, Don Blakeslee was having trouble keeping his aircraft together in dense cloud; the 4th had been selected to lead the Berlin show and when the bombers did not materialize the fighters turned for home, meeting a large force of enemy fighters while so doing. Combat under difficult conditions resulted in the 4th losing four of its own for only five kills.

Meanwhile Jack Jenkins groped his way to Berlin; although his charges were experiencing their almost routine spate of engine troubles there were no actual losses. Jenkins himself was nursing a sick Allison and at one point was forced to outrun fifteen enemy aircraft. Back at base, freezing cold and not a little fed up with the way the mission had turned out, Jenkins was surprised to find the Nuthampstead Lightnings famous. Thawed out after his gruelling sortie there was a flurry of press interest — the 8th Air Force had

flown over Berlin for the first time. It was not a great deal to shout about, as the 55th's pilots knew, although it was some compensation for the hard work they had put in on the P-38, and no-one could change the fact that the Lightning would henceforth be known as the first American fighter over Berlin. A record is a record.

The following day the Berlin mission was rescheduled, Blakeslee again leading the fighters. There were 770 of them to cover 502 Fortresses and Liberators, the 8th AF fighters being joined by five groups from the 9th AF. As expected the Luftwaffe rose to defend the Reich capital — but the outcome was not as had been hoped for by the Americans. In conditions just as bad as those of the previous day, the fighters lost 23 of their number, the worst casualties being suffered by the 363rd Group of the 9th. Only three groups, the 4th, 354th and 357th, reached Berlin.

Lieutenant Colonel Jack S. Jenkins standing with his P-38J 42-67825/ CG-J of the 38th FS, 55th Group. Texas Ranger IV *was the first US aircraft to fly over Berlin (USAF).*

In 48 hours' time the 8th was again to attack Berlin, a terrifying ordeal that was to end in the worst bomber loss the 8th ever suffered — 69 aircraft MIA. On the credit side the AAF fighters destroyed 81 enemy aircraft, just over twenty per cent of the 400 the Luftwaffe committed to defend the city. This number was estimated to be half the available fighter force in the west, and included night fighters.

Major Kit Carson, flying with the 367th Group, commented on Luftwaffe tactics during this operation:

'On the 6 March run, our group shot down twenty of the Luftwaffe interceptors without a loss. We were getting better. The enemy was still attacking in a "gaggle" of fighters, using hit and run tactics with the basic formation seeming to be two or three sticking together as a unit and going into a vertical dive from 25,000 ft, toward the deck, on the break-away.'

The phenomenal leap in enemy fighter kills was what Pointblank was all about. This was the way to whittle down the Luftwaffe prior to D-Day and further proof (if such was needed) of the lethal qualities of the P-51 even in the hands of relatively inexperienced pilots, such as those of the 357th. The Mustang force of 100 machines drawn from the 4th, 357th and 354th Groups, did better with its 43 kills than no less than 615 P-47s which knocked down 36. That did not in any way denigrate the Thunderbolt, but the fact remains that the North American fighter was quickly building up a reputation second to none and at the same time engendering a pilot loyalty that was not to wane for the duration of the war.

Its first five missions to the 'Big City' cost the AAF bomber force dearly: before March was out these raids alone had stricken 141 B-17s and B-24s from the unit rosters, plus 56 fighters. Berlin was, as the RAF also found, one of the most well-defended targets in Europe. But the 8th Air Force could justifiably point to its perhaps more tangible results, over and above bombs showered on targets within a vast urban metropolis which may or may not have succumbed totally to the rain of high explosive and incendiaries. The AAF fighters destroyed 168 enemy fighters in aerial combat, the vast majority on the 6 and 8 March raids, the last Berlin mission of the month taking place on the 22nd. While these day fighters and, more importantly, a percentage of their pilots, would not rise to challenge future AAF raids, the RAF could claim no similar satisfaction from the number of night fighters its heavy bombers managed to shoot down during its own 'Battle of Berlin'.

There again, three of the Berlin raids of March were not nearly so costly as the early ones, the one on the 22nd recording no fighter combats. It could not therefore be assumed that every strike on Berlin was going to be expensive in terms of lives and aircraft; time and again the Luftwaffe surprised the 8th AF with its widely varying degree of response to a threat to primary targets which on the face of it had to be defended at all costs.

On 8 March the fighters claimed 79 enemy aircraft. The Wolfpack emerged top dog, with 28 for five lost, beating its nearest rivals at Debden by a considerable margin. The Eagles came home with scores of sixteen for the loss of one. The combats took place at all heights up to 25,000 ft. LeRoy Schreiber, an eventual twelve-victory ace in the 56th, watched the battle unfold:

'About fifteen enemy aircraft came through the

bombers from the left in a frontal attack. These all hit the deck, chased by red-nosed Thunderbolts. I led my Flight against another group of about twenty Focke-Wulfs that had come through the bombers. About five or six bombers that had been hit were circling down with the crews baling out.'

Bob Johnson surprised three enemy fighters attacking a lone Fortress and also making runs on crewmen on parachutes.

'I attacked and ended up chasing two of them for some time, gaining rapidly. I could see their black smoke pour out. I gave a short burst at 50 yd and missed. I finally got a good burst at 3,000 ft altitude and one of them hit the ground in fire and smoke.'

Bud Mahurin's flight, covering the rearmost boxes of bombers, had not seen any action until it was almost time to turn for home. 'But we were reluctant to return without firing a shot, especially with all the shooting going on around us. I looked over the side of my ship at an aerodrome, to see an Fw 190 circling the field. We immediately started down to attack.'

Mahurin's aim was true. The Fw he had singled out crashed into a tree under the fire from his eight .50s. He climbed.

'As we pulled up from this attack we spotted an Me 110 which had taken off.' Donovan Smith, Mahurin's number three, made short work of this one, which 'slid into a forest and spread timber like falling matchsticks'.

'I saw a Ju 88 and went down on him. I closed very fast and hit him from 200 yd to point-blank range. The right engine caught on fire, the ship let down and exploded in a field.

'For the fourth and last time we passed over the aerodrome. Another Fw 190 was circling for a landing, and again we bounced. He saw us coming and started off right on the tree tops. Whenever he would come to a field he would drop down, pulling up only to go over the trees. Finally he pulled up to avoid some high tension wires and I was able to get in a good burst. I had expended all my ammunition and I broke off. The Jerry rolled over on his back and plowed into a field.'

The combats of March once again changed the table of top scoring aces in the 8th. After the 6 March Berlin show the scoreboard read as follows: Bob Johnson and Bud Mahurin had seventeen each for the 56th to boast the two top fighter pilots in the ETO in terms of aerial kills. Then came the 353rd's Glenn Duncan with fifteen, Francis Gabreski and Gerald Johnson each had fourteen; Hub Zemke counted eleven and Dave Schilling and Leroy Schreiber, ten. The 56th's predominance in aces was not entirely one-sided, as Duane Beeson of the 4th had been quietly getting on with the job of flying the P-47 to good effect and had fourteen kills at this time.

Don Blakeslee was singularly unimpressed by the 56th's record and the attendant press publicity. Not even when on the 8 March Berlin mission Bob Johnson raised his score to 21 to stand clear of the field did Blakeslee think that the revitalized 4th would not get its chance to even the score with the Mustang. He knew, as did every other astute group commander, that being in the right place at the right time usually made the difference between a good bag and nothing. Fortunes changed; it had happened before, it would happen again, perhaps sooner than he knew.

As the war progressed, the innovative fighter pilots of the 8th got more than a fair hearing for their ideas and techniques that would result in even more misery

Left *Purchased by War Bond subscription, 'Bud' Mahurin's P-47D-5 was lost on 27 March 1944. Mahurin evaded capture and returned to the UK.*

Right *Covering their aircraft in a cloak of anonymity had no attraction for the flamboyant pilots of the Wolfpack, as this photo shows. Originators of some of the wildest fighter schemes in the 8th Air Force, this 61st Squadron mix of razorback and bubble canopy models includes only one that comes anywhere near regulation markings — 42-29520/HV-P (IWM).*

Above *Duane Beeson on the wing of his P-51B Boise Bee, 43-6819/QP-B, 334th FS, 4th FG.*

Below *The energetic leader of VIII FC through its most critical period, William 'Bill' Kepner was no chairbound General. This Thunderbolt, 42-25637, was maintained by 2 Base Air Depot for his personal use (USAF).*

for the enemy. Colonel Glenn Duncan sought the ear of General Kepner with an idea which stemmed largely from the loss of Walter Beckham in February. The 353rd's CO reasoned that the highly dangerous business of ground strafing should be made as safe as possible for the attackers while meting out maximum hurt to the enemy. To make attacks more efficient, Duncan offered to form a special unit within his group. Composed of volunteers, this unit would become the 353rd's 'C' Group and be headed by Duncan.

The idea was highly agreeable to Kepner when he heard that its object was to become thoroughly familiar with the behaviour of the P-47 at low level, study the known defences and layout of the target and the surrounding terrain — and then go in and wreak maximum havoc, preferably in one pass. The last was stressed, as was the need to keep low after the strafing attack had been made. The special unit was composed of Duncan and sixteen pilots, one quartet each from the 353rd, 355th, 359th and 361st Groups, who became known as 'Bill's Buzz Boys', 'Bill' being the nickname of General Kepner.

Between 26 March and 12 April, these pilots honed their concept of the lightning surprise attack, carrying out a total of eight missions against airfields in France and Germany, river traffic, flak towers, locomotives and installations. The unit experimented with bombing attacks as well as gunnery,

using M4 fragmentation clusters. It was, however, found that guns did the most destruction — when the target could be clearly identified and ammunition used sparingly. Glenn Duncan's encounter report for an attack on 29 March highlighted some of the problems of making very high speed passes at zero feet. Fortunately such attacks appeared to give the German gunners their share of problems in judging the range and speed of attacking fighters:

'We began our dive from about 10,000 ft from out of the sun and hit zero feet about two miles from the field (Bramsche A/D). I pulled up to about 150 ft as I crossed my check point on the edge of the 'drome and began squirting a few bursts. No matter how hard I looked I could not see any E/A parked or hidden. The only thing of interest was a light flak tower on the north-west side of the field that shot to beat hell but couldn't figure the correct deflection for 400 mph on a P-47. We four pulled up to about 5,000 ft on the far side of the field and surveyed the situation. A little bit of flak followed us but was not too great a bother.'

Duncan then led his twelve fighters to Vechta A/D, which held numerous aircraft:

'Due to the close proximity of the 'drome and our position, I called to the rest of the flight and told them

Highest scoring ace of the 353rd Group, Colonel Glenn E. Duncan on the wing of one of his P-51Ds — named (as were his P-47s) Dove of Peace, serial number 44-14416.

to stay up and go around to the edge of the field as I was going down. I passed across the front of the hangar line and saw many twin-engine and single-engine aircraft parked on the 'drome. I lined up two of the twin engines and let go. The first one lit up quite well but never did blow up or catch fire while I was coming on it. The second one took quite a number of strikes and consequently caught fire. There were single-engines dispersed in a line across the field from these two, and I was able to pick up many of those in my sights and get a few hits on each. There were about five or six of the single-engines that I could see at the time. However it is very hard to pick out a great number of objects going along lickety split.'

Duncan pulled up and joined his flight again, dodging the flak that was by this time coming up quite heavily. But the German gunners still did not seem to be able to reach the circling Thunderbolts with 40 mm fire. They did, however, concentrate their aim on one machine, that of First Lieutenant Kenneth Chetwood — who, quite put out by this attention, promptly dived and blasted the flak tower.

Picking up a third aerodrome, at Twenthe/Enschede, Duncan's flight went in again:

'. . . a very likely target as a staff car was speeding across the end of it and there were several twin-engine and single-engine aircraft parked, clearly visible from our great range. I called for the flight to go

down and believe me, the boys were really flying good this day. They stayed together very well. We dove down to the deck and came across the 'drome in good four ship line abreast, each individual picking a likely target. The staff car caught quite a lot of .50-cal from both the man on my left and myself, at which time my guns ran dry.'

Duncan also spotted an Me 410 which would have been a good target had he had anything to shoot with, but the Flight turned for home at that point, with fuel running low. One pilot was forced to bale out over the sea to be rescued by ASR and Lieutenant Chetwood landed with a damaged wheel which gave him little problem.

Kepner himself put an end to the 'Buzz Boys' on 12 April, his message to them including a 'thank you' for the work in developing new fighter tactics. The results would be put to good use in larger scale strafing attacks in the future. The special strafing unit had not been sent out purely on ground attack operations, and most of these had been undertaken after the regular escort duty had been completed. After Big Week and Berlin, the bombers drew a series of long and short range targets with ports and airfields figuring prominently. Equally numerous were targets of opportunity although the primary was invariably a production centre of some kind important to the enemy war effort.

Fighter support for the late March-early April bomber strikes gave the Eagles a new lease of life in the aerial victory tables, the group finding repeated success during the period. During the latter part of March the 4th was able to claim a hundred kills and the 56th only ten under the arbitrary fortunes of war. Having all but ignored incursions into Berlin's

airspace on the 22nd, the Luftwaffe rose in force to defend Brunswick the following day — whereupon the well-placed Eagles despatched thirteen for no loss to themselves. Among the victims was Wolf-Dietrich Wilke, *Kommodore* of JG3, a 162-victory ace. His loss together with that of JG2's *Kommodore* Egon Mayer (102 kills) earlier in March, was a grim portent for the *Jagdverbände*, which had, as the AAF had anticipated, had one of its worst months of the war.

While individual Allied pilots' victories would never come anywhere near those of their opponents — many of whom had served continuously since the earliest days of the war — due to the rotation system, beating such men in air combat gave just cause for celebration. Actions against some of the world's best fighter pilots enhanced the reputation of the ETO as the toughest theatre there was. Records understandably remain sketchy as to exactly who shot down who in the confusing mêlée of a dogfight often involving fifty to a hundred aircraft at a time, and AAF pilots rarely knew at the time — or subsequently — whether they had scored against a novice or an *Experte*. Much depended on the circumstances of the combat but the days of the one-to-one dogfight were long since over. And even when a victory was scored, there were numerous instances of the 'half score' where more than one pilot fired at and hit the same aircraft. It was often hard to tell who had delivered the coup de grâce.

The American wingman system helped to provide supporting evidence of a victory claim, and to give two pilots a mutual second pair of eyes. The battles of March 1944 brought to the fore two pilots who practised this cooperation to the full — Gentile and Godfrey.

8 Watch on the wing

'It was not until 19 August 1942 that I got my first German planes, one Junkers 88 and a Focke-Wulf 190. That was Dieppe, at the time of the great raid on that port — the time our side was turned loose on the offensive, if only for a day.' Reviewing his combat career in the spring of 1944, Don Gentile had, along with other fighter pilots, 'sweated out' the build up of the 8th Air Force until it was better able to take the offensive.

'We prepared to take the offensive away from the Germans and then with the Thunderbolts, really started to go out and get it. The big bombers were the heavy guns in this phase of the war. Their job was to beat the German Air Force out of Western Europe, and our job was to keep the Germans from stopping them. In those days we flew close support for the bombers. When the German fighters came in on the bombers — not before — we turned into fighters and shot at them. As soon as an individual plane or a single formation broke off the attack, we hustled back to the bombers.

'The thing was, it was a limited offensive. We couldn't go all out. We had to peck and peck at them until they were weak enough to be trampled on. In those days I got some ''probables'' and some ''damaged''; we could not follow the enemy fighters past the point at which they broke off the attack. We had to climb back to the bombers to make sure they were not hit from another side. So we could not follow the ''smokers'' or the partially clobbered to see them crash, or if more shooting was needed, to do that and finish them off. The score of the whole group was low in those days and it stayed low. It was 2 April 1943 when the group quit Spitfires for Thunderbolts, and about June or July of that year when we started noting a kind of faltering in the Luftwaffe. The pecking of the bombers and ourselves was beginning to take effect.'

Gentile's backtrack on the gradual change in the enemy continued, 'It looked as if the time would soon come when we'd be turned loose to trample them down. But the German is a crafty foe and he began then one of those planned retreats of his. He took many of his planes out of France and Holland and Belgium, and there we were sitting in our Thunderbolts, unable to follow them. The Fortresses and Liberators barrelled right into Germany after the Luftwaffe. We could go along with them only so far and no further. The Luftwaffe just waited for the bombers to go past our sphere of action. Then they hit and didn't stop hitting until out bombers were back with us. Then the Luftwaffe strutted home like dogs which chase a marauder out of the front yard and are content to let it go at that.

'Meanwhile our home front was busy on the Mustang. With the Mustang there was no place for the Luftwaffe to retreat. That plane put the Huns right back up against the wall but we did not have enough fighter cover in the latter part of the last year [1943] and the early part of this [1944], to give anything but close support to the bombers.

'Fighter planes had to fly close support to our bombers, to protect one another and devote themselves to breaking off enemy attacks, but still could not follow through on the Hun making his getaway. This was the old pecking days over again. But this time there was this important difference — when we could get strong enough to start trampling, he would have no place to run. He would have to stand and fight. The time finally came for us in late February of this year. There was no more need to put up all our planes in close support of the bombers: there was no more need to keep the formation at any cost. We were sent out there to go and get and clobber the Nazis. If they wouldn't come up, we would go down against their ground guns and shoot them on the ground. Get them, that was the idea. Kill them, trample them down.

'It was this time I personally was ready for. I had been waiting to fly and flying was practically my whole life. In the two years of mixing it with the Germans I had learned a great many things that you can't learn in any but the hard way.

'Colonel Blakeslee's team became, in seven weeks of the happiest, craziest hayriding ever, the highest-scoring outfit in the whole league. In all this time of

Among the virtuosos of the P-51B was the 4th's Don Gentile, a pilot who quickly saw the new fighter's potential (IWM).

the rising and falling of the tide for us, the Luftwaffe had deteriorated steadily, but it has been a thing about which I have been slow to make up my mind. The Nazis all seemed like champs to me at first, but as I started to learn my business, I began to notice that some of them did not know their business as well as others.

'In recent days I have noticed more and more Huns who do not known their business. This may be because the older I get in this game the more critical I become and the easier it is for me to spot a boy who is green at the trade, worried, not sure of himself and on the defensive all the way. But I don't think that's the whole reason. I think it is true that the Luftwaffe consists more and more of new boys as the old hands get killed. However, there are still quite a lot of the old hands still around. And they are real hot shots. They know two things you need to know in this business: how to kill and how to keep from being killed. There is nothing defeatist about this attitude — nothing that I can notice anyway.

'So, by and large, I don't think this team I'm on

would have run up the score it has if things hadn't broken just right for it — if the bell hadn't rung to go all out at exactly the time when it was ripe to do just that. I know that's true in my case. I have a feeling now, looking back over the last few weeks, that all my life, everything I have done in it has gone to fit me to take advantage of the weeks between 20 February and 8 April 1944.'

By the latter date Don Gentile had claimed 30 air and ground victories (later adjusted to 27.8) to make him the leading ETO ace. Recently teamed with John T. Godfrey, the pilot from Piqua, Ohio, had his patience rewarded. Not only patience but a firm 'press on' attitude. There was, for example, the time when he was cornered over Paris on 14 January — at least the two Fw 190s who bounced him thought they had him cornered. Gentile, out of ammunition, described the incident as 'a pretty tight spot. As tight as I ever got in.'

With his aircraft taking hits Gentile's instincts took over. He made a turn and came head-on at his two adversaries, right into their line of fire. Unnerved and expecting an answering hail of bullets from the American's guns, the German pilots broke. Gentile took his chance and fled.

Such quick thinking and reflex action on the part of his comrade in arms were much admired by John Godfrey:

'It's his aggressiveness. He's got a split-second jump on any other fighter I ever saw. Your ordinary good flier sees a flock of Huns below him, and he counts them. He picks out the one in the rear and dives for his tail. Gentile sees a flock of Huns below, and he's after them at the same instant. He'll hit any one he can get to quickest. Reflexes, I guess. When it comes to the pinch, he's got a little something extra.'

The Gentile-Godfrey team came together by accident. By 6 March Godfrey had four kills in ten and a half months' service in the AAF. Three of these had been made with the Thunderbolt, one with the new P-51, at a time when his hours on the type were numbered in minutes — sixty to be precise. On the next Berlin mission the early afternoon sweep by the 4th brought Gentile and Godfrey together. In clear weather Gentile led a flight, with Godfrey taking number three slot in another. Due to aborts, some of the week-old Mustangs succumbing to technical troubles, Godfrey found himself number three in Gentile's flight and he moved to the number two position as the fighters met up with the bombers at 26,000 ft.

Overhauling the bomber stream the Mustangs were positioned over the lead box just as twenty-plus Bf 109s attacked. Some thirty more were in the area, waiting their time. Gentile and Godfrey picked out one pair and pursued them after making six or seven turns. All four fighters had reached 20,000 ft before Godfrey made the first kill.

'I managed to get on this '109's tail but I couldn't get the right deflection. I closed to 75 yd astern and noticed strikes. He rolled over and I really clobbered him. The pilot then baled out.' Godfrey looked round to see Gentile spiralling down with the other '109, trying also to get inside the enemy aircraft. But the American did not have it all his own way. Gentile finally lined his victim up:

'I had a hard time getting inside him; then I closed to 75 yd and clobbered him. He rolled over and went down, streaming white smoke. He was spiralling out of control and almost obscured by smoke.' The duo then attacked another '109 from head-on, Gentile leading and Godfrey tucked in close, covering.

'Don was going up to another '109. I followed him, giving him cover. He shot this one down and the pilot baled out. We joined up and climbed to 20,000 ft again.' Then two more Bf 109s were spotted, flying almost abreast of each other, 2,000 ft below.

'You take the one on the right and I'll handle the other bastard,' Gentile called over the R/T.

Gentile was an advocate of getting close enough to his victim so that there was little chance that he would miss. 'Stick your guns up his coat tails and pull the trigger' was an expression he used. He employed such tactics on this next kill.

'I opened fire at 250 yd and closed in until I almost rammed him. I got good strikes. The plane went down spinning and smoking badly and the pilot bailed out. Jim's target exploded.'

Godfrey reported, 'We closed in and both opened up at the same time. They both had belly tanks, and the one I fired at blew up. Don's strikes were right in the cockpit and they both opened up at the same time.' Godfrey then found himself in trouble. 'At 4 o'clock I noticed one coming in on us and told Don to break.'

Two top pilots flying in such harmony was a distinct advantage. If one had to momentarily break off an action, the other was invariably able to take over. Gentile and Godfrey became famous for 'handing' enemy fighters to each other. Having made his break on this occasion, Gentile joined Godfrey again. 'We turned into him and got him between us. I fired first and got strikes but overshot, so I told Jim to take over.' The German pilot headed for the deck with the two Mustangs latched on to his tail. Both Americans took turns firing at him. At 500 ft his aircraft began to smoke but it still flew. Godfrey fired again and ran out of ammunition, by which time the '109 was very low, trying to evade his pursuers by hedge hopping.

Gentile delivered the coup de grâce: 'I told Jim to cover me while I finished him off. His belly tank

The deadly duo. John Godfrey (left) and Don Gentile pose for another publicity shot in front of the latter's P-51B Shangri-La *(IWM).*

caught fire and he climbed to 1,000 ft and bailed out.' Godfrey witnessed his leader's victory. 'His plane crashed in the woods and his 'chute opened at about 500 ft. We picked up a lone Fort about fifty miles west of Berlin and escorted it to the English coast. Don and myself were together during all this engagement giving each other cover alternately.'

By 5 April 1944 the third ranking ace was Major James A. Goodson who then commanded the 4th's 336th Squadron. Desk work did not interfere in any way with combat flying although it brought one advantage, as Goodson himself put it: 'Being squadron commander is a great relief. You don't think about yourself in the air. You're concerned with your boys and what they're doing.' Goodson also shared Don Blakeslee's view that married men lose something of their fighting edge over bachelors. He felt that marriage tempered a man too much: 'The cautious pilot is doomed; with one exception, I've never seen a fighter pilot get married and keep on the way he was. He gets careful, thinking about his wife. First thing you know he's thinking about her and a Hun bounces his tail.'

Goodson was also conscious of the need for his pilots to keep physically up to par. 'I don't take any more 48-hour leaves. You go out and have a good time, too good a time, and lose sleep and perhaps hoist one too many. For a few days after a 48, I notice I'm not up to snuff. Little things. I'm not on top. So no more 48s for me. Or the first thing you know, some Jerry will notice it, too. We're fighters. We've got to keep in trim just like any other fighter.'

Goodson also gave his views on the 4th's new Mustangs — how much, he was asked, did it figure in the current round of success?

'Personally I preferred the Thunderbolt. But few others in the group did. You see, we'd flown the Spits. This new Mustang is a great deal like the Spitfire.' Asked which was better, Goodson said: 'They both have their good points. It's better, in my opinion, than the early Spitfire. The Spitfire has been improved. The Mustang has more range, and we're able to follow the Hun down on to the deck in it, a thing the British never do. But there we have the difference of training.

'The RAF teaches you never to be too keen, or you might not come back. They teach percentage flying. The Americans astonish them, the way they'll peel off and bounce anything they see, in any numbers, and keep right on down on to the deck.

'The Mustang took up where the Thunderbolt range ended. And we've got the Hun flat-footed again. They never expected us to be strafing the Berlin area. My squadron bounced an airfield and caught them totally unprepared. Planes were scattered all around. We made a pass over. Then we came back for another pass. We kept right on coming over until everything was done we could do. Planes destroyed and hangars burning. There was flak but the planes couldn't get up to meet us. We nailed them to the ground.'

Goodson excelled in the art of 'nailing them to the ground'. His prowess at ground attack earned him the title 'King of Strafers' and he ended the war with fifteen confirmed ground victories as well as fifteen downed in aerial combat.

Recalling a hectic mission late in March Goodson remained undaunted in the face of one of the Mustang's early drawbacks. 'I led my squadron down on twenty-plus enemy aircraft. As soon as we attacked they went into a steep spiral dive, dodging in and out of cloud. During this chase my windscreen and finally my whole cockpit frosted up, leaving me on instruments at 1,000 ft.

'When I was able to scratch some of the ice off, I found myself near an aerodrome full of Ju 88s with some in the circuit. One was going in for a landing and I gave him a burst with considerable deflection. I got strikes but he continued to land. I came back and hit him again as he was taxying. This started him smoking, but due to the frost condition of my windscreen it was not until after the fourth pass that I considered him blazing sufficiently to call him destroyed.

'I then observed another '88 flying around. I had trouble getting behind him, but finally got a few strikes on him from ninety degrees. He was very close to the deck, and promptly crashed into a field, but although it was a good prang, I returned and got some more bursts on him, leaving the crash burning.'

At this time, it looked very likely that an 8th AF pilot could beat the top score of 26 made by Eddie Rickenbacker in World War 1. That figure had not yet been equalled by any American in this war and it was a positive goal to aim for. With the fresh spirit of 1944, the 'ace race' took on new significance. But it was not always the cool, calculating approach that paid dividends. More than a few fighter pilots hit the headlines by being quite the opposite — wild and woolly might be an apt way to describe such characters. In their own way they too contributed materially to the downfall of the Luftwaffe and foremost among them were the Poles. Ever since their country had been ravaged by the invading Germans, individual Polish airmen had been striking back at the enemy with a vehemence others could appreciate, if not feel in quite the same way. Polish pilots were numbered among the ranks of most Allied air forces and although they tended to predominate in the RAF which had eventually formed squadrons composed almost entirely of that country's nationals, the AAF had its own colourful band. The majority were in the 56th Group: men with such tongue-twisting names as Mazimierz Rutkowski, Abigniew Janicki, Tadensc Anderz, Tadeusz Sawicz, Witold Lanowski and Mike Gladych.

These men found an affinity with such 56th stars as Francis Gabreski who was himself a second generation Pole. Strings were pulled to keep the Polish pilots in action with the AAF, even though some of them had to fly unofficially. Such was the tangled web of his military service since being forced to leave his homeland, Witold Lanowski was initially denied the chance to fly on operations, although he had as much flight time as, if not more than, some of his contemporaries. The problem stemmed from the fact that he was technically a serving officer with the Polish Air Force and could not hold rank in the AAF at the same time. This detail did not however prevent Lanowski flying operationally with the 56th.

Another man who did so was the flamboyant Mike Gladych. He was another Pole not officially on the roster of the 56th, as he was in the spring of 1944 still a flight commander with No 302 Squadron, RAF. But Gladych managed to get himself posted to the 56th 'on loan'. On 8 March he attacked three Fw 190s and shot down one, then went down to strafe an enemy airfield. Dave Schilling said of him, 'A wild man in the air, if I ever saw one. I don't see how he has lasted so long.'

Wild, but clever too. On that 8 March mission Gladych showed it was possible for the Germans to work for the Americans, albeit unwittingly.

'We were over Germany escorting some bombers when a fight developed fairly close to the ground. I suddenly found three Focke-Wulfs off at right angles to me and above. I tried to jump them but they kept away.

'I then went right down to the deck among the trees. They followed me and that is exactly what I wanted. A rat race developed and they started shooting. Finally I got on the tail of one of them. He was a dead pigeon. To shoot him I had to straighten up and one of the planes above me put some holes in my wing. I started going home because my gas was running low, but the two remaining Focke-Wulfs started to fly in formation with me. They must have thought I was out of gas because they beckoned me to land. I motioned OK and kept on flying just ahead of them until we reached a German airfield.

'I knew what to do. I gave the field a short burst and all the ground guns opened up with everything they had. The two Germans were flying less than ten yards behind me and the anti-aircraft fire landed right among them. I didn't stay to see what happened but headed for England.

'Just as I crossed the British coast, the Thunderbolt ran out of gas. There were heavy clouds and I couldn't see the ground, so I was forced to bale out. I hit the stabilizer getting out and it set me spinning. I tried all the tricks to stop the spin before I opened the parachute but they didn't work. At last I pulled the ripcord but the parachute cords were tangled. I thought I had had it when I shot out of the clouds, but at the last minute I manged to straighten the cords. I hurt my leg landing and sat there until a couple of British Army officers came up.

'They were very suspicious and wouldn't believe I was Polish. They asked me various things and when I mentioned the London 'Blitz' of 1940, they asked: 'were you over London in 1940 and 1941?' I told them I had been over with the Polish fighter squadron. It took a lot of argument to convince them. Finally they said,'Well old boy, you disappointed us terribly. We hoped you were a German.'

The six Polish pilots comprised a special Flight within the 61st Fighter Squadron, each man taking it in turn to lead. All were highly experienced and each undoubtedly scored a number of kills — but they were reluctant to disclose exactly how many, for understandable reasons; Gladych got at least 18½, ten of them while flying with the 56th, and Lanowski added four to his two RAF victories while flying the Thunderbolt. The Polish Flight of the 56th ended in August 1944 when most of its pilots were posted. Lanowski, however, remained and was eventually given a commission in the USAAF.

★   ★   ★

Harassment of the Luftwaffe's airfields and installations led in April 1944 to yet another new idea to take the war to the enemy from bases in Britain. This resulted in the deployment of the P-38 in a new role, that of formation bombing. Flights of Lightnings were led to their targets by a machine outfitted as a bombing leader, complete with bombardier located in an elongated nose section known as the 'droop snoot'. By April 1944 the Lightning groups were flying the improved P-38J-10 model, with more refinements on the way from Lockheed. Three groups were then operational and on 5 April VIII FC despatched 456 fighters on strafing attacks against airfields in Germany. Between them the 20th and 364th Groups put up 96 P-38s for the mission. The 20th had drawn airfields in the Münster/Berlin area and Colonel Harold Rau led fifty machines into the air at 13:07 hr. Heavy cloud was threatened as the group crossed the Dutch coast at 15,000 ft between layers of overcast. Soon the pilots were on instruments as these layers merged into a solid wall. After an hour or so the P-38s began to see the bursts from radar-predicted flak and at 14:40 hr Rau decided to abandon the mission.

It appears that just before Rau called his decision to his pilots he was distracted by other P-38s (from the 364th) plunging directly through his own formation. The Lightnings were still receiving attention from the flak and one burst caught the aircraft of Rau's wingman, First Lieutenant Jack Yelton flying his *Cactus Jack* as part of the 55th Squadron formation. The next few minutes were eventful for Yelton.

'I was Colonel Rau's wingman and ''Pappy'' Hower was leading the second element. We started our descent between Münster and Berlin and entered a heavy overcast at around 10,000 ft. We had only been in it for a few seconds when the whole world exploded for me. The next thing I knew was that I came to in an upside-down dive at — I should estimate — 2,000 ft.

'I more or less automatically jerked back the wheel and brought the ship out of the dive right on top of the trees; in fact I felt the tail hit some trees. I cleared my head and took note of what happened. Obviously I had been hit by flak because both windows were

broken and the cockpit was a mass of pulp and glass
from shattered instruments: no compass, no nothing.
Both engines were streaming oil and prop juice but
the thing was still running. I had some cuts on my face
and neck and there was a lot of blood, but as far as I
could tell, nothing serious.

'I looked up and noticed that the base of a dark
overcast was about 2,000 ft and no more P-38s were
in sight. I was not surprised since Colonel Rau had
said at briefing that we would not go down if the
clouds were lower than 5,000 ft — so I figured that,
still in the soup at that altitude, they had turned and
gone back up.

'My problem was to know which way to go as long
as the engines kept running. It was a very dark day
and without a compass I had no idea which way.
Using the eeny-meeny-miny-mo system I started in
some direction. It seems I had hit among a maze of
German airfields in that area and within the next four
or five minutes I shot down two aircraft which were
low and obviously in the traffic pattern. The first was
an Fw 200 with wheels down at about 500 ft. I got it
broadside from stem to stern and the thing exploded
and came apart. I kept going and about two minutes
later I saw an Fw 190 in front of me and right on the
deck; he was obviously taking a little low-level
pleasure cruise. I crawled to within 2,000 ft of him
before he noticed me. He then pulled the dumb
manouevre of beginning a gentle straight climb. I
crept on his tail, keeping the trigger down for what
seemed thirty minutes, and at about 900 ft he caught
fire. As I whipped away I saw the pilot climbing over
the side.

'I went down on the ground and immediately saw
the outline of a big looking burg ahead. With my

Sights like this did nothing to boost the reputation of the P-38 — and there
were many of them as pilots struggled to bring back aircraft suffering from
damaged or sick engines. This forlorn returnee was a P-38J-5 (42-67232) of
the 384th FS, 364th Group.

usual brilliant thinking I figured this must be Berlin
so I made a sloppy one-eighty and started back the
way I came. Having done this, only a few seconds
later both engines — both, not one — started to quit.
Having lost a bit of speed I tried the prop controls and
everything else as I gained a little altitude. However,
the props were through and both were just wind-
milling.

'I didn't have enough altitude to bale out and as the
countryside looked damn rough around there I
decided to crash-land on another German strip which
was close to my left. I figured on making a nice rough
belly-landing on their runway and stepping out with
no injuries to myself but with the ship definitely
messed up. However, as I came in dead stick, I must
have gone crazy for I pulled the act which I shall
always regret, no matter what the nice Air Corps
brass hats have said.

'It was a wide runway and as I started in I noticed
two Me 110s sitting in a very tight position on the
right side, getting ready for a nice classy take-off in
formation. When I was about 500 ft from the runway,
I must have gone completely batty because I kicked
right rudder and aimed straight for them. The last
thing I remember was looking into both cockpits and
then — wham! The whole world exploded again. The
crash and explosion must have been simultaneous
because the next thing I knew I was lying on the
runway a few hundred feet from the burning wreck-

age with a few rosy-cheeked Hitler Youth kicking me in the ribs!'

Jack Yelton's amazing escape from death was due to the fact of him being flung out of the cockpit of his Lightning as it stuck the Messerschmitts. He landed some distance away and broke both shoulders, injuries aggravated by the fact that he was confined for fifteen days without any medical attention. Then he was operated on and in October 1944 passed the International Repatriation Board, enabling him to be returned to the USA on 21 February 1945.

This story had an unusual end to a day's combat but it speaks volumes for the durability of the P-38 and perhaps, reflects the widespread trait in American fighter pilots not to be daunted by the odds — whatever the circumstances. There were numerous examples of sheer guts and determination and the aforementioned, seemingly reckless tackling of far superior numbers of enemy aircraft undoubtedly paid dividends. Such tactics served to unnerve the enemy and were later exemplified by one pilot who responded to a radio call as to where he was, with: 'I'm down here. I've got twenty Messerschmitts surrounded!'

The 5 April mission netted nearly a hundred enemy aircraft, honours being shared pretty evenly between the 4th (which hit five aerodromes) and the 355th (six). The latter group had a particularly successful mission as it also destroyed eight enemy aircraft in the air for the loss of three. On the same day, the 339th Fighter Group occupied Fowlmere, Cambridgeshire and began working up on an unfamiliar new type. Having trained on the P-39 in the US, the group pilots were given a few weeks to get used to the P-51 under the command of Colonel John B. Henry, Jr, the man who was to lead the 339th until the end of the war.

The good work the fighters were doing received due recognition in the form of Distinguished Unit Citations which were awarded for separate actions or for a number of successful missions over a period of time. On 5 April the Steeple Morden group was cited for a DUC for its ground strafing skills, and on the 8th of the month the 20th Group was similarly honoured for its contribution to the VIII FC total of 88 enemy aircraft shot down and a further 49 destroyed on the ground. On the debit side that day's loss figures included Captain Virgil Meroney, then leading ace of the 352nd Group with nine kills.

9 More muscle

On 10 April the first 'Droop Snoot' Lightning mission was flown by the 20th and 55th Groups. While the bulk of the fighters supported a heavy strike by the bombers against a number of enemy airfields, these two P-38 units undertook to test a new fighter-bomber experiment on airfields in France. The 20th put up 39 aircraft, 29 of them carrying bombs which they were to drop on the signal of the lead aircraft. The rest were conventional P-38s acting as escort to the 'B-38' formation. The primary target was Florennes/Juzaine airfield. Meanwhile, the 55th sent out 34 P-38 bombers and thirteen escort Lightnings to attack St Dizier. Area support was provided by P-47s of the 353rd Group.

Brainchild of Cass Hough and 8th AF ordnance and armament specialist Colonel Don Ostrander, the droop snoot idea was enthusiastically received in the command's top echelons, particularly by Doolittle. It was thought that a bombing leader P-38 would be more economical due to its speed and two-man crew compared to a Fortress or Liberator — and on paper that was certainly true enough. The saving in manpower was potentially immense if fighters could undertake some of the missions otherwise requiring heavy bombers.

It was known that on some short-range missions a P-38 could carry the load of a heavy bomber while needing only one man in 98 per cent of the aircraft and no more than two in the remaining two per cent, which were the droop snoot lead ships. Also, P-38 bombers retained their heavy defensive armament, thereby reducing the need for separate escort fighters.

Major Herbert E. Johnson, Jr, led the 20th Group mission, with Lieutenant Herschel 'Easy' Ezell, Jr, occupying the bombardier's position in the nose of his modified P-38J. The rest of the formation, armed with two 1,000 lb bombs apiece, lifted off at 07:30 hr. Unfortunately, as they neared the target Ezell, crouched over his Norden, realized as countless bombardiers before him, that the weather was not going to be kind: solid cloud obscured the designated target and the group had little recourse but to wheel about and head home, toggling their bombs into the Channel en route.

The 55th had more success at Coulommiers, its secondary target. Finding St Dizier similarly 'socked in', the droop snoot formation released seventeen tons of bombs. Not to be outdone the 20th set out again in the afternoon, this time sending 27 aircraft to Gutersloh to drop thirteen tons of bombs, led by Lieutenant Colonel Harold Rau. Again Ezell was up front with the bombsight — a familiar crew position for him, as he had previously flown 25 missions as a B-17 bombardier.

The 8th AF officially viewed the droop snoot concept as a mixed success; the element of surprise had certainly been achieved but the decreasing threat to the heavy bombers led the 8th eventually to abandon such missions. One result of the idea was perpetuated in paint on the vast majority of the 8th and 9th Air Force P-38s. To fool the Germans, each of the bomb-carrying Lightnings in a droop snoot formation had had its nose cap stripped of camouflage and highly polished so that the reflection gave the impression of being a glass nose. Henceforth the Germans could never be one hundred per cent sure that a formation of P-38s was armed merely with guns. . .

The first ten days of April 1944 were typical of what the 8th Air Force fighter groups were to experience, virtually to the end of the war; each mission, while generally adding to the inexorable wearing down of the Luftwaffe, held the risk that experienced fighter leaders would go down, particularly as ground strafing now presented odds that few could anticipate or plan for. There was always the chance that an alert gunner would 'get lucky' in the way that was becoming increasingly difficult for the average German fighter pilot. On 5 April the 4th Group had reason to mourn the loss of Duane Beeson, one of its most accomplished and popular aces.

Right *Camera's eye view of Steeple Morden airfield showing the runways and 'frying pan' shaped revetments for each fighter* (355th FG Association)

German intelligence was well aware of the names of the leading 8th AF fighter pilots and managed to compile comprehensive dossiers on most of them, interrogators being able to quote a quite startling list of facts about commanders, base, fellow squadron pilots and so on, to downed fliers. Fortunately, the majority of AAF pilots were handed over to the custody of the Luftwaffe before being sent to PoW camps. It is on record that at one time Hitler wanted all captured airmen shot but the German air force, horrified at this suggestion and no doubt aware of the sort of retribution it could bring among its own personnel, successfully blocked any such move. Being passed into air force hands was indeed fortunate and the methodical Germans, soldiers and civilians alike, invariably observed this rule of war. Mercifully, the murder of pilots by undisciplined civilian mobs was rare, but this was always a risk, particularly so at the end of the war when the established order of things began to break down.

As the leading aces began to go down, largely as a result of ground strafing, the Germans were able to

Left *First ace: Captain Walter Koraleski claimed the distinction for the 354th FS nicknamed the 'Bulldogs'. He is pictured with his P-51B, WR-L, shortly before becoming a PoW on 14 April 1944 (355th FG Association).*

Below *Sharing the grass with a 38th Squadron P-38, this Thunderbolt is believed to have been from the 56th Group, one of the earliest to change its nose marking from white to red — as indicated here. Slinging M-41 frag clusters from the belly shackles was not so common as putting them under the wings, due to limited ground clearance.*

cross each man off their list and it became something of a game to guess who would end up 'in the bag' next. Being 'welcomed' as though he was expected to arrive sooner or later, gave the enemy a psychological advantage over a newly captured pilot. Subtle interview techniques and generally fair treatment put the unwary off their guard and led them, however unwittingly, to add to the enemy's information. There was fortunately very little the Germans could do to turn this knowledge to their practical advantage.

For Duane Beeson the morning of 5 April began normally enough; with other 4th Group pilots he piled out of a Dodge weapons carrier and strapped into his Mustang *Boise Bee* on the Debden flightline, assisted by his crewchief, Staff Sergeant Willard Wahl. A last wipe of the windscreen and then Beeson was off, rolling out for take-off on another Jackpot — a strafing attack on an aerodrome in a defined area. In this instance the area was near Berlin.

It was 15:45 hr by the time Beeson's section of the 334th was orbiting Brandenburg and looking for Briest aerodrome, the specified target. German flak was alert and a burst hit Allen Bunte's aircraft which crashed into a lake. Bunte narrowly escaped drowning as the Mustang sank. The hunting Eagles found

At the latter end of its 8th AF service the P-38J notched up a useful record on ground-attack sorties, where its heavy armament had few peers. Lieutenant Glasgow and his crew seem well pleased with 364th Group P-38 The Rebel Kids *(USAF).*

the 'drome, which was full of parked Ju 88s. Beeson's fire consumed the first of three he lined up in his sights. A second took shells without burning, while the last of the trio exploded violently.

Heading out, the Mustangs came upon an airborne Ju 88 and several pilots queued up to shoot at it. Beeson saw his strikes hit the cockpit and engines, and the aircraft crashed, bursting into flames. Then another juicy airfield target was seen: Gardelegen, also loaded with Ju 88s. Fellow pilots confirmed Beeson's destruction of one, plus holes in six more as the red-nosed P-51B swept down the enemy flight-line. At the end there loomed the giant bulk of an Me 323 and Beeson gave this a squirt, breaking off to climb over it at fifty yd range.

It was almost as though the Germans had parked the Me 323 there deliberately and the flak was just waiting for the American fighters to hop over it; *Boise Bee* staggered from a mortal hit in its vitals. His radiator smashed, Beeson weaved violently to avoid more damage. Following him, Chuck Carr's aircraft was also hit. Beeson climbed to 1,000 ft with his Merlin streaming glycol; rapidly the engine seized and the propeller froze to a stop. There was nothing for it but to jump and with a heartfelt 'Damn it' he parted company with the wrecked Mustang. Carr, his machine also losing coolant, did likewise on a bad day for the Eagles. A fourth pilot was killed in the later stage of the mission when he went down in the North Sea and died of exposure.

During April there was a number of base moves by

Dangerous mishap for a P-38J of the 364th Group on 4 May 1944. The fuel in the ruptured starboard drop tank ignited but prompt action by firefighters saved 42-67224 for repair (USAF).

fighter groups as the 8th Air Force was integrated into the air support plan for the invasion. Some fighter airfields were required by bomber units and on the 5th, the 353rd moved to Raydon, the 55th occupied Wormingford and the 56th bid adieu to Halesworth and packed its bags for Boxted, a not entirely unfamiliar locale, as this was where the group had first made its home in the ETO.

The month saw the 4th, 352nd, 355th and 359th in the process of converting to the P-51, while the 78th, 353rd, 356th and 361st were still primarily P-47 groups. The 20th, 55th and 364th continued to fly P-38s and the 357th and 339th were the two original P-51 groups. The 56th remained loyal to the P-47 and its longevity in the theatre allowed the group considerable leeway when it came to the aircraft it flew. The reaction to a suggested switch to Mustangs was not pressed...

Although things went the way the 56th wanted in this regard, the 354th which had done so much to introduce the Merlin Mustang to long-range escort, was chagrined to find itself a Thunderbolt outfit at the end of 1944. By then back under the control of the tactical 9th Air Force, it was logical enough to have all ground attack groups flying one type, although the P-38 squadrons did not necessarily agree with this line of reasoning either! The 'Pioneer Mustang Group' had earned its title many times over and it finally got its P-51s back, in February 1945.

As ground attack prowess increased the 8th AF fighter groups developed their own tactics for dealing with various types of target. That the P-38 could be a particularly effective weapon at low level had already been demonstrated and on 8 April the 20th Group flew an operation which was to earn it considerable distinction. The day started as a routine bomber escort to Oldenburg, but bad weather prevented the group taking off. About noon conditions improved and Colonel Rau, reluctant to waste the rest of the day, obtained permission for a fighter sweep. The Lightnings would go to central Germany and seek

aerodromes and ground targets in the Hannover-Salzwedel area, eighty miles west of Berlin. It was a 'first' for the 20th as this one group would carry out the mission alone, unsupported by other aircraft, to a location known to be well defended.

Rau organized each squadron into White, Yellow, Red and Blue Flights of four aircraft each and the 48-ship formation took off from King's Cliffe at 14:02 hr. Arrival over Salzwedel was at 15:54, whereupon each squadron separated to hit its briefed target. The 79th, led by Rau, went for an airfield south of the town, the 77th sought out one to the south-east and the 55th dropped down over Ulzen to see what airfield activity there was there.

The target list unrolled as the 20th went to work. He 177s and Ju 88s were destroyed by the 79th together with an He 111 and other twin-engined types not positively identified. The squadron's Red Flight caused carnage on a parade ground and killed an estimated 300 troops, while Colonel Rau's White Flight moved on to the railway and blasted two locomotives.

Jumped by seven Bf 109s, the squadron sustained two losses, one when an enemy fighter crashed into a P-38. Three '109s were shot down. The 77th worked over its selected airfield, claiming eight destroyed and 21 badly damaged while losing one P-38 to ground fire. An Fw 190 was quickly despatched as the marauding Lightnings strafed their way home, opening fire on anything that seemed to be serving the cause of the Third Reich, including another locomotive and its twenty-car oil tank train, left in flames.

The 55th Squadron, unable to locate an airfield, roved the area, beating up a variety of worthwhile targets. Eight more locomotives succumbed to this assault and the P-38s also hit three large oil and gas dumps, flak emplacements, factory buildings and a bridge.

All told the 42 pilots used 21,475 rounds of .50-cal ammunition and 3,850 rounds of 20-mm. A fourth aircraft, this from the 55th FS, failed to return. This mission and others carried out subsequently, gave the 20th a reputation as a train-busting outfit and the appelation 'The Loco Group'. The 20th's outstanding record was a tribute to the air and ground crews — and to an aircraft that had found its true forté in the ETO.

The second week of April 1944 saw the 8th's bombers returning to one of its most notorious targets — Schweinfurt. The mission to the ball-bearing production centre scheduled for 12 April was scrubbed due to bad weather but the following day's unlucky portents did not bring the casualties they had in 1943. Even so a long range mission could, despite cover from 871 fighters as on this occasion, still exact a toll. To drop just over 200 tons of bombs on the industrial area cost fourteen B-17s from 154 aircraft that reached the target. Slightly worse in terms of losses were the eighteen Fortresses that failed to return from Augsberg and these plus six B-24s lost from the strike elements sent against Oberpfaffenhofen made the day's total MIAs 38.

The bombers were intercepted by the Luftwaffe and the AAF fighters claimed 42 of them destroyed in the air. Strafing attacks added another 35 and nine friendly fighters failed to return. From the total the

Landing accidents could be nasty. This one involved one of the 56th Group's distinctively camouflaged P-47Ds and a Mustang. The Thunderbolt has ten kills chalked up and is a 62nd Squadron machine, 42-76303.

4th Group counted two P-51s and on return to Debden a third aircraft had to be added. Don Gentile, on his final mission before returning home to the US, came in low for a spectacular buzzing of the Essex base — but the farewell did not go according to plan. Misjudging his height Gentile flew *Shangri-la* into the ground. It came to rest with a broken back, a total write-off. The incident was the more embarrassing as the press corps had gathered to cover the story; it was said that Blakeslee was livid. In his book, anyone who pranged a kite while buzzing had no place in his outfit. . .

Results continued to vary on fighter missions and were not always directly in proportion to the number of aircraft despatched. On 22 April, for example, the 359th had a score of seven enemy aircraft shot down for the loss of one P-47, the East Wretham group being part of an 859 fighter support mission to bombers attacking Hamm. The following day the group sent seventeen aircraft on a dive bombing mission with seventeen Thunderbolts supporting them. Results were unspectacular. The command put up a total of 382 fighters drawn from ten groups to carry out strafing attacks on airfields in France, Belgium and Germany, the 361st and 356th also carrying bombs on a proportion of their aircraft. The total claims for the day amounted only to 11(destroyed)-0(probable)-24(damaged), seven 8th AF aircraft being lost.

The best day in terms of Luftwaffe fighters destroyed for the remainder of April was the 24th when the bombers selected various targets in Germany. Fighters drawn from all 8th and six 9th AF groups participating in post-escort ground attacks ran up a

score of 58 to add to the air combat claims of 66. The 357th and 355th put in claims of 22 and 19 respectively, the 4th coming a close third with 18 downed; the day cost 17 American fighters MIA.

More droop snoot missions were flown during the remaining days of April, other groups also using their aircraft as dive or glide bombers against airfields. By the 30th a new German threat in the form of the V-1 flying bomb had been recognized by Allied intelligence and the 8th in common with the 9th and the RAF began an intensive effort to locate and destroy the launching sites. That day, the combat debut of the 339th Group, saw the fighters attacking 'No-ball' targets, the freshman Mustang group sweeping the area chosen for attack by the 353rd. All 128 aircraft despatched returned safely.

The overall fighter losses of early May were also small, but on occasion the bulk of them were suffered by one group. On the 4th of the month, the fighters escorted bombers to Berlin, Brunswick and other targets in central Germany. Cloud cover frustrated the majority of the bombers releasing their loads as briefed — in fact only one wing was able to do so. Fighters engaged and the 356th lost two P-47s. Claims of six aircraft shot down for the loss of two aircraft, plus a third wrecked in a crash-landing, were small compensation.

Four days later the fortunes of war changed yet again when a big air battle ensued over the German

capital. As was now commonplace VIII Bomber Command divided its available force, sending bombers to Brunswick and Brandenburg, the secondary targets. The 2nd Division's B-24s went to Brunswick as part of this two-pronged strike. The raids were hotly contested by the Luftwaffe, estimates of the numbers engaged varying between 180 and 200. These fighters attempted to intercept, primarily in the vicinity of Hanover.

The 352nd Group, the self styled 'Blue Nosed Bastards from Bodney', did an excellent job of escort that day. Having caught up to the lead boxes of heavies over Nieburg, the group met the diving onslaught of Fw 190s and Bf 109s, which levelled off to deliver head-on attacks on the bombers. Always difficult to combat, as their high speed dives left precious little time to close and knock them down, the Americans could not catch this initial pass, despite two squadrons trying to do so.

The Luftwaffe fighters would invariably re-form at low altitude and climb for a second attack. Colonel Joe Mason sent the 328th and 487th Squadrons down after them. This move resulted in claims of 27(destroyed)-2(probable)-7(damaged) for the loss of only one Mustang. Among the successful pilots was First Lieutenant Carl Luksic, who brought down three Bf 109s and two Fw 190s to give VIII FC a new 'first' of five kills on one mission. The announcement of another ace was not a new occurrence in the 8th, but the spotlight fell more on the top pilots, those whose kills had by then passed the twenty mark. The 8 May mission raised the stakes even higher when Bob Johnson got two to raise his score to 27, equalling the air-to-ground record then held by Dick Bong in the Pacific. Johnson's view of the 8 May combat was recorded at the time:

'About thirty Huns were over the bombers, their contrails snaking out in the sky. Smoke was coming from the bomber box, and one was going down. I started after the Jerries, and then saw an Me 109 diving at me. I rolled and fired at him, but missed. Then he squirted at me and missed.

I made another turn, and he tried to outrun me, the damned fool. He went down, rolling and turning to evade, and I hit him every half roll.'

Johnson had developed the art of watching the exhaust trail of the enemy fighters, waiting for the gases to stop when the pilot reduced power for a sharp turn. When he saw the exhaust trail thin, Johnson took his chance: 'I kept hitting him on every turn. When his wing came off I figured he'd had it.

'We started back up for those contrails above the bombers. I was down to about 3,000 ft now, in the spotty clouds. Hartney, my number three man, yelled that a couple of Fw 190s were diving. He took off after them under a cloud, and I told him I'd jump them when they came out. Then he began yelling for help.

'I saw two FWs come out, then Hartney's Thunderbolt, and then four more Jerries chasing the Thunderbolt. I came head-on at these four. One of them was blinking at me with those .30s, and I let him have it. It got his engine and he went down smoking and blew up. The other three broke away.'

This action was typical of Johnson and other pilots, who would try to protect each other when the enemy got one of their own cornered. The wingman system was vital in the heat of a big battle and there were few aces who did not acknowledge that their second pair of eyes was often the difference between a kill and the enemy living to fight another day.

With VIII FC lauding the fact that the new leading American fighter ace was based in the ETO, it was time for Johnson to go home, leaving the limelight to a fellow Wolfpack pilot, Lieutenant Colonel Francis Gabreski. 'Gabby' Gabreski's score stood at twenty when Johnson bade farewell to England.

On 12 May the 8th Air Force struck oil targets in Germany for the first time on a major scale, the bombers going after a number of refineries. In support were 735 Mustangs, Thunderbolts and Lightnings drawn from all groups. The 56th had an excellent day, with eighteen enemy aircraft to its credit; the 4th got ten and the 357th an impressive fourteen. The Wolfpack, ever ready to employ new tactics to foil the enemy, used the 'Zemke Fan' for the first time. The idea was that the 56th would fly to a predetermined point and split into three elements. The left and right groups would apparently leave the main force — but both were briefed to watch and render assistance the minute the main element was attacked in strength. The effectiveness of the manoeuvre was such that Captain Bob Rankin came home with five kills to his credit, becoming the second 8th AF 'ace-in-a-day'.

That the 8th's fighter force could now handle the longest range escort mission with almost routine ease was illustrated on 13 May when the bombers flew to targets in eastern Germany and the western areas of Poland. Of the groups in support, the 355th flew the longest distance, its Mustangs being seen as far afield as Posen, 1,470 miles from home. 'Seven league boots' also enabled the 361st to extend its range with its new P-51s.

On 15 May 1944 the last fighter group assigned to the 8th Air Force arrived at its home base of Wattisham in Cambridgeshire. The 479th brought with it many months of experience and a familiarity with the P-38 which was to stand it in good stead in the ensuing months. With the invasion of Europe mere weeks away, the 479th had scant little time to conclude its theatre indoctrination, and Group CO Kyle L. Riddell set to work with a will. 'Riddell's Raiders' were ready for their first mission on 26 May.

Among the men who took the P-38J into action with the 479th was Lieutenant Robin Olds, later to become famous in another war in another aircraft — Vietnam and the F-4 Phantom. Olds shot down eight

Left *Other groups, not boasting the comforts of Debden, Duxford and other more permanent bases, had to protect themselves from the elements — witness the mud-encrusted boots of these groundcrew men at Bodney. The pilot is also well cushioned from the effects of long-range flying* (via Paul Coggan).

Right *English colloquialisms crept into American speech and were perpetuated on aircraft. The well-known expression for a good aircraft was used by Jack A. Beckman of the 358th FS who transferred from the RCAF, during the 355th Group's P-51B period* (355th FG Association).

enemy aircraft before the group transitioned to the P-51 in August, making him ETO top scorer on the P-38.

Although airfield strafing was by the spring of 1944 an integral part of VIII Fighter Command operational planning, it was not until 21 May that the first 'Chattanooga' mission took place. As the name implies the intended target was the European railway system, particularly those lines which would ideally be used by the Germans to move supplies to the front when the invasion came. That day the command put up 617 fighters which ranged across Germany to attack 225 locomotives, stations, installations of various kinds and also river traffic. So successful was this and subsequent strikes that the railway system was virtually strangled in time for the invasion.

As well as 91 locomotives positively destroyed, the fighters had an excellent day against enemy aircraft with 83(destroyed)-0(probable)-67(damaged) claimed on the ground as Mustangs, Thunderbolts and Lightnings cut swathes of destruction across Germany. The three operational Lightning groups did particularly well in this line of business, the heavy cannon of their aircraft proving highly effective against locomotives and rolling stock.

On Chattanooga number one the 55th showed its oldest rivals from King's Cliffe that the latter had no monopoly on this type of work by receiving credit for 23 locomotives destroyed and a further fifteen damaged. The group also made life unpleasant for German river traffic and an Hs 129 unfortunate enough to blunder in front of the guns of the marauding P-38s was blasted out of the sky.

Six of the 55th's pilots failed to return out of a total of 27 MIAs for the day — a grim reminder that strafing brought hazards, and not only from the guns of the enemy. More than one pilot limped home with pieces of exploding target embedded in his aircraft. With mere seconds to identify a likely target a pilot following his lines of exploding shells at an average 350 mph had even less time to avoid the resulting conflagration. He also had no sure way of knowing the pyrotechnic effect his fire would have and at such closure speeds, was often over the target at the exact moment it went up. Even more at risk were following aircraft, whose pilots, seeing few immediate results from the first pass, might make a second run. More

than one found that his comrades' bullets had indeed found their mark and that the chain reaction was complete the second he was in range and the world exploded in his face. At best a singed and scorched airframe would carry him home, but the transportation of fuel, bombs and ammunition by a variety of methods continued to give strafing fighters some nasty surprises as innocuous-looking vehicles, barges or trains blew up. And even worse was the fact that in the spring of 1944 the Germans were obliged to transport flying bomb warheads from the factories to launching sites on the French coast.

On 23 May it was the P-51's turn to fly as a fighter bomber for the first time when the 359th and 361st Groups despatched 103 aircraft to destroy a railway bridge at Hasselt. Each Mustang of the bombing force of 89 carried a pair of 500-lb bombs, fourteen aircraft acting as escort. Of the total, 75 machines dropped their bombs on the bridge, the result being that 17.5 tons was enough to destroy it. One 361st aircraft was missing in action.

As Allied preparations to gain a foothold on the coast of France were being completed, the fighters of the 8th Air Force were consolidating their superiority over the enemy homeland to a degree that would not have been thought possible twelve months previously. Not only was it the distances flown by single-seat fighters that were vast: US industry had proved itself more than capable of providing front-line squadrons with excellent aircraft in sufficient numbers, so much so that the 8th was able to send out over 700 aircraft on 27 May and well over 600 on each successive day to the end of that month. With the 479th completing the allocation of groups, as May ended the 8th had just under 900 fighters available for operations on D-Day. Added to this total were 2,000 or so fighters of the 9th Air Force and the RAF — some 3,000 to oppose a nominal strength of 400 serviceable single- and twin-engined fighters available to the Luftwaffe. But the long range of Allied fighters meant that this total was whittled down a bit more virtually every day that operations were flown.

Another German train goes west under the guns of an American fighter. The European railway system was laid waste before D-Day, virtually strangling the enemy's ability to move supplies up to the Allied bridgehead.

Staff Sergeant Robert McCord assisting Second Lieutenant Alvin Juchheim into his 78th Group P-47D on a steel-plating dispersal put down to prevent the heavy machine from sinking into waterlogged ground at Duxford (USAF).

Although Germany's output of fighters hardly paused even in the face of repeated attacks on her factories, training pilots to fly them effectively in battle was, by mid-1944, becoming a daunting task. Training airfields had to be widely dispersed away from the likelihood of American fighter attack — but by that time, there were very few locations that could feel completely immune to being bombed or strafed.

At the end of May the German fighter force was distributed thus: 1, 2 and 3 *Jagddivisionen* in north Germany had about 175 single-engined and some 35 twin-engined; 7 *Jagddivision* in southern Germany had approximately seventy Bf 109s and Fw 190s, and *Luftflotte* 3 could count on at least 125 with others based in Austria. The decimation of the *Zerstörergruppen* at the hands of 8th and 9th AF fighters had led to their removal from the northern European battle zones to ostensibly safer locations in the south-east.

Those remaining to face the might of the 8th included elements of ZG76 equipped with anti-bomber 30 and 50 mm cannon-armed Me 410s at Vienna-Seyring and Prague, while 7 *Staffel* of ZG26 was also using Vienna. This pitifully meagre force was boosted by pulling single-seater *Geschwaderen* back from the East, IV/JG54 arriving from the Leningrad area during the month. The *Jagdwaffe* was finding it increasingly difficult to transfer more than single *Gruppen* from active sectors, although the release of three *Gruppen* of the crack JG27 from Austria to central Germany made the picture look a little more encouraging.

It was at this time that the Germans also formed special anti-bomber formations which it was hoped would inflict devastating casualties on the B-17s and B-24s. Adolf Galland as Inspector of Fighters meanwhile made plans to conserve a force that would, when ready, overwhelm the defending fighters and result in the destruction of entire combat boxes of Fortresses and Liberators from a single raid. More significantly as far as the 8th Air Force was concerned, the Germans were working to bring the first Me 163 rocket and Me 262 jet fighters into operational service.

10 'Planes overhead will be ours'

That the previous months' pounding of German airfields, railways, installations and waterways in France and the Low Countries had been devastatingly effective, was more than apparent in the first five days of the momentous month of June 1944. Such sorties continued prior to the invasion, primarily to ensure that the enemy would have little chance to recoup his losses while Allied troops established a bridgehead. On 2 June the bombers attacked French airfields and the Pas de Calais area, giving weight to the deception that the main assault would be in that region rather than in Normandy.

Cloud hampered these pre-invasion strikes to some extent but the 8th dropped well over 7,000 tons of bombs between 2 and 5 June. Fighters found meagre 'trade'. The escort of 412 aircraft destroyed but one enemy aircraft on 4 June and none at all on the following day when 372 covered the bombers on their short-range missions. From the early evening of Saturday, 3 June, it had become apparent that D-Day was on. Fighter bases, in common with those which operated medium bombers, transports and reconnaissance aircraft, received orders to virtually shut down. No-one — and that meant *no-one* — was allowed to leave or enter. And by 01:00 hr on Sunday morning each aircraft would be ready to fly, having been fully armed, fuelled and serviced — and painted with broad black and white recognition stripes around the wings and fuselage. Each machine also had to be covered up lest the secret be leaked to the unsuspecting enemy across the Channel.

It turned out that there was far more time for this preparatory work than had been expected. All Sunday. And Monday as well. Air and ground crews, fully aware that this was what they had been fighting for since the beginning, made few complaints — quite the reverse. Nobody wanted to miss this. Men with their tours complete found both the time and inclination to fly just one more mission — provided they had the rank. Flight Officers and Second Lieutenants who would normally have flown found themselves grounded because 'the brass' had stepped in and filled their places.

Each of the groups was assigned a particular patrol area if it was not engaged on fighter-bomber missions, the orders for VIII FC being to 'provide escort and continuous patrol throughout the day'. Most groups flew from dawn until dusk to maintain the air umbrella over the Channel shipping and invasion beaches. The task of flying cover to ships, the gun crews of which had notoriously itchy fingers when any aircraft, whatever its nationality, came anywhere within range, was given to the P-38. It was thought safe enough to put the P-38s over the ships as its unique configuration could hardly be confused with any other aircraft type, Allied or enemy. This phase of the air operation, plan 'Neptune', was led by the 55th Group. One of the pilots airborne that day was Robert P. Tibor:

'Our job was covering the ships in the Channel. The P-38s were assigned to that because not even the most trigger-happy ack-ack gunner on the ships could mistake the twin-tailed Lightning.

'The clouds were low, and we couldn't see far. I was disappointed at first. It didn't look like the show was so big after all. But as the limited horizon unrolled we kept seeing ships. Ships and more ships. Big and little ships. They were spread from England to within fifteen miles of the French coast, creeping under the cloud cover as darkness came. Out in front were the destroyers, cruisers and battleships, and behind moved the concentration of troop and supply ships.

'When we got back to the base Monday night, we knew this was it. Nothing happened in the air. We didn't see a Jerry plane. With the weather, the clouds, and the air-tight security regulations, it looked like the big show was going to be another surprise to the Jerry.

'We went in for interrogation by Intelligence, and when we came out we said nothing at all to anybody about what was going to happen tomorrow. It didn't matter whether a guy was your best friend or not. When anybody asked what we saw, we just shrugged and said "It was a milk run".'

The 55th had lifted off at 16:51 hr on 5 June and

Above *Everett Stewart, one of the war's outstanding leaders, flew with three Groups — the 352nd, 355th and 4th. This shot is believed to show him during his time with the 352nd* (via Paul Coggan).

Above right *In common with Stewart and many other pilots, Henry Brown flew a number of aircraft during the course of his combat flying. This photograph shows a P-51B with part of Brown's final score of 17.2 — making him the top ace of the 355th.*

Below *The ground crew spent a lot of time decorating* Arkansas Traveler *even down to adding the diamond pattern of the 353rd Group to the elevator trim tabs and a single diamond on a yellow square to the rudder hinge. The aircraft was regularly flown by the 350th Squadron CO Dewey Newhart although he was not at the controls of this aircraft when he went down over France on 12 June 1944. The* Traveler *passed to another owner* (USAF).

throughout the next 24-hour period other groups were alerted for their first missions in order to relieve those returning and maintain the shield. Everything was carefully planned and executed without trouble, the ground controllers having to cope with the exacting total of some 11,000 aircraft airborne from English bases at various times throughout 6 June. This was an all-time record either in war or peace. D-Day sorties by Allied aircraft were to total well over 14,000 for the day.

Tibor's observations continued: 'When we took off it was still dark, and we used navigation lights to keep formation. We flew at 3,000 ft, under the cloud cover. We couldn't see much on this mission because we were blinded by the broadsides from the Channel below. The ships were throwing everything they had at the beaches. Those huge flashes would come, and then the explosions inland. We were flying on instruments, and the glare of gunfire hurt my eyes and made it tough to see the little navigation lights of adjoining planes in the formation. Collision in the air was a danger. The sky was full of planes... I didn't see any answering gunfire from the beach. There didn't seem to be any big guns there.'

Captain Paul E. Hoeper was in the second group of Lightnings put up by the 55th: 'It was light enough to see the pattern developing, on the second mission. The troopships and landing craft were now at the beaches, with the big Navy ships behind throwing broadsides and recoiling through the water leaving white wakes. There were still no Jerry planes.'

Ground crews achieved very quick turnrounds of aircraft required for subsequent missions. Paul Tibor went up a third time during the morning.

'On my squadron's third mission the weather was better. We came over at five in the afternoon and the water off the French coast looked like the jam at Piccadilly Circus on a Saturday afternoon. The coast was black with ships and landing craft. A thousand craft were heading back for England, streaming across the Channel, and a thousand were heading for France.

'One Me 109 carrying bombs appeared. We dived for him but somebody else got him; he didn't last long. The only other enemy plane we saw was another '109 which dived out of the clouds. Three Spitfires screamed into view after him. He swooped down toward the water and up into the clouds again, the Spits right on his tail.

'Over the beach-head tanks were crawling in, streams of them like an invasion of beetles. Gliders that had carried our men were lying all over the landscape. Some of them were broken. The ground was spotted with coloured parachutes which had dropped guns and supplies. Five squadrons of Lightnings flew cover all the time over the ships.

'This was the big show, but we weren't doing anything. We all thought the Jerry would throw up every plane that would get a wheel off the ground. And it was just a milk run for us. Coming back I saw a big ship concentration moving out of the Thames estuary behind a smoke screen.'

The 20th Group flew 147 sorties on D-Day, the 55th Squadron taking off at 03:46 hr and the last aircraft of the 79th Squadron not touching down until 00.16 on June 7. Again, no enemy activity was noted. This was reflected thoughout VIII FC which put up 1,813 sorties; only a few groups were able to share in the total score of 26 enemy aircraft destroyed in the air and four on the ground for the day.

Sortie rate varied within the overall plan: the 353rd Group flew seven patrols, the 352nd nine. The 357th put up eight patrols and the 356th seven for 134 sorties, its missions including ground strafing with trucks, goods wagons and locomotives included in the score. Ground targets were also hit by the 355th which flew six missions before the day was out, the group's bag including fifteen from the total of enemy aircraft shot down.

An example of how the pendulum of luck could swing away from one group even on a day when enemy activity was at a minimum, was sadly shown to the boys at Debden. The group mounted six patrols and ended the day with seven Mustangs down for the destruction of four Fw 190s. The worst damage was done by at least fifteen '109s and '190s which bounced Don Blakeslee's evening patrol to the Rouen area. All four aircraft of the 335th's Blue section were shot down in quick succession, their pilots being killed. Mike Sobanski, 335th Squadron ace, was also killed soon afterwards, as was Edward Stepp of the 334th. Two other pilots came down but survived while the group's seventh loss was a pilot from the 339th, over to Debden to fly a D-Day mission with his old group.

The 56th put up its first sorties at 03:30 hr just as dawn was starting to break. The task of the P-47s, and most of the Mustangs, was to rove inland ahead of the invasion forces and attack communications, troop movements and airfields. Robert J. Rankin was one of the pilots of the 61st Squadron who flew on D-Day:

'Weather was bad, but there were some holes in the clouds over the Continent. We beat up everything we could see. We came over an airfield and seven planes were lined up. We'd developed a new strafing technique which entailed diving instead of coming in level. This made us harder to hit. When we got down to about 3,000 ft we started to pull out of the dive, and open up with those eight .50-cal guns at the same time. As the nose of the plane swung in the pull out, the guns swept the field. We plastered those sitting planes and went on.

'We ran into some Mustangs strafing a convoy of motor trucks. There were about 25 trucks lined up and when we got there the P-51s were sweeping across giving them hell. We joined in. Some of the trucks carried gasoline and some munitions. When we made our first pass we had to circle around waiting for another. So many of us were after that convoy that we had to queue up for our turn. The truck crews were running for cover as the gas was going up in flames and the munitions exploding. The flaming gas spread over the ground under the trucks, and a great column of black smoke billowed up. Up ahead, some Jerry planes hit the Mustangs and there was a dogfight. We only saw one, and Zemke chased him.'

In the days following 'Operation Overlord' the 8th Air Force was engaged primarily on support for the invasion forces, the fighters mixing in their own ground attack operations with escort to bombers sent to a wide variety of tactical targets in areas likely to be used for any German counter-attack and further afield. Airfields figured highly during this period and in fact the bombers did not fly against strategic targets again until the 18th. Fighters continued to find a reduced level of Luftwaffe activity on the ground as well as in the air, the best days being the 8th and 12th. But there was an upsurge of enemy fighter intercepts on 20 June, when VIII BC sent more than 1,800 heavy bombers to more than fifteen target areas while

Left *Groundcrew work on 42-106923 of the 364th FS, 357th FG, at Leiston. The group made a practice of flying 'half and half' painted P-51B/C models when natural aluminium finish became the norm, retaining a degree of camouflage. Invasion stripes compromised this — but by then, it didn't really matter. . .* (via Paul Coggan).

Left *Parked on a wooded dispersal, the 339th ground men check the degree of damage suffered by* Sally *during a ground strafing run. Fighters and flak were by no means the only hazards to contend with and in this case low-strung telephone cables were the culprits* (via Paul Coggan).

Left *Lieutenant Amos H. Bomberger of the 361st Squadron, 356th Group, flew 42-26649/ QI-B,* Miss Carriage, *from Martlesham Heath.*

Above right *Down in the rough with its wheels up is a Mustang of the 358th FS assigned to the 2nd Scouting Force, as indicated by the bar over the squadron code* (via Paul Coggan).

fighters escorted and mounted their own fighter-bomber strikes.

Challenging this 8th AF effort in varying numbers, the Luftwaffe again suffered badly; fighters attempting to hit 2nd Division B-24s met 271 P-38s and P-51s and lost 28 destroyed from a total for the day of 41 plus eighteen on the ground. Many fighter missions during this period were flown under code names which instantly identified the type of sweep to be carried out, among them 'Stud', 'Royal Flush' and 'Full House'.

It was also in June that the later model Thunderbolts and Mustangs began to be operated by the squadrons. In the P-51D the most significant change apart from the all-round vision canopy was a re-designed wing gun bay which incorporated three .50-cal machine-guns on each side. Each weapon was set in an upright position with the ammunition feed being designed to lie as flat as possible, all but eliminating the stoppage problem that had been experienced in the P-51B and C models.

Despite the time of year, 8th AF bomber operations were still being frustrated by weather conditions. These frequently were manifested by a dense build-up of cloud over the target area. In an on-going battle in which the AAF often had to admit defeat, the elements forced instigation of an intensive programme to develop radio navigation and radar aids aimed to circumvent nature's cloak which all too often shrouded the relatively tiny points in Europe that the bombers were trying to destroy. Throughout the war the famed Norden bombsight was utilized by most 8th AF heavies and this ingenious piece of precious equipment always worked best when the target could be clearly seen by the bombardiers. Another difficulty was the time-lag between weather reconnaissance and actual time over target. This varied but was never less than hours old. In the interval cloud could mass enough to result in unsatisfactory concentrations of bombs, diversions to secondary objectives and a general waste of the massive effort required every time a sizeable mission was mounted. One solution was therefore to obtain more immediate weather reports.

The answer was provided by an idea put forward by Colonel 'Bud' Peaslee who recommended forming a force of fighters flown by bomber pilots to fly ahead of the formations of heavies and report the conditions they found in the target areas by radio. Bomber pilots were chosen because they understood the difficulties faced by navigators when confronted by solid overcast just as the formation reached the primary. If a change to secondary targets was called for, they needed to know which of these was clear.

Peaslee's plan for a scouting force was outlined to Doolittle in May 1944. The response was enthusiastic and a call went out for volunteers from among lead or command pilots who had completed one or more tours in bombers and who wished to try their hands at the controls of a P-51. Peaslee himself was an experienced bomber leader who would test his idea at first hand.

Transition of suitable pilots was remarkably quick. After a conversion course in the T-6 each man put in about twenty hours' flying time on the Mustang. For administrative purposes it was decided that the scouting force aircraft would be attached to regular fighter groups, one in each air division. Peaslee's original unit in the 1st Division went to Honington to use the facilities and aircraft of the 385th Squadron, 364th Group. The 355th Group's 354th Squadron provided similar accommodation for the 2nd SF at Steeple Morden and the 3rd SF was attached to the 55th Group's 338th Squadron at Wormingford.

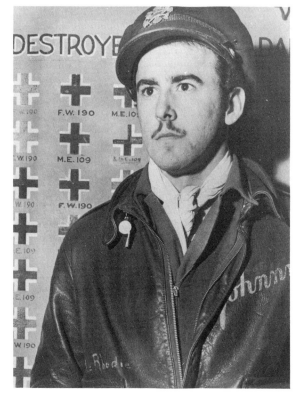

P-51D 44-14460/WR-R of the 355th was a 2nd Scouting Force machine named Hi Nell. *The pilot shown is believed to be Lieutenant Bill Whalen, the only SF pilot to achieve ace status.*

Captain John Godfrey in front of the scoreboard of the 4th Group at Debden (IWM).

Peaslee himself led the first SF mission on 16 July and although it was initially found that the P-51 pilots, lacking a navigator, had some difficulty in locating targets, the 'advance weather forecasting' they were able to provided was invaluable. Also, a fully-armed Mustang was well able, if necessary, to fight its way out of trouble, and as happened on occasions, provide escort to straggling bombers.

★　　　★　　　★

Despite early hopes that 8th AF bombers could gain some respite from enemy defences by flying on to more distant Allied territory and thereby avoid a dangerous flight back to England, it took many months of negotiations with Stalin before agreement was reached on the use of Russian bases for shuttle raids. Limited support facilities had hitherto prevented a repeat of the first shuttle mission to North Africa on 17 August 1943 and the more direct routes to Russian territory appeared to offer an ideal solution.

The date chosen for the first 'Frantic' shuttle was

21 June; Berlin, Potsdam, Stendal and other locations were on the target list for the bulk of 1,234 heavies from all three divisions. Of this total 163 3rd Division B-17s were briefed to hit oil installations at Ruhland/Schwarzeheide and fly eastwards to bases at Poltava and Mirgorod. In support of this force was the 4th Fighter Group, its strength boosted by a fourth squadron, the 352nd Group's 486th — 61 Mustangs in all. Don Blakeslee was very keyed up before this prestigious mission for the 8th. He told his pilots, some of whom stared incredulously at the long red ribbons on the operations map in the Debden briefing room:

'Now look, before we all get excited about it — I'll say the whole trip is about 7½ hours. We've done them that long before. We'll be throttled back so by Christ, we can stay up for eight hours. There'll be 1,000 bombers acting as a diversion for our Forts.

'We'll take the bombers up to the Russian frontier — from there it's 258 miles to base. We shall be met by Russian fighter planes — Yaks.'

Optimistically Blakeslee added, 'On the way to

Russia we will not do any fighting. You will not drop your tanks. If for any reason you should have to drop your tanks before Berlin — you've had it. You will have to return to East Anglia.

'No one will abort because of lack of oxygen. You'll be at 15,000 ft. You don't need it. You have no business in the group if you have to have oxygen at 15,000. If you get dizzy, go down under the bombers for a while.'

When they had swallowed all this, their CO added a little more encouragement.

'This whole thing is for show. That's why everything must be pansy. It's not what you do, but what you seem to do.'

In order to ensure that the mission was just that, Blakeslee stowed sixteen maps in his cockpit. His was a big responsibility. The vast featureless Russian terrain was no place to stooge about in a single-seater fighter low on fuel. If anyone could find the designated landing ground at Piryatin, Blakeslee could.

An early take-off saw the Mustang force make contact with the B-17s at 11:13 hr over Leszno, the synthetic oil target having been bombed. A little over an hour later 25 Bf 109s made a head-on attack on the Forts. The P-51s warded them off as best they could but the pilots dared not indulge in too much fuel-consuming combat manoeuvring. Two of the interceptors were shot down before the rest retired. One 4th Group aircraft was lost. Characteristically forgetting all Blakeslee had said, Kidd Hofer went tearing off after the diving Germans, his non-appearance resulting in him being listed MIA.

Blakeslee's navigation was right on the money as the Mustangs banked over Piryatin dead on time. A traumatic night lay ahead. A German reconnaissance aircraft had revealed the Americans' intention and a well co-ordinated and executed strike took place. The B-17s at Poltava bore the brunt of the attack and on the 22nd the fighters were dispersed to other bases lest the Germans repeated their success. It was back to Piryatin the following day and it was the 26th before Blakeslee led his ships on the first leg of the flight back to Debden. En route the 8th AF Mustangs landed in Italy; Hofer turned up on Malta, having 'overshot' Italy, finally arriving at Foggia on the 29th.

On 2 July the 4th's shuttle formation joined the 15th AF's fighters on a mission to Budapest and met the enemy in aggressive mood. Combat resulted in eight destroyed for five P-51s lost. Sadly, Hofer was one — this time his 'lone wolf' exuberance had proved his undoing. Last seen climbing to engage twenty-plus '109s, his body was subsequently found with the wreckage of his aircraft at Mostar, Yugoslavia.

Further sorties from Italy took place before Blakeslee led his depleted force back to Debden on 5 July, having logged 6,000 miles, ten countries and 29½ hours of operational flying. Ten enemy aircraft were claimed for the loss of seven P-51s.

The 4th mourned the loss of Hofer; his colourful antics and total disregard of orders — bordering on the courageous with a man like Blakeslee at the helm — left a gap even in a group which was no stranger to extrovert characters. Also sorely missed was Jim Goodson. Another victim of ground fire, he had bellied in after strafing New Brandenburg the day before the shuttle mission. Goodson jumped out and watched resignedly as his colleagues shot up his new Mustang. The Germans could cross another 8th AF ace from their 'wanted' list.

11 New threat

As soon as forward areas in France had been secured by Allied ground forces, engineer battalions prepared emergency airstrips for the use of aircraft, it being a great advantage for crews not to have to face the Channel crossing if their machines had been damaged. Numerous diversions were recorded in the weeks following the invasion as pilots sought a welcome haven. Plans had also been implemented for some 8th AF fighter groups to operate from Continental bases for short periods to meet operational eventualities, although support of ground forces was vested in the RAF and 9th Air Force, aircraft of both quickly moving into newly liberated aerodromes and temporary strips.

Bomber targets continued to be mainly 'No-ball' V-1 launching and storage areas, airfields, bridges and transport. On 4 July the 8th put up 952 fighters, all but the 359th participating, to escort 558 B-17s and B-24s attacking airfields and bridges. The 56th claimed twenty enemy aircraft for the loss of one P-47, these victories taking the group past another milestone — 400 enemy aircraft destroyed in air combat. Gabby Gabreski then led VIII FC aces with 28 to his credit.

July 1944 was a month of changes, some positive, others far less so. On the 7th the box score for the day was 75 kills, one probable and nineteen claimed as damaged, with the 55th Group taking the lion's share with 19½. Among the six fighters missing from the day's escort duty was that of Colonel Glenn Duncan, CO of the 353rd Group.

Both the 55th and 364th began their conversion from the P-38 to the P-51 in July, the latter aircraft introducing to service the 'No-miss-um' gunsight, the K-14. A gyro computing sight, it enabled very much more accurate deflection shooting and was rightly to become known as the 'ace-maker sight'.

In July the 20th Group began conversion to the P-51 and flew the last full mission with the P-38. On the 20th the 55th Squadron, flying as the 20th 'B' Group, initiated Mustang operations. One day later the 77th Squadron followed suit, leaving the 79th to close out the P-38 period as 'A' Group on the same mission, No 138. Escort was provided to 1st Division B-17s bombing various targets in south-west Germany. No less than 1,110 bombers of both types were despatched that day, the mission boards including Saarbrucken marshalling yards, the Messerschmitt plants at Regensburg/ Obertraubling and Regensburg/Pruffening, Schweinfurt's ball bearing production centre and Munich. The 20th Group returned unscathed.

On the 18th of the month, one of the up-and-coming Mustang pilots had an excellent day when he shot down four on one mission, George Preddy of the 352nd Group being the victor. The group overall claimed 21 that day, later adjusted to twenty.

By no means all personnel were pleased to see the back of the P-38; one man who had cared for the aircraft since his training days in 1941 was Max Pyles. Joining the 79th Fighter Squadron at the time of the arrival of the first P-38s in 1941, Pyles was among a number of engineering personnel who had taken the opportunity to attend Lockheed ground school at Burbank:

'Having been a mechanic before joining the AAF, I really enjoyed the chance to go to school there. Lockheed ran an Allison engine course at that time and as I had by then completed aircraft maintenance and engineering school at Curtiss Wright, I appreciated being able to learn more about the aircraft the squadron was then flying, along with P-39s and P-43s.

'I was a Flight Chief to start with in England. Due

Above right *George Preddy and his crew chief Lew Lunn discuss a technical point at Bodney early in 1944. The black ID bands on the rudder and tailplane were subsequently removed* (via Paul Coggan).

Right *It was evidently a good day at Burbank when Lockheed completed the P-38J that became Lieutenant Arthur Heiden's* Lucky Lady. *Under the skilled hands of Master Sergeant Max Pyles this 79th FS aircraft never aborted a mission by the 20th Group as a result of engine failure. Here Heiden congratulates Pyles on being decorated for his technical ability with the Lockheed aircraft and its Allison engines* (Max Pyles).

to some disagreement with the Line Chief, I was assigned as Crew Chief to the Squadron Commander, Major Franklin. His aircraft, I believe it was a J-15 model, had about twenty hours on it when I started crewing it. After Franklin, Arthur Heiden took it over. I discussed with him some of the things I thought he should watch for to make the plane and engines do their job. I told him I was interested in one thing — to get him over Germany and get him back.

'The thing I stressed most was lean mixture fuel/air ratio to the engines. Most engines were lost due to fouled spark plugs — they became unbalanced when the plugs did not fire. When power was applied the engine literally blew apart. We tried to explain the problem but with little success. Our gas was heavy with lead to increase the octane for high power output.

'I told Heiden to pull the mixture controls back until the engine rpm started to drop, to move them back until the lost revolutions were back to the original setting, then to leave them unless they went above 40 in of manifold pressure. Then he should go to auto lean only. Lean mixture burns hotter and keeps the spark plugs clean.

'On checking the plugs after flight this proved to be true; also flight times were increased by forty per cent. I believe that if our group had had more knowledge of the Allison engine's performance settings, and improvements on the production line had been made faster than they were, we might have kept the P-38 — but other groups were having the same problems.

'But as the records show, when the P-38 was really put into action it didn't come up short. I would say that a lot of our problems stemmed from a general lack of knowledge of the aircraft. It required a greater understanding of its technicalities than other aircraft — but with that knowledge and the ability to apply it in maintenance, the P-38 was a great flying machine.

'I crewed for five pilots during my time in the 20th — two in P-38s and three in P-51s. I 'lost' one P-51 pilot when he took a direct flak hit just behind the engine. I did not find out what happened until after the war when the plane was found bellied-in with him still in the cockpit.'

★   ★   ★

While the 8th Air Force fighters were enjoying a marked superiority over the Germans 'in their own back yard', tragedy, only indirectly attributable to

combat, was never very far away. Sometimes it would strike at home where it was least expected, as the 78th Group found on 19 July. After a successful day's hunting, the Mustangs accounting for twenty of the enemy during strafing attacks on aerodromes, a returning B-17 limped into Duxford for a crash-landing. The Fortress touched down and burned, the resulting fire killing thirteen of the 78th's personnel.

Disaster of a different kind occurred on the following day when the 56th's Gabby Gabreski was shot down whilst strafing. His loss to the group was the sadder as he had not needed to make the mission, having finished his tour. But while waiting for a seat on a transport to take him home, the Wolfpack drew a strafing mission to the Frankfurt area. Reasoning that one last crack at the enemy would be worth the risk, Gabby saddled up and went. Like most aggressive fighter pilots, he had come to terms with the risks and as everyone knew, disaster 'always happened to the other fellow'.

Having crossed the Ruhr the squadron spotted a number of He 111s on an airfield just west of Frankfurt. These were duly attacked, Gabreski himself accounting for two. Then, perhaps because this was his last combat flight for the forseeable future, Gabby decided to make another run, and literally go out with a bang, all guns blazing. This he did, coming in just above the deck. The bullets were overshooting; down a bit — too low!

Probably it was the propeller striking the ground, or the belly. Whatever it was, the impact set up terrific vibration. The Thunderbolt would not stay in the air much longer, and there was every chance that a prowling fighter would spot an easy kill. A bale-out was possible but Gabby had no way of knowing how long his aircraft would stay in one piece — a climb to bale-out height could prove fatal. That left him one choice. Belly it in and take his chances. At least he should survive a crash landing.

The Wolfpack ace found a couple of open fields bordered by trees. He dropped in fast, at about 180 kt indicated. In order to stop before he reached the trees, Gabby had to drive the P-47 into the ground. He kicked full rudder to dig a wingtip in. At least that way his machine would loose momentum. Then there was little to do but brace himself against the gunsight and hope. The careening Thunderbolt stopped and Gabreski realized he had forgotten to open the canopy. Smoke from up front added strength to the adrenalin needed to shove the canopy back and get his head out. Divesting himself of the encumbrances of combat clothing, he 'slithered' out and ran. For a man not given over-much to physical exercise, Gabreski's exit speed was impressive. He ran even faster when he realized that two German soldiers were doing their best to shoot him. Dropping down

when they stopped to fire and running when they ran, the American pilot headed for his goal, a building that looked like a covered shrine on stilts. He made it and the soldiers passed by.

There followed five days of relative freedom, deep in enemy territory. Befriended by a group of villagers he was eventually handed over the Wehrmacht. For the 8th's leading ace (31 victories — later corrected to 30.5 including 2.5 destroyed on the ground) the war was over. Back home at Boxted, Dave Schilling would take the reins of the Wolfpack.

Another event for VIII FC on 27 July was not very positive, although it stood as a record nevertheless. The 20th FG was en route when one Mustang was struck by lightning. The pilot baled out and it was found that he had left his damaged aircraft at an altitude of no less than 28,000 ft. Elsewhere, the day recorded the bombers plastering targets in Belgium and Holland, including gun batteries on the coast, and fighter-bombers seeking rail traffic. Total fighter strength put up from England was 368. Sorties included the first in Mustangs for the 364th, in the process of converting from the P-38. A squadron of Lightnings made up the group's full complement for the mission.

American fighter losses paled in comparison with those of the enemy, whose statisticians had little choice but to report 472 fighters lost during April. Despite the downing of valuable leaders such as Gabreski, there was little likelihood that the Luftwaffe could reverse the trend. But the Germans had an ace or two yet to play. On 28 July Colonel Avelin

P. Tacon, Jr, met the first of these over Merseburg: Tacon was leading the 359th Group when... 'I encountered two Me 163s. My eight P-51s were furnishing close escort for a combat wing of B-17s, and we were flying south at 25,000 ft when one of my pilots called in two contrails at six o'clock high some five miles back at 32,000 ft. I identified them immediately as jet-propelled aircraft. Their contrails could not be mistaken and looked very dense and white, somewhat like an elongated cumulus cloud some three-quarters of a mile in length. My section turned 180 degrees back toward the enemy fighters, which included two with jets turned on and three in a glide without jets operating at the moment.

'The two I had spotted made a diving turn to the left in close formation and feinted toward the bombers at six o'clock, cutting off their jets as they turned. Our flight turned for a head-on pass to get between them and the rear of the bomber formation. While still 3,000 yd from the bombers, they turned into us and left the bombers alone. In this turn they banked about eighty degrees but their course changed only about twenty degrees.

'Their turn radius was very large but their rate of roll appeared excellent. Their speed I estimated was 500 to 600 miles per hour. Both planes passed under us, 1,000 ft below, while still in a close formation glide. In an attempt to follow them, I split S'd. One continued down in a 45-degree dive, the other climbed up into the sun very steeply and I lost him. Then I looked back at the one in a dive and saw he was five miles away at 10,000 ft. Other members of my

flight said that the one which went into the sun used his jet in short bursts as though it was blowing smoke rings. These pilots appeared very experienced but not aggressive. Maybe they were just on a trial flight.'

On the following days, 8th AF fighter pilots made contact with the little rocket fighter again. Fully aware that the Germans were working on revolutionary new aircraft, VIII FC circulated known details to all groups without delay. As soon as the 359th's combat reports were analyzed, Kepner wired his command, giving a full summary of the contact. A drawing of the Me 163 had already been circulated and this was referred to in the message, which said that it appeared to be reliably accurate and useful for recognition training. Kepner's text continued:

'. . . It is believed we can expect to see more of these aircraft immediately and that we can expect attacks on the bombers from the rear in formations or waves. To be able to counter and have time to turn into them our units are going to have to be in positions relatively close to the bombers to be between them and our heavies. It is believed that these tactics will keep them from making effective, repeat effective, attacks on the bombers. Attention is called to the fact that probably the first thing seen will be heavy, dense contrails high and probably 30,000 ft above approaching rear of bombers. Jet aircraft can especially be expected in Leipzig and Munich area or any place east of nine degree line.'

On 29 July, VIII FC credited P-38 pilot Captain Arthur J. Jeffrey of the 479th with the first Me 163 destroyed in aerial combat. Post-war examination of

the records of the Me 163 unit in action that day showed that the aircraft, last seen diving away, had not in fact crashed. The unit was the famous JG400 commanded by Wolfgang Späte, whose unenviable task was to turn the rocket fighter into a worthwhile combat aircraft in the face of extreme difficulty not the least of which was the inherent instability of the aircraft's fuels.

It was August before the fighters were able to claim a decisive victory over the Luftwaffe jets; (rocket and turbojet fighters were classed as 'jets' in contemporary accounts, Allied intelligence only suspecting that the Me 163 differed significantly in terms of its power source. To US fighter pilots the difference held little significance.) The month also recorded the first losses of AAF bombers and fighters to such aircraft.

★   ★   ★

On 1 August 1944 command changes brought Brigadier General Murray C. Woodbury in to take over 8th AF fighter responsibility at Bushey Hall. Major General Kepner's absence from the head of the command would last until 3 August the following year, when he would return briefly after the end of the war. Woodbury's appointment was only temporary for on 3 August, he handed over to Brigadier General Francis H. Griswold, in whose hands VIII FC would be until October of that year.

The first days of August saw the now almost routine posting of maximum effort fighter support for bombers striking both tactical and strategic targets on a broad front across continental Europe. That the quality of the enemy was deteriorating under the punishing weight of attack both by bombers and fighters which had come of age as a force in their own right with their individual target list and variety of tactics and weapons with which to destroy them, was being proved on an almost daily basis.

On 4 August the Thunderbolt-equipped 356th Fighter Group from Martlesham got among the enemy — who did not employ the most sound tactics against the Americans. Bounced by the Americans at 38,000 ft, the Bf 109s dived — a classic mistake against P-47s. With their seven-ton 'juggernauts' almost literally falling out of the sky the 356th had little trouble in catching its quarry. No less than fifteen German fighters fell — and not always directly to .50-cal machine-gun fire. Manoeuvring into position behind a pair of '109s, Lieutenant Westwood Fletcher and his wingman were in hot pursuit while the two Messerschmitts frantically weaved at low level to evade an impending hail of bullets. Both German pilots tried too hard. One misjudged a turn and collided with an oak tree and the other hit the ground of a meadow, momentum carrying the aircraft some distance before it exploded.

It was not quite so easy for Second Lieutenant Robert Gleason who tangled with one of the more experienced pilots in the enemy formation. Although finally despatching his quarry, Gleason counted 77 holes in the airframe of his aircraft when he arrived back home. These shots had come from a second Bf 109 which had latched on to his tail while Gleason was intent on his kill. The 356th was much elated at the day's work which resulted in victories of 15 (destroyed)-0(probable)-2(damaged).

Over at Bodney, on 5 August the 352nd pilots were indulging in a little off-duty card playing. The chips mounted in the Officer's Club and George Preddy had Lady Luck at his shoulder. Aided and abetted by his friend Harry Kidder, Preddy swept the board to the tune, some said, of $1,000. The game broke up as nobody had any money left. But by chance August was the start of the 8th Air Force's War Bond Drive, with each station being set a target sum. Bodney's was $53,000 and Preddy started the ball well and truly rolling with a bond purchase of $1,200.

As there seemed little likelihood of a mission that day, the weather being predicted as 'rotten', the pilots had a party. Having imbibed a little heavily, Preddy headed for the sack. He was interrupted by the Briefing Officer of the Day who imparted the bad news. A mission the next day (or rather later today), briefing in twenty minutes. As it was Preddy's turn to lead the 352nd, it was SOP for him to take the briefing. Shrugging off attempts to cover for him,

Preddy somehow got through the ordeal, telling the pilots that they would in a few hours' time be over the German capital escorting the bombers in attacks on oil refineries and factories. All the fighter groups were tasked to go, the 352nd making up part of the 740-strong element of Little Friends.

Precariously balanced on the platform in the briefing room, Preddy could not hide the fact that the party had run its course, either from his pilots or Group Commander Joe Mason. George Meyer and the others plied Preddy with coffee and the mission took off on schedule.

Much has been written about George Preddy's prowess as a fighter pilot — but few incidents illustrate this as well as the events of 6 August 1944. On oxygen at 32,000 ft Preddy had his party spirit come up, a pretty unpleasant experience in the confines of a Mustang cockpit. But the day was clear with fine visibility and the enemy was up. Perhaps making an extra effort to overcome his condition, Preddy tore into intercepting '109s with a vengeance. His encounter reports tells what happened next.

'We were escorting the lead combat wings of B-17s when thirty-plus Me 109s in formation came into the third box from the south. We were 1,000 feet above them so I led White Flight, consisting of Lieutenant Heyer, Lieutenant Doleac and myself, in astern of them. I opened fire on one near the rear of the formation from 300 yd dead astern and got many hits around the cockpit. The enemy aircraft went down inverted and in flames.

'At this time Lieutenant Doleac became lost while shooting down an Me 109 that had gotten on Lieutenant Heyer's tail. Lieutenant Heyer and I continued our attack and I drove up behind another enemy aircraft, getting hits around the wing roots and setting him on fire after a short burst. He went spinning down and the pilot baled out at 20,000 ft. I then saw Lieutenant Heyer on my right shooting down another enemy aircraft.

'The enemy formation stayed together taking practically no evasive action and tried to get back for an attack on the bombers who were off to the right. We continued with our attack on the rear end and I fired on another from close range. He went down

Above right *One of the most tragic losses to VIII FC was that of George Preddy, leading ace in the ETO at the time he was shot down on Christmas Day 1944, by American AA fire. This photo shows his penultimate P-51D which was exchanged for a later model on 6 August 1944, when Preddy took command of the 328th Squadron*

Right *Preddy's ground crew servicing his 487th Squadron aircraft. Five more kills and groundcrew names were added to the nose before Preddy transferred to the 328th (via Paul Coggan).*

Left *More work for the groundcrew as a result of a nose-over by a P-51D of the 357th FS, 355th Group (via Paul Coggan).*

Below right *Demonstrating the Berger G-suit effectively required someone to take the place of the P-51's vacuum system to show how the suit inflated to maintain blood pressure. Captain Charles Netherway obliged for Lieutenant Donald Johnson at Fowlmere, where the 339th Group's pilots became willing guinea pigs for the 'ace maker suit' (USAF).*

Far right *Tucked in close to an RAF ASR Warwick, 44-13899/5E-E displays the late-war markings of the 384th FS, 364th Group.*

smoking badly and I saw him begin to fall apart below us.

'At this time four other P-51s came in to help us with the attack. I fired at another '109, causing him to burn after a short burst. He spiralled down to the right in flames. The formation headed down in a left turn, keeping themselves together in rather close formation. I got a good burst into another one causing him to burn and spin down. The enemy aircraft were down to 5,000 ft now and one pulled off to the left. I was all alone with them now, so went after this single '109 before he could get on my tail. I got in an ineffective burst causing him to smoke a little. I pulled up into a steep climb to the left above him and he climbed after me. I pulled it in as tight as possible and climbed at about 150 miles per hour. The Hun opened fire on me but could not get enough deflection to do any damage. With my initial speed I slightly out-climbed him. He fell off to the left and I dropped down astern of him. He jettisoned his canopy as I fired a short burst getting many hits. As I pulled past, the pilot baled out at 7,000 ft.

'I lost contact with all friendly and enemy aircraft so headed home alone. CLAIM: Six (6) Me 109s.'

For this extraordinary feat George Preddy received his nation's second highest decoration, the Distinguished Service Cross. His score stood at 29 when he went on a well-deserved leave.

As the Allies advanced through France and the Low Countries, there was a bonus for the air forces: as enemy-occupied territory shrank there was more chance that damaged aircraft could make it to their side of the lines and pilots baling out would have less

ground to cover to reach friendly forces. A slight disadvantage was that Allied AA units were also in place — and very few of them had had a great deal of experience, particularly in recognizing friend from foe. There were numerous incidents of Allied aircraft being fired on by both sides and all group reports contain mention of such incidents. Fortunately relatively few resulted in losses. But there are exceptions to every rule . . .

Among the technical advances introduced into USAAF service at this time was special clothing designed to alleviate pilot discomfort during violent high speed manoeuvres. In August 1944 the 339th Group had begun battle testing the Berger G-suit which incorporated inflatable pads to equalize pilot blood pressure and prevent blacking out as blood drained from the brain. Early in 1944 VIII FC had acquired enough examples of the Berger suit to run comparative trials with a British model, the Frank suit. This latter worked on water pressure and was found to be equally effective although the 4th Group which participated in the trials highlighted some of the drawbacks. Paramount among these was the discomfort if the Frank suit happened to leak, and it was also bulky, hot and heavy to wear.

Berger suits were not immediately available, but the first were in the UK from 3 June 1944. These were also issued to the 339th at Fowlmere and although they were praised by pilots, there were inevitably some teething troubles. Maladjusted pressure valves caused considerable discomfort and individual incidents of men being 'practically squeezed to death' showed that care had to taken in this regard. Once the valves were correctly set, pilots felt they were 'free to pull the wings off the P-51' — the ace-maker suit had arrived. There was apparently considerable fascination in watching the Mustang's accelerometer registering 5, 6, 7 even 8 G — so much so that pilots found it hard to keep their eyes on the gunsight. G suits became highly prized by the 339th, and they were worn on all subsequent missions. By November, there were enough suits to equip the rest of the VIII FC groups.

★　　★　　★

On a typical day when full bomber and fighter missions were mounted, there would normally be a considerable level of 8th AF air activity over and around the UK. As well as photographic reconnaissance force aircraft leaving for their allocated target areas on the Continent, both fighters and bombers — plus the numerous liaison and training types employed by the 8th — would undertake their important second-line duties. A typical day was 12 August 1944 when the 25th Bomb Group also despatched four Mosquitoes to act as scouts for the bombers, three Mosquitoes and one B-26 undertook weather recon-

naissance of the Continent, and two B-17s were sent off on weather recce of the seaborne approaches to the UK, their flights taking them out over the Atlantic.

Fighters were routinely requested for radio relay missions to support specially equipped bombers; one of the most interesting being the ill-fated 'Aphrodite' mission which primarily involved time-expired B-17s and B-24s in 'flying bomb' experiments. An 'Aphrodite' on 12 August required 47 aircraft although this was primarily a US Navy operation under the code name 'Anvil'. The force took off from Fersfield bound for the site of the third of the German V-weapons, the long range guns known as V-3, at Mimoyecques in France. The 'bombing' force was one PB4Y-1 Liberator and two PV-1 Ventura mother ships, covered by 26 Mustangs and nine P-47s carrying out the radio relay task. As the force headed for the coast of England to fly out over Southwold, the Liberator, or 'baby', exploded in mid-air. Very little was found in the wreckage and Lieutenant Joseph P. Kennedy, brother of the future President, was killed, as was Lieutenant W.J. Willy, the radio operator.

On 6 August Frantic V was flown by B-17s of the 96th and 390th Groups, accompanied by P-51s of the 357th. Unmolested, the bombers hit a Focke-Wulf assembly plant in Poland en route to Russia and bombed a Polish oil plant on the way home via Italy on the 8th. Luftwaffe activity was slight, one Bf 109 being shot down. Of the seven Frantic missions, the 8th AF was to fly four before the plan was terminated in September 1944.

The 12 August losses among the fighter groups engaged on escort and ground attack on transporta-

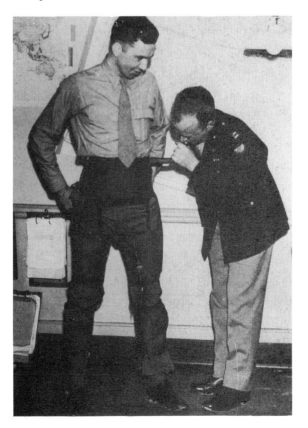

Left and below left *Port and starboard views of 44-13345/C5-I of the 364th Squadron, 357th Group, after an emergency landing at Lomma, Sweden, on 25 August 1944. The less controlled landing in the latter photo was also by one of the same group's aircraft.*

Right *Striking interim markings were carried by 55th FG Mustangs for a time, including* The Millie G, *one of six aircraft flown by Ed Giller. Although not the only 55th FG Mustang so marked, it was probably the most famous, being the subject of many photographs* (via Bruce Robertson).

tion targets was relatively heavy — eighteen aircraft were listed as MIA with three more listed as Category E and a further four damaged. To offset these figures the fighters claimed thirteen enemy aircraft destroyed on the ground, and six in the air. Among the losses in 361st FG was Tom Christian, who was killed; VIII FC had an equally bad day on the 13th, with thirteen aircraft down. One of the hazards of having that 'friendly' AA below was shown on the 14th when the 356th lost Lieutenant Louis G. Alphonse to American ground fire over Avranches.

A far happier conclusion to another shoot-down came on the 18th when the 355th's Captain Bert Marshall was downed by German flak some twenty miles west of Soissons. Belly-landing his P-51 in a field, Marshall was beginning to think that his luck had deserted him when there came the unmistakeable sound of a Merlin engine, throttled back to land. Marshall lost no time in exiting his own aircraft and running to the machine piloted by Second Lieutenant Royce Priest. Scrambling in and wedging himself on to Priest's lap, Marshall had an unusual return to Steeple Morden. Mouths dropped open when not one but two pilots climbed down from the Mustang.

★   ★   ★

Heavy cloud prevented full operations during the latter weeks of August, bombing missions including

the use of PFF aircraft to assist bombardiers deprived of clear conditions. But low cloud could help as well as hinder; the four remaining P-47 Groups despatched 163 aircraft on the 23rd, the object being to shoot up rail traffic in the area between St Omer and Rheims. All aircraft returned without loss on a day when there were no bomber operations. The Thunderbolts carried bombs and dropped 21 tons on their selected targets.

Two days later the weather cleared enough for the bombers to undertake a major assault on aircraft component plants, Luftwaffe experimental establishments and oil-related targets. Rechlin and Peenemünde were among the aiming points for B-17s of the 1st and 3rd Divisions, these and 2nd Division B-24s being ably covered by nearly 1,000 fighters. The most successful group was the 479th with seven air-to-air victories out of a total of 11(destroyed)-2(probable)-3(damaged) for the day. In addition the American fighters denied the Luftwaffe another forty machines on the ground, and damaged a further thirty.

Towards the end of August tangible evidence that the Luftwaffe had brought a twin-jet fighter into operational service was brought back in the gun cameras of P-47s of the 78th FG. From the operational viewpoint the Me 262 was a far more practical proposition than the often-lethal (to its pilots) Me 163 rocket fighter.

12 Contingencies

As the size of the striking forces allocated to the 8th increased, so too did its support services, both flying and non-flying. One of the former was the Air Rescue Spotter Squadron, formed in May 1944 and subsequently retitled the 5th Emergency Rescue Squadron. Equipped primarily with P-47 Thunderbolts fitted out with release gear to enable them to drop life-rafts to ditched aircrew, this unit was composed of pilots who had volunteered for a second tour once a tour with a first-line squadron had been completed. One man who took the option to transfer to the air-rescue squadron was Jack Bateman, formerly of the 359th Fighter Group.

'When the 359th switched to the P-51 Mustang, I had 500 hours on the Thunderbolt and a high regard for it. Not welcoming the prospect of flying the new type, I elected to stay with the Thunderbolt and left the Group on 1 May 1944.'

Arriving at Boxted, Bateman soon realized that although the rescue squadron was unlikely to meet the enemy in combat, there were plenty of other hazards. Lives often depended on these fighters flying, and England was no place to have lost, fatigued and occasionally wounded pilots blundering about the sky, invariably in inclement weather. The squadron was a helping hand, a voice in the overcast which would do its best to lead them home — pilots quickly realized that there were other hazards awaiting the unwary crew than enemy fighters and flak. An air-sea rescue tour brought its own excitement and no little drama. Bateman recalled an occasion when he was up looking for a B-24 stooging around, lost over southern England.

'As Duty Flight Leader for the day, I had to sit around, waiting for a call. Few other fighters were airborne as the weather was so bad — but this was the very time that the emergency squadron Thunderbolts were required to fly. This particular B-24 was located, but the pilot refused to do what I asked him. We would try to guide the cripples into the 8th's emergency aerodromes such as Manston or Woodbridge, which had the runway length and the facilities to deal with the worst situations. It was far better for a damaged aircraft to avoid its home base if there was a risk of a crash and resultant blocking of runways, damage to other aircraft on the field, and so on.

'But this B-24 pilot would have none of this, at least at first. But I eventually convinced the Liberator pilot that Manston was his best bet and the boy duly brought the aircraft in for a landing, with one engine out. Lining up on the runway myself, I couldn't see the other end of it and went round again, on instruments almost immediately. I broke cloud at less than 500 ft altitude with my wingman still close. Suddenly the lost B-24 loomed up.

'I took violent evasive action and lost him, by climbing but I picked him up again at 5,000 ft. The Liberator was this time guided back for a safe landing at Manston, and our Thunderbolts followed suit.

'A return to Boxted looked to be out of the question; there were no direction-finding aids in operation and the fighters had only their beacon homing and radio compass equipment. But the controller informed me that there were three more aircraft calling in on the emergency frequency, one of them heading for Manston. Due to the weather, only the south coast airfields were open.

'There was nothing for it but to try to make Boxted and refuel (ERS P-47s had up to five hours' duration with belly tanks and minimum power settings) for another search mission. The vectors back to base warned us that there was no break in the cloud and that our two fighters should fly south of Colchester reservoir, a well-known landmark.

'The Thunderbolts groped their way to Colchester and made two circuits of the town; a dark spot reflecting through the murk was thought to be the reservoir. Another circle was followed by an ILS instrument climb.

'I asked for a return vector to Manston, ETA thirty minutes. We would refuel and then have another crack at reaching Boxted. Visibility was by this time about 100 ft below the cloud layer.'

Both Thunderbolts finally made home base after flying over the reservoir at Colchester to pin-point their position. After landing they reflected on the flight — the two pilots had barely seen the steeple of Colchester church and one P-47 had passed each side of it . . .

'The ERS Thunderbolts maintained constant group communications with Boxted control and called RAF rescue launches to the vicinity of downed flyers. These Seagull launches pulled numerous crews from the drink and were powerful enough to get to a rescue position with all speed. Our Thunderbolts affected many rescues in this way as they were able to relay all the information on aircraft position and crew state in a very short time.

'One of my most vivid memories concerned a B-17 in bad trouble. Coming out over the Dutch coast with two engines out, the bomber was at 4,500 ft when his call was received. For some reason, only my circling P-47 picked up the signal from the Fort. I asked for all information from the bomber crew to relay to his own control, making a minute-by-minute up-date on a tri-angulation fix.

'I then realized that there were two B-17s in the

Right *Showing perhaps the power of the press, Tom Raines, 359th FG/5th ERS PRO, holds up Jack Bateman during a little off-duty horseplay at Boxted in 1944. The nose art behind is that of Bateman's P-47D* (Bateman).

Below *Jack Bateman in the cockpit of one of the two dozen or so P-47 Thunderbolts operated by the 5th Emergency Rescue Squadron for approximately one year beginning in May 1944. Bateman's mount is 42-8693/ 5F-E Miss Margaret, the aircraft he regularly flew* (Bateman).

area plus a P-38. When the Lightning was intercepted, I remained with the most badly damaged
bomber. Control advised me to direct it into Woodbridge — although I knew that a Fort had already put
down there and was partially blocking the main runway. The second bomber was so low by this time that
the pilot couldn't see the base until he was virtually
over the runway threshold. The pilot landed in 1,200
ft and turned off before the wreck. He barely made it
as a third engine quit just as he touched down.'

Control — 'Keyworth 50' — was very appreciative
of the rescue fighters' efforts. Afterwards, the fighter
pilots were personally thanked by the Fort crew —
had they not been able to make a straight-in approach
and landing at Woodbridge, it was doubtful if they
could have made it. As if to highlight what might well
have happened, a B-17 crashed at Woodbridge the
following day.

'On occasions, we advised the bomber crew to
ditch rather than try to make a landfall and risk a far
more hazardous landing. In making this decision for
a bomber crew, the fighter pilot had to make a quick
judgement based on wide experience, of the prevailing sea conditions and the known location of rescue
launches. In one particular case a ditching was considered to assist the co-pilot's chances of survival. His
condition was such that his chances were said to be
slight and the captain had to put the rest of the crew
first. A bale-out would undoubtedly have resulted in
the loss of the co-pilot.

'But a ditching was not undertaken lightly; I
always stressed that the pilot and co-pilot had only a
slight chance of getting out of the aircraft before it
sank. It was no time to build up any false hopes — but

it was the crew's decision. Only the captain of the
aircraft could make the choice to save his crew and
run a high risk of losing his own life. This crew elected
to ditch. Nine men scrambled into a dinghy and I
dropped markers and smoke floats to guide the
launch to it. The Seagull picked up nine but as I had
feared, both the pilot and co-pilot of the B-17 failed to
get out.'

★   ★   ★

An American fighter group was a vast entity, with the
pilots and aircraft at the tip of a very large pyramid of
ground support and administrative sections all
geared to putting the maximum number of aircraft
into the air to meet operational requirements, looking after the health and welfare of the flyers, paying
them and carrying out the thousand and one tasks
that added up to a smoothly run organization
virtually independent of the country in which it
happened to be based. In England with its relatively
modern facilities, this task was less arduous than it
was in almost any other theatre of war. Early on, of
course, the USAAF relied heavily on assistance from
the RAF and the goodwill of the British populace for
the provision of inumerable items which were initially in short supply from the other side of the
Atlantic.

As the war progressed and the 8th Air Force established its own place in the supply chain, American
provisions and equipment came into Britain at an
ever-increasing rate, to the point that the visitors
were able to bring much-sought-after 'luxuries' to
their hosts, labouring under the exigencies of war.

Below left *A sight Landers and other 78th Group pilots would have been glad to see — the identification letters of Duxford airfield, heralding warm quarters, good food and company.*

Right Isabel III *was one of the numerous P-51D-5 models that were built without fin fillets issued to the 357th. This one was on the strength of the 363rd Squadron in 1944* (via T. Bennett).

Countless acts of kindness and consideration in sharing this bounty forged lifelong friendships between individuals of the two nations.

Social events were held regularly on the bases and Christmas was the ideal excuse to throw lavish parties for local children, many of whom had ever seen the abundance of 'goodies' let alone missed them because of the war. That the Americans were welcome was hardly in doubt. True, the wildness of the young men was at times a source of annoyance, especially as many inhabitants of England's sleepy villages and hamlets had not, at that time, even made the acquaintance of their own countrymen from Wales, Ireland or Scotland — let alone someone who hailed from Ohio, Texas or Nebraska. Few towns situated near a US air base would ever be quite the same again.

American fighter pilots frequently had the chance to air any grievances or make observations on the progress of the war as they saw it, to visiting US Congressmen and Senators; to members of the British Royal Family and to numerous high-ranking officers from their own and other nations' armed forces. On occasions these personages would request informal talks with fighter pilots — who were, in their turn, only too willing to 'tell how it is' in the time honoured, democratic way. US Assistant Secretary for War for Air Robert A. Lovett paid such a visit to the UK in 1944. During his tour of USAAF establishments he requested a chat with men from a 'hot fighter outfit'. The spotlight fell on Duxford and the pilots of the 78th Group.

General Hunter asked every pilot who had made a kill to gather in the base projection room, where gun camera film was screened for Mr Lovett's benefit. He shook hands and to put things on an informal footing, said: 'I know how you probably feel about people who come over here from Washington to talk to you. But I would honestly like to help where I can. Now suppose you knew that your brother, your kid brother, was a pilot back home, and coming over here. What things would you want us to do to the Thunderbolt back home before your brother had to fight in it against the Focke-Wulfs?'

That kind of approach brought forth spontaneity from the boys; the comments were both laudatory and critical — not too much, but enough to give the Assistant Secretary food for thought and, through this and other channels, the manufacturers got the feedback from the men in the front line and in the fullness of time, changes were made on the production lines. In summary the pilots didn't necessarily want aircraft of super performance — rather they wanted small improvements and reliability. Equally important to most of them was an assurance that an adequate flow of replacement aircraft and parts would be forthcoming.

Although procedure varied to some degree in each fighter group, the train of events that resulted in the despatch of a mission from the UK followed a similar pattern throughout the war. VIII Fighter Command procedures were initially patterned on those of the RAF and were progressively modified as the 8th Air Force gained autonomy. Alerted by 8th AF, VIII FC headquarters passed warning of an escort mission the following day during the afternoon of the day preceding it, in the form of a Field Order. Each FO carried a sequential number which, although beginning for VIII BC on 17 August 1942 with Field Order 1, allowed for the early deployment of US fighters in conjunction with RAF operations and were numbered accordingly. Thus prior to April 1943 when VIII FC began issuing its own Field Orders, a fighter escort or sweep would invariably carry the RAF numerical sequence as *Rodeo 200* and so forth.

Field Order 1 for VIII FC was not issued until April 1943, by which time Bomber Command had reached FO 50.

The Field Order was sent by teletype to the operational stations by the evening of the day preceding. It gave all relevant data on the route, the target, check points and size of the force involved in the mission, each group being detailed to provide a number of aircraft to fulfill the total required. The group then checked the availability of pilots and aircraft among its three squadrons to meet the requirement. Assuming it was an escort mission, each fighter group would supply aircraft for penetration, target or withdrawal support of the bomber force involved, this in turn depending on the type of fighter with which the group was equipped, and the degree of experience it had. Groups fresh to the ETO would invariably be placed on withdrawal support for their first few missions, in order to minimize contact with enemy fighters until their 'theatre training' was deemed complete. Once the selection had been made, this data was telephoned to 8th Air Force, followed by teletype confirmation. Headquarters responded with details of timings — when the bombers were to be at each rendezvous/checkpoint, when they would cross the English coast and when they would penetrate enemy airspace, and the altitudes at which they would fly.

With the FO prepared, senior officers discussed the details, assimilating known enemy strengths and locations, the likely reaction by the enemy in proportion to the importance of the target, the weather and other factors relevant to the mission. The order was then drafted and sent via the teleprinter to the three fighter wings and the groups. Alternatively, if the details were complex and the final order took consid-erable time to appear in final draft form, the details would be telephoned. The wing headquarters super-imposed the mission route on the map of Europe and again checked the details, including its relation to any friendly ground activity — depending again on the period of the war. Weather was checked and re-checked and authorization given for last-minute weather reconnaissance flights if these were felt necessary to add to the information already to hand.

From wing the order was transmitted to the fighter groups where the station operations rooms would distribute the mission requirements through their own local chains of command in order to put the operation into practice. The Group Duty Officer informed the squadron duty watches who would in their turn, alert the various specialist sections of the units to prepare aircraft for the day's mission. This brought the armament, flying control, engineering and messing sections into action, ideally up to four hours before the mission take-off time, and approximately two hours after the bomber bases had begun their own preparations.

Fighters would invariably have been readied the previous evening in order to save time on the following day — but the weather on the day would often be the deciding factor for a mission actually taking off. On numerous occasions missions were prepared only for the weather on the morning in question turning out to be bad enough to delay flying, or for the operations to be scrubbed entirely.

Each fighter had its own Crew Chief, Assistant Crew Chief and Armourer — who often replenished more than one aircraft. Ground crew duty was structured differently to that of flying personnel, and their tours of duty were often for the duration of

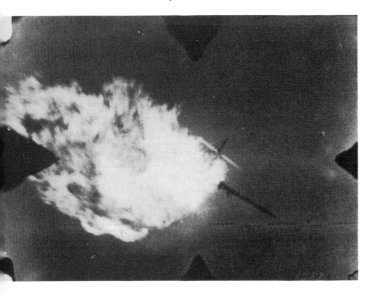
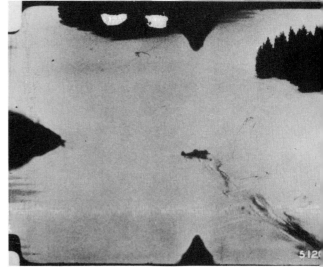

hostilities. Thus a single crew could look after a number of fighters during their time in the ETO, with individual aircraft carrying the names of different pilots over an extended period of time. The ground crew names were invariably painted on the aircraft adjacent to the name of the pilot and these men were responsible for that machine throughout its service life.

The ground crew first removed the protective covers from the canopy and engine, depending on the time of year. In winter efforts were made to shroud the aircraft as completely as possible during periods of intensely cold weather bringing heavy frost or snow. The propeller was then pulled through to clear any residual oil in the cylinders. If conditions were particularly damp, a check might have to be made on the state of the spark plugs and the electrics in general.

The armourers, meanwhile, uncovered the guns and the Crew Chief started the engine. When it was warmed up he made a thorough pre-take off check to ensure that everything was functioning as it should, paying particular attention to the oil pressure, electrics, hydraulics and magnetos. Previously he would have satisfied himself during a visual walk-round check that the aircraft was in good shape. During this he looked for properly inflated tyres, that all inspection panels were firmly fastened, that the canopy and all glass areas were free of scratches, dirt or oil and that the cockpit floor was clean.

The armourer's responsibility extended to the gunsight, which he looked over to see that it had not been damaged since the last flight, or had been properly set up if it had had to be replaced or serviced. He checked that the guns were properly seated in

their mountings, that the firing solenoids were in good order and that the ammunition feeds were free of obstructions. He then supervized the loading of the gun bays with the maximum amount of ammunition, made up according to previously determined ratios of armour-piercing, ball or tracer. The aircraft then had its drop tanks topped off, as the main internal tanks would have been filled the previous evening. The oxygen was replenished with new bottles delivered to all dispersals by a cart. Then, depending again on group procedure and the time available, the ground crew would get their breakfast and kill time before take-off.

When the pilot arrived at his aircraft, the Crew Chief accompanied him on another walk round before helping him strap in and assist with engine starting. Care had to be taken not to flood an already-warm engine and drain the battery in repeated attempts to restart. Most pilots appreciated this but inevitably some were a little heavy-handed. Although the pilot invariably outranked his Crew Chief there were few who did not take notice if the Crew Chief was seen to wince during the pre-take off check and modify his technique accordingly. The pilot knew that he depended on a good ground crew to complete the mission safely and ensure that his aircraft was in tip-top shape mechanically.

About an hour before the main briefing for the mission the fighter leaders would be in Group Operations, studying the details, and planning the procedures to be followed. Three hours before take-off the pilots were woken up and each man would be taken to the Officer's Mess for breakfast prior to attending briefing.

The main briefing was conducted by the Duty

Far left and left *Victim: American fighter pilots occasionally caught enemy fighters with external tanks — and the results were spectacular if their fire ignited the fuel. This Bf 109 ended up in a snow bank after the exploding tank put it out of action* (via Bruce Robertson).

Right *Ticking over under the guiding hand of a groundcrew man,* Heavenly Body *was part of the 78th's 83rd FS.*

Left *Armament sections of all groups worked hard to ensure that fighter guns worked when required. These men are making up ammunition belts at Honington on 4 Sept 1944* (USAF).

Right *'With the aid of models, the group leader discusses last minute tactics before the mission. Pilots here are fully kitted up and have only to 'mount up and plug in'* (355th FG Association).

Below right *Unsung hero of the air war from the UK was the humble bicycle, invaluable mode of transport on the ground, particularly on a muddy airfield. This scene at Steeple Morden shows group pilots getting the last word on tactics before mounting their steeds and heading for the flight line.* (355th FG Association).

Intelligence Officer, the Weather Officer and the mission leader, each of whom imparted all the details the pilots required for all aspects of the operation. For a group to be efficient these officers, plus those whose responsibility was communications and flying control, had previously to brief themselves thoroughly as to the contents of the Field Order. This saved time in answering any questions the pilots may have had as the briefing progressed.

The Intelligence Officer's responsibility was awesome; he had to have a full picture of the mission as a whole, including the strength, route and target of the bomber forces involved, take-off time, time over target, rendezvous points and so forth. Also to be imparted was the planned return route and estimated times of arrival back at base. All call signs were given, as were flight compositions, identified by letters and colours. These, and call signs, quickly became familiar with each base, group and squadron using terminology that changed little.

To assist recognition of friendly bomber groups, considerable use was made of illustrative material showing group tail symbols and/or coloured markings, each fighter group being responsible for escorting a known number of Bomb Groups in the Wing to which it was assigned. Any special instructions were also passed on by the Intelligence Officer and an indication of the size and location of enemy fighter forces was noted.

A touch of humour was invariably injected by the Weather Officer — a man with an unenviable job at the best of times. He would give information as up to the minute as possible on local conditions, what change there might be as the formation crossed the enemy coast and what could be expected in the target area. Winds, cloud formations and the presence of icing conditions were detailed, complete with weather maps. Visibility at all operating altitudes was duly noted, as was the possibility that the bombers would meet condensation trail air temperatures en route.

The pilot who was to lead the mission then summarized the task ahead, in the light of operational conditions the group had previously experienced. There had to be some assumption at this point as to what the enemy would do, and contingency plans were made to deal with attacks as they developed. Much depended on the strength of the opposing forces, but most eventualities were covered. Each of the squadrons in the group was allocated flank, front, rear and close escort positions, the last being the least enviable as it usually meant sticking with the bombers and not engaging unless absolutely necessary. Close escort was taken in turns by each squadron.

The mission leader outlined the tactics to be followed if the enemy attacked and stressed the need to keep flight integrity. No pilot should become separated from his wingman, but radio channels should be used economically without unnecessary chatter. Finally, any questions were answered, and the time checked.

Briefing over, Group Chaplains offered a blessing to those individuals requiring such spiritual reassurance for a safe return. Then everyone departed to travel, by various means, to his aircraft.

When the group returned in some five or six hours time (again depending on the distance to the target) the mission was the subject of a thorough analysis by the Intelligence Officers. Everything that happened or was merely observed was drawn out of the pilots, so that an accurate account of the day's work could be compiled both for 8th AF records and that of the group. It was at this time that every man could help to build the picture, even the novices. Perhaps they personally had had an uneventful flight — but they may have seen enemy aircraft shot down by other members of the group. Their verification could make the difference between a 'probable' or a 'confirmed' claim both in the unit's own records and the personal score of a fellow pilot. It was the Intelligence Officer's task to sort this mass of (often conflicting) data into a coherent report, assisted by the Flight, Squadron and Group Commanders, who would go over the entire mission with the aid of blackboard, maps and diagrams. If the mission had involved ground strafing, this post-mortem was a lengthy process — it would have been pointless and unnecessarily risky, for example, to have the group (or others) attack an airfield again, if the day's results had been decisive. If there were still worthwhile targets there, the IO wanted to know. Natural tendencies to talk over and 're-run' the mission helped here, and pilots were urged to maintain close liaison with the interrogators in case vital points were overlooked. Records were updated accordingly.

When the results of the day's mission were committed to paper, checked and edited, a summary was teletyped to VIII FC. From this, procedures would where necessary be modified, personal accomplishments recognized through the award of decorations and the results put into files ready for the next Field Order to start the entire process over again.

13   Jets and shuttles

Twelve days after the first 8th AF victory over the Me 163 came the first recorded encounter with the Me 262. One victory resulted, this being shared by Major Joe Myers and Lieutenant M. Croy, Jr, both of the 78th Group's 82nd Squadron. Flying at 11,000 ft above Termonde, Belgium, the pilots sighted a '262 heading south at 500 ft. Both Thunderbolts initiated a dive after it. Lessening their dive angle from 45 degrees in order to make the interception, Myers and Croy saw that they had built up speed to 475 mph IAS by the time they passed through the 1,000 ft mark. At that point they were seen by the German pilot, who

began taking evasive action. He made three or four very flat turns before Myers opened fire. Almost immediately the enemy aircraft hit the ground at high speed.

This 28 August victory heralded an increase in sighting reports of enemy jet fighter activity for the month of September, although there were no victories over either the '262 or Me 163. One aircraft was credited as a probable and one as damaged in 26 encounters reported by the fighter groups. Bomber crews had 121 encounters — but it was a significant measure of the risks the Germans ran in attacking the heavily-defended formations, even in superior aircraft, that these resulted in the loss of but one bomber and one fighter. The Germans found that the high

Lucky Wabbit II *hailed from the 343rd Squadron, 55th Group.*

speed of their jet aircraft tended to nullify many of the advantages this seemed to bestow; keeping their sights on bombers flying at half their speed or less was extremely difficult as they dared not slow down for any length of time lest they fall victim to not one or two enemy fighters but by that stage of war, whole squadrons of them.

The last ditch formation of Me 262 units for interceptor duty resulted in a gradual increase in the frequency of this type in 8th AF reports compared with those mentioning the Me 163. The Me 163 force was never very large, JG400 being lucky to have more than half a dozen aircraft available at any given time.

★   ★   ★

September 1944 was to record a new high in destruction as the 8th's fighters roamed across Germany virtually at will shooting at any worthwhile targets that presented themselves. Airfields always had a high priority and although strafing was hazardous on occasions, not all of them were bristling with flak. Trains were also important to the enemy, who could hardly move the many tons of supplies and spares needed by his hard-pressed ground forces if the prime mover, the locomotive, was not available. The 8th Air Force and its 9th and RAF colleagues did their best to deny the Germans their trains. And when they took to the roads and waterways these too were interdicted to a degree unparalleled in the history of warfare.

With the Allied armies primed and ready to strike into Reich territory, its air umbrella, so vital for the success of the final battles of the war, was overhead every day, weather permitting. On 1 September the four groups still flying the Thunderbolt went out after locomotives and rolling stock, as did 513 Mustangs and 47 P-38s, a total force of 866 aircraft being despatched. The bulk of the force was made up of Mustangs which provided escort to bombers attacking various targets in Germany, while the P-47s were split into two forces to sweep the Brussels/Antwerp areas on the one hand, and to seek out railway traffic in north and north-east France. When the mission was over, the command credited the fighters with 94 locomotives destroyed, 537 pieces of rolling stock destroyed or damaged, plus 382 road vehicles including fifteen tanks attacked. Four groups shared the destruction of five enemy fighters.

It was the Luftwaffe's turn to suffer heavily on the 5th when the score reached 192 aircraft destroyed on the ground and 21 in the air. The lion's share went to the 56th and 479th Groups, the latter then under the able leadership of Hub Zemke who was instrumental in getting the last VIII FC fighter group among the kills: Robin Olds summed up his service with the 479th at that time by saying that his memory retains 'Mustangs, Zemke and London, in that order'.

In the air that day, Lieutenant William H. Allen's four Mustang element of the 343rd FS, 55th Group, was returning from bomber escort when enemy aircraft were spotted taking off from the airport at

Below *Full invasion stripes were short-lived, but underside markings remained for some time. By September 1944 the 84th FS, 78th Group, had a mix of razorback and bubble canopy P-47s.* Roger the Lodger *was the mount of Captain Gerald E. Budd (USAF).*

Right *Stylish P-38J name is* Gallant Warrior, *Lieutenant Wilson of the 364th Group obviously being proud of his educational background. Wilson's kit is virtually complete apart from the oxygen mask (USAF).*

Left *Relatives and squadron colleagues welcomed the news that a 'missing' pilot had put his aircraft down and been captured. This happened to Captain Thomas E. Joyce when he had to ride QP-K down for a belly landing near Darmstadt on 12 September 1944 to become another loss to the 334th FS, 4th FG (Bundesarchiv).*

Left *Bombed-up Thunderbolt from the 353rd FG ready to go for a ground-attack mission, 11 September 1944 (USAF).*

Below *Lottie of the 78th Group's 83rd Squadron pictured after a heavy landing, apparently at Poltava, Russia, one of the Shuttle raid bases (USAF).*

Goppingen. The Mustangs dived on them, Allen's *Pretty Patty II* accounting for five to give VIII FC another ace-in-a-day. The small force racked up sixteen of the enemy for no loss to itself. Two days before, the 55th had begun an intensive period of operations which would result in the award of a DUC for nine days' work from 3-11 September. The 479th was similarly commended for its exploits on the 5th and the 339th, 78th, 356th, 353rd and 56th also became DUC recipients during the month.

The 11th saw the sixth 'frantic' mission, the 20th Group covering the bombers on their long haul into Russia after bombing synthetic oil plants and refineries. While the Luftwaffe chose to offer spirited resistance for the first time since May, the King's Cliffe Mustangs were not involved in air-to-air combat either into or out of Soviet territory. 'Frantic' missions were always tinged with uncertainty about what the unpredictable Russians would do next and it did not behove American single-seat fighters to stray far from the designated areas to find out. Their Allies were not averse to being very trigger-happy and numerous incidents in the past had proved that their recognition of friendly aircraft was not of the highest order. But conditions sometimes were beyond mortal man to control, as the 20th's Lieutenant Harold Horst found out.

Having negotiated a weather front with dense cloud which separated two of the fighters from the main body, Horst pressed on alone to find Piryatin. Unable to do so, he approached an alternative airfield, only to find a Russian fighter on his tail. Making three attempts to land, he finally decided to abandon the idea and had to force-land as the last of his fuel drained away. Finding a suitable clearing, Horst landed without injury — and realized he had been airborne for an amazing nine hours and twenty minutes.

While the 20th took elements of the 3rd Division on to Russia, more than 500 enemy fighters challenged the incursions of the rest of the 3rd, 1st and 2nd Division forces. Bomber losses amounted to seventeen and the US fighters were heavily engaged. Highest scorers were pilots of the 359th, who notched up 26 from the day's total of 115(destroyed)-7(probable)-23(damaged). The group received a DUC for its actions that day and the Luftwaffe could count another 42 aircraft destroyed on the ground by fighters strafing on the way home.

The bombers returned to oil targets the following day and again the enemy attempted to blunt the weight of the attack. His reward was 54 fighters lost. All but the 20th Group, which remained on Soviet territory until returning to England on the 17th, were involved in the mission.

If the air situation was well in hand, the course of the Allied ground advance was not so; having decided to cross the Rhine at Arnhem, the assault forces had run into unexpectedly stiff German resistance. On 18 September the situation worsened and frantic appeals for help were answered by VIII FC. Led by the CO of the 63rd Squadron, Harold Comstock, the 56th, 78th, 353rd and 356th Groups were detailed to knock out flak threatening to decimate supply-dropping B-24s tasked to bring aid to the beleaguered troops. It was an 'at all cost' operation to try to save the day — and it proved one of the blackest days for the Wolfpack. 'Flak busting' was an unenviable task and the briefing was a rowdy affair with pilots showing their feelings about the job ahead in no uncertain terms. Their spirited reaction was understandable.

The Nijmegen support mission was only part of the day's activity, although it was the major part. 'Frantic VII' was mounted, B-17s flying east (for the last time as it was to transpire) after dropping supplies to another force in the greatest danger — the Polish underground army fighting in the suburbs of Warsaw.

As well as the 185 P-47s despatched on their gun hunting trip, Mustangs and Lightnings covered the vulnerable B-24s, which had to make their supply runs from ultra-low level to avoid ground fire. Where the P-47s found the flak emplacements, their .50-cal guns and fragmentation bombs were effective, all but a small number of the guns being silenced. But the cost was high: eight P-47s were downed during the mission, and a further eight were forced to land or crash-land with varying degrees of battle damage. On the credit side, only one pilot was killed.

A repeat mission was laid on for the following day, when the 56th had cause to take it a little easier on escort duty. The Luftwaffe was still active over the battle front flying both interception and fighter-bomber sorties. It was the job of the 8th's fighters to keep the latter away from Allied positions — which the 357th Group did with a vengeance on the 18th. A low-level combat resulted in a very respectable 26 for 2 in favour of the Americans, the clash taking place some fifteen miles north-east of Arnhem.

Deteriorating weather brought some slackening of pace in the following days but as troop carriers and gliders was primary targets the requirement for close escort were paramount to prevent the Germans slaughtering the hapless transports and their charges. As the week came to its end it was, however, obvious that the German ground forces were too strong and by Saturday 23rd, the venture was all but over. The British force withdrew having sustained heavy casualties. The major part played by VIII FC groups had prevented these being even worse, but the cost was high — 73 fighters MIA.

The Arnhem operation marked the last opera-

tional use of the P-38 Lightning as a fighter in VIII FC; Hub Zemke, leading the 479th, had a mix of P-51s and P-38s under his command, and the final missions of the latter were highly successful. Low down, where the Lockheed fighter had few peers and a heavier punch than either the Thunderbolt or Mustang, these final missions saw the Luftwaffe fighters suffer heavily at its hands. Zemke, flying a P-51, added to his personal score and P-38 pilots who were successful included Lieutenant Colonel Herran who claimed three during a sweep on 26 September.

★   ★   ★

As the weather over Europe gradually deteriorated to culminate in one of the worst winters for many years, VIII FC activity reduced accordingly. The Luftwaffe was conspicious by its comparative absence in the air, although more encounters with jet fighters were recorded. On 7 October the 356th reported its first contract with the Me 262 when Don Strait's flight observed one in the vicinity of Kassel.

The month brought changes in the command structure pertaining to the 8th's fighter force when, from 10 October, the three wings were placed under the jurisdiction of the three bombardment divisions, a move which had begun on 15 September. This change was primarily to ensure that there was a better ratio of fighters to bombers for escort than had occasionally been the case before when the fifteen groups had been spread thin with consequential bomber losses.

Henceforth, the 1st, 2nd and 3rd Bomb Divisions would control the 67th, 65th and 66th Fighter Wings respectively, making for a simpler chain of command and enabling each bomber force commander to marshal his fighter forces more directly in accordance with operational requirements, rather than in liaison with VIII FC during planning of missions for the entire force, as before. In practice, fighter groups were not tied to escort only bombers from their assigned divisions and their own operations, unique to fighter aircraft, continued to be planned and executed as before. Arnhem had been an example of a priority shift from escort to ground support, and the coming weeks would see an equally urgent need for fighters to concentrate on ground targets over the battle line.

The winter would also see some changes of home base for the 8th AF fighter groups, albeit temporary in most cases. One of the most nomadic was to be the 361st, which began its moves on 26 September when it vacated Bottisham for Little Walden. Although the group subsequently took 'French leave', ground support was vested in the groups of the 9th Air Force and the RAF squadrons based on the continent — these were able to handle most of the direct tactical ground support missions required until the war's end, leaving the 8th to continue with its primary task of bomber escort.

While October's level of air fighting was less than the previous months of 1944, there were milestones reached. The 357th chalked up its 400th kill on the 12th when First Lieutenant Charles 'Chuck' Yeager bounced a score of Bf 109s and routed them to the tune of eight, five going down under his guns. The 364th also had a good day's hunting considering the paucity of targets, and claimed eight more but for the loss of four of its own. Enemy claims by all the groups involved in escort to 2nd and 3rd Division bombers totalled nineteen for five lost.

While Allied fighter pilots had an ever-narrowing area in which they risked capture should they be forced to bale out or crash-land, there was always the chance of being apprehended by hostile civilians, sometimes with grim results. This happened to Paul 'Pinky' Roberts of the 356th Group on the 7th and it was later confirmed that he had been killed by a mob.

The increasing risk of collision in inclement conditions was also highlighted on this day when two 20th FG Mustangs were known to have run into one another. Overall, the force lost eleven aircraft for a score of 29(destroyed)-0(probable)-4(damaged) — even on a bad day the USAAF fighters maintained their marked superiority over a much depleted and demoralized enemy force. But that is not to say that the Luftwaffe was a force to be ignored; production of fighters continued a steady climb despite the devastation visited on the factories, repair depots and airfields. And the remaining *Experten*, Adolf Galland among them, still dreamt of marshalling a force strong enough to overwhelm the escort and knock down hundreds of B-17s or B-24s on a single daylight raid. Such a plan was implemented and, by the early part of November 1944, there were 28 *Gruppen* based

in central Germany, with another sixteen training or resting. Much faith was pinned on Me 262s spearheading this spectacular operation, and given a degree of technical reliability from the aircraft's notoriously troublesome engines, there is little doubt that such a combat could have been very one-sided. The weather continued to be kind to the Germans, and cloak much of this clandestine activity from Allied eyes. Other factors would, however, have much more bearing on the idea of a 'last ditch' interception.

The Me 262 had still not been encountered in any numbers by late September and although the Me 163 was reported at infrequent intervals, the twin-engined type was seen to be potentially the most dangerous to 8th AF operations in that it had the endurance to take on and beat the best the Americans had. The Me 163 was seen as not so much of a threat once its shortcomings were recognized; despite being even faster than the Me 262 under full power, its effectiveness decreased sharply once it had exhausted its lethal mixture of fuel and had to make a virtually power-less glide back to earth.

As far as the Me 262 was concerned, it was obviously faster in level flight than its piston-engined counterparts, and the most reliable mode of attack was the high speed dive from above and behind, designed to catch the enemy pilot unawares before he could employ superior acceleration to leave his would-be attacker standing. More effective was the cat and mouse approach whereby the Mustangs could be positioned behind the jet as it approached base. Committed to the landing, the enemy aircraft had little chance of evading the inevitable fusillade of fire.

Firstly, though, the airfields used by the jets had to

Lieutenant Frederick Jurgens, 79th FS, 20th Group, in the cockpit of his P-51D. The man on the wing is holding what appears to be an item of the fighter's radio equipment.

Above Morphine Sue II *was one of many examples of a pilot liking his aircraft nickname enough to carry it over to a number of machines he flew regularly. This one was the mount of Lieutenant Donald McNally who was lost on 15 November 1944 while on a weather flight with Lieutenant Lawrence McGraw. The exact circumstances were never established and both pilots had to be assumed killed by causes other than flak or fighter attack on the 355th FG roster (355th FG Association).*

Left *Nose of Ben Drew's aircraft of the 375th FS, 361st Group, showing the striking red bomb outline to the nickname. It was in this aircraft that Drew shot down two Me 262s on 7 October 1944.*

be located; there was also a need for pilots to gain a better insight into the capabilities of turbojet-powered aircraft, and once again the RAF came to the assistance of the 8th. The Gloster Meteor was then entering squadron service and arrangements were made to deploy five of them to American fighter bases for familiarization training. The performance and configuration of the Me 262 and the Meteor were not dissimilar and the tests, which began at Debden on 10 October, were valuable in helping pilots of conventional fighters understand what was then a very new concept.

Increasing numbers of jets were reported in October, some 25 being seen on the 7th when the kill record stood at two. Lieutenant Urban Drew of the 361st doubled that score when he manoeuvred behind two of them taking off from Achmer. The same day three 364th Group pilots worked together to destroy a single Me 163.

Accidents continued to happen, as on the 19th when the 479th lost a Mustang to friendly AA fire over Calais. The pilot fortunately baled out. Winter flying has always held hazards for pilots, and over Europe in 1944 clear conditions over the UK could very quickly deteriorate by the time fighters reached Germany and throw a well-planned operation into disarray. This occurred on the 30th and was the direct cause of the loss of Hub Zemke to the 8th Air Force for the duration of the war.

The fighters were tasked to escort bombers of all three divisions to Hamburg, Bremen, Hamm and other locations where oil targets were situated. The weather got so bad that both the 1st and 3rd Divisions were ordered to bomb secondary targets rather than plough on in the teeth of ever-threatening clouds. The build-up showed no sign of thinning out and elements of the fighter escort had no choice but to penetrate it, just to see how bad it was. They soon found out. Violent updraughts and general turbulence lurked within and the flimsy single-seaters became so much chaff.

Leading the 479th A Group, Zemke was, ironically, on the last of his 155 missions before being transferred to an HQ desk job. While bombers had little choice but to bulldoze through the soup, the fighters did try to climb over it. Even so, the tops were so high that some of the fighters had to try their luck at an altitude of 24,000 ft. It was hopeless and Zemke called for an about-turn. He banked left to make the turn — but the Mustang was snatched by the turbulent air, hurled on to its back and dropped like a stone. Losing altitude fast the aircraft began to break up.

Zemke's wingman fared slightly better. Plummeted some 14,000 ft, his Mustang came back under the pilot's control just above trees after a terrifying spin. The pilot, Lieutenant Dick Creighton, had thought the aircraft doomed and attempted to bale out, but the vicious G forces imposed kept the canopy firmly shut. As he regained control Creighton saw that the ASI read 550 mph and the accelerometer 8 G! Other pilots were caught in the turbulence; Lieutenant Walter Drake, leading the second element in Zemke's flight lost both drop tanks before inadvertently stressing his P-51 to 9 G. Lieutenant Colonel Jim Herren bettered even that with 9.6 G after a pull-out at 3,000 ft, with his aircraft slightly buckled and wrinkled but in one piece.

Zemke's aircraft was lost, as was that of Lieutenant Doug Holmes; both baled out to become prisoners — their survival under such taxing flying conditions being directly attributable to the remarkable Berger G-suit.

★　　★　　★

Among the incidents of October was another attempt by a Mustang pilot to pick up a downed colleague; this had been achieved successfully before but there was always the risk that not one but two pilots and aircraft would be lost if it failed. On the 3rd Captain Henry W. Brown of the 355th became a victim of German flak and was forced to put his Mustang down in a cow pasture near Nürnberg. The fighter made a successful crash landing and Brown was just beginning to think his war was over when he saw a P-51 approach with its wheels down. This second machine was piloted by Major Charles W. Lenfest, 354th Squadron Operations Officer and Acting Squadron Commander.

Lenfest put his aircraft down on the soft surface of the meadow and Brown scrambled aboard. But when Lenfest gunned the engine he found that the aircraft was stuck fast in mud. Both men could do little but wait inevitable capture, which occurred about five hours later. With Captain Brown, the Germans had yet another 8th AF fighter ace as their guest for the duration — this time the man who led the entire air force in kills with a score of 17.2

Lenfest was sent to Stalag Luft 3 at Sagan and determined to escape. He attempted this three times and on the fourth managed to elude recapture. It was then 17 April 1945 and the war in Europe had but weeks to run.

Clever interpretation of the well-known American epithet Big Ass Bird *is displayed here on a Mustang of the 364th Group on 17 October 1944 (USAF).*

14 'Clobber 'em'

There was little sign that the temperature would rise as November 1944 brought another bout of inclement weather to the continent of Europe. On the second of the month George Preddy moved up to the leading ace slot with the loss of Captain Henry Brown of the 355th. With most of the 'old hands' rotated home or lost in action, men with less time in the 8th were dominating the scoreboards. Not that length of service had a great deal to do with the success rate in air combat — many pilots spent many hours of combat time without scoring kills, or even being in an ideal position to do so. It was invariably a case of the luck of the draw — being in the right place at the time the Luftwaffe put in an appearance.

Air-to-air kills were not the only contribution the fighters made; the 8th was one of the few US Army Air Forces to count ground victories towards the achievement of 'acedom', primarily because the work was invariably hazardous. Equally, the credits received by individual pilots were divided into air and ground kills and some men derived more personal satisfaction from gaining the upper hand in the air, while others found a particular penchant for the exacting art of destroying aircraft on the ground.

William J. Cullerton of the 357th FS, 355th Group was by no means atypical. His final record was five aerial kills and thirteen destroyed on the ground, the first two air victories occurring on 2 November. The bombers were out, primarily after oil targets, covered by 968 fighters from all the groups. More than 400 Luftwaffe fighters rose to challenge, their first appearance in any numbers since September. Cullerton's group ended the day with eight. The Americans observed Me 262s as well as Fw 190s and Bf 109s, Cullerton picking off one each of the latter types. His combat took place at low altitude, a Bf 109 falling first and the '190 being shot out of the landing pattern of an airfield it was trying to reach. After the victory, the 357th strafed the airfield in the face of intense flak. The squadron was credited with 26, Cullerton claiming six of them.

Early November saw the 356th at Martlesham Heath exchanging P-47s for P-51s. The transition was not without its problems, pilot unfamiliarity with the very different Mustang resulting in nine accidents during the month, most of them during landing. There was also some problems with freezing gun mechanisms. The month also saw the introduction of operational pilot training at operational group level; previously pilots had received theatre indoctrination with two separate training groups established in the 8th, the 495th and 496th. It was felt that a pilot would more quickly pick up procedure, tactics and 'spirit' of a first-line group if he flew with it from the start. Thus were born the 'Clobber Colleges'; staffed by experienced combat pilots who passed on all the latest information on technical matters and the current operational situation, these were highly successful and laid the groundwork for training programmes in the post-war USAF.

Technically, the 8th AF fighter units were very well equipped. Moves made at the end of the previous year had aimed at standardizing on a single aircraft type to ease maintenance, servicing and mission planning in both the fighter and bomber forces. In consequence the fighter groups hitherto flying P-47s were re-equipped with Mustangs and the bomber groups the B-17. This standardization was not completely achieved although the fighter units were predominantly Mustang-equipped by the war's end. The exception was the 56th, which was itself slated to receive the P-51H in May 1945.

The Mustang, long-range fighter, without equal, was, in its D-model series, one of the aircraft which represented the ultimate in mass-produced piston-engined fighters. While other types, notably the British Tempest, the late model Spitfires and German Fw 190D series, could equal or better the P-51's performance, their roles were different. Mustang pilots also had G-suits to assist them materially in combat; plus the excellent K-14 gunsight, introduced on production lines with the P-51D-25NA/D-25NT series; and a range of bombs and rockets with which to devastate ground targets. The Mustang carried extra ordnance on the wing racks on frequent occasions, mainly GP bombs and clusters of

Above *Echelon starboard by Mustangs of the 383rd FS 364th Group. Nearest the camera is* Caroline Moon, *complete with fetching art-work.*

Right *Trio of aces of the 352nd Group are (l to r) Clayton Davis (final score 5), Carl Luksic (8.5) and John Meyer (24) (via Paul Coggan).*

Right *Peaceful Digby, Lincs catches P-51D, 44-13630/VF-R,* Rebel, *of the 336th FS with a member of the groundcrew.* (RAF Museum).

20 M-41 frag bombs, although it was not considered a primary ground-attack type by the 8th. Rather, the P-51D was an all-round fighter which did everything required of it extremely well including the paramount task of escort and interception at extreme ranges.

In the spring of 1945, a few groups received kits to enable Mustangs to carry high velocity aircraft rockets on 'zero length' launchers outboard of the racks, although rockets were not used by 8th AF units to any great extent. The weapon most used during strafing was the reliable M2 .50-cal Colt Browning machine-gun, and although other Allied fighters were fitted with cannon, the 'fifty caliber' fired ammunition which, while not having the penetrating power of a cannon round, was significantly heavier than a light (.303 or 7.62mm) machine-gun. Its reliability and ability to accept ball, armour-piercing, incendiary and tracer ammunition made it one of the foremost weapons of World War 2. It proved, set in wing bays in banks of two, three or four, to be more than up to the task required of it.

The P-51 may have been equal if not better than all conventional fighters it was likely to meet in combat — but it was outclassed by the new generation of jet fighters which the Luftwaffe was using increasingly. November 1944 was to bring 137 encounters and 29 occasions when USAAF fighters were in a position to attack. Weather conditions were, however, in the Allies' favour in that although the bombing effort was consequently reduced, so too were actual losses directly attributable to jets — only two fighters fell victim to these enemy fighters. The 8th Air Force commanders nevertheless experienced their greatest worry since the bloody unescorted raids of 1943: it did not take a great deal of imagination to envisage what even a small number of Me 262s could do to a Fortress of Liberator formation, given surprise and clear conditions. The question was — how best to deal with this threat with existing equipment?

In practical terms there was little: no Allied jet fighters were ready for combat in sufficient numbers to meet the '262s on equal terms and initially the only solution was to increase the size of the fighter escort so that every two heavies had a Mustang covering them. Otherwise efforts had to be made to pin-point the bases used by the jet fighters and destroy them — or at least maintain continual surveillance on them so that fighters could be positioned to attack jets at their most vulnerable time, taking off and landing.

The 8th Air Force consequently raised the number of fighters in each group to a peak of 135 and maintained the established practice of groups operating two separate A and B formations of three twelve-plane squadrons each. Steps were also taken to ensure where possible, that US fighters had a significant height advantage in areas where Me 262s had been encountered.

Gradually, the threat of the Me 262 became quantifiable: during the first big air battle of November, some individual aircraft had fired their batteries of R4M rockets into a Liberator formation. Although without scoring any hits, this new tactic meant that the jets could not only intercept at speeds higher than conventional escorts, but could stay well out of range of defending guns to destroy their targets. But November and December were to show that Germany's jet fighter programme was fraught with numerous operational and technical difficulties. The paucity of sightings was an understandable relief to Allied air commanders but at the same time the possibility of the Germans planning something spectacular at the 'eleventh hour' could not be ignored.

Fighter encounters with the German jets met with varying degrees of success; they were by no means one-sided but now more than ever before catching the quarry depended on how the opposing forces came upon each other. The old adage 'he who has height controls the battle' was even more relevant in jet

versus piston-engined combat than it was in conventional fighter engagements.

Two more Me 262s fell to the 8th on 6 November. Lieutenant William J. Quinn's flight of Mustangs, which included the aircraft of Captain Gerald Montgomery, were on operations over Germany when two jets appeared 5,000 ft below them. The Eagles from Debden dived on them. 'One suddenly turned into me', Lieutenant Quinn subsequently reported, 'and I opened fire. I saw my bullets hitting his canopy and he immediately peeled off and went into the ground.'' Captain Montgomery chased the second jet, which escaped. Better results came to Captain

'Chuck' Yeager of the 357th. Leading Cement White Flight north of Osnabruck, three Me 262s were seen by the pilot who was later to win fame in high speed test flying. The enemy aircraft were at 180 degrees to the Mustangs and about 2 o'clock low. The flight of Mustangs dived from their 10,000 ft altitude to head off the last jet in the trio. Yeager got in a hit or two before the loose V-formation pulled away. There was no evasive action. Yeager subsequently found the jets again, flying under an overcast. At 420 IAS he fired a high deflection burst at the leader. After two or three bursts he saw hits registering before the jet again used superior speed to outpace the P-51.

The combat did not end inconclusively, as Yeager found an airfield with a lone '262 attempting to land. Pouring on the coal to overhaul it the Mustang got into firing position. With 500 mph on the clock Yeager made sure. A short burst registered hits on the enemy aircraft's wing. Accurate flak made the American break off but he saw the '262 crash land short of the airfield, with a wing off.

One of the leading exponents of the Me 262 was *Major* Walter Nowotny and his death in action on 8 November was a serious setback to the Luftwaffe, which had few pilots with the requisite experience of combat operations available for training on a demanding new type. The apparent inexperience of the pilots of Me 262s encountered thus far helped foster a new spirit of aggressiveness in 8th AF pilots. They relished the chance of hunting aircraft which were, due to their theoretically superior performance, the biggest challenge yet to their own prowess in combat.

The ensuing weeks saw a reduction in the scale of bombing by the 8th, due primarily to bad weather, but those operations which were mounted resulted in more losses for the Luftwaffe. However small these were, the war of attrition continued to work against the German effort. But on 18 November scores

Left *John D. Landers flew at least one Mustang named* Big Beautiful Doll *while he commanded the 357th Group at the end of 1944. As with his other ships, he included his six Japanese aircraft kills in the scoreboard. Serial number of this 363rd FS aircraft is unknown.*

Below *Lieutenant Colonel Gail Jacobsen's* Burn'n Burnie *of the 434th FS, 479th Group.*

climbed into double figures in terms of aerial victories, plus 69 on the ground — the sort of figures the command was well used to. There were no bomber escorts that day, leaving the fighters free to sweep airfields in the Langenseebold, Weissenborn and Freiham and Neuburg areas.

On the 20th the 356th Group mounted its full first mission with the P-51, and lost one aircraft from a relatively small force of 558 fighters despatched. The following day the total escort for 1,291 B-17s and B-24s was a more typical 954 fighters. All groups operated, primarily on escort for another trip to Merseburg. This was the first of three raids contested by the Luftwaffe in numbers approaching earlier, more confident days.

Chancing on several hundred Fw 190s, the Mustangs fought their battles somewhat hampered by cloud cover; other enemy aircraft were caught

Four frames from gun camera film record the demise of another Fw 190 under the guns of an American fighter (USAF).

during forming up. The result was a series of combats in which top honours went to the 352nd (19½), 364th (18) and 359th (17). Bill Whisner of the 352nd joined Claude Crenshaw of the 359th with joint membership of the 'ace in a day' club, both pilots destroying five apiece. Crenshaw made note of the advantages bestowed by both the G suit and the K-14 gunsight in his combat report of the engagement. Bringing down five still ranked as a feat of marksmanship during the course of one mission, and by the end of the war the 8th could count nineteen men who achieved it. The 21st also highlighted the risk of a pilot getting lost. Separated from his parent 360th Squadron, Lieutenant Walter O. Hedrick flew on, ever onwards until his Mustang ran out of fuel. Bellying it in on a convenient piece of flat ground, he found he was near Haro, Spain. After this, his eventful first mission, Lieutenant Hedrick returned to Martlesham Heath.

Following two days' break, the 25th saw plenty of action for the 356th which was undertaking escort to the Lutzhendorf region followed by strafing. Five of the nine victories recorded for the day by 8th AF fighters went to the 356th, as well as a number of aircraft damaged during strafing. Lieutenant Freeman Hooker of the 361st Squadron went off on a freelance search for rail traffic and found and attacked two locomotives in the marshalling yard at Zwickau. The group's 359th Squadron added another twelve locos destroyed and Lieutenants Jack Cornett Brown and Robert Carr shared a B-17. This bomber had put down near Fulda and the Mustangs' attack (to prevent its capture intact) caused an engine fire.

Nine destroyed for six Mustangs lost did not constitute a good day's hunting — but 114 enemy aircraft shot down for the loss of nine Mustangs did. This occurred on 26 November when the bombers went to hit oil supplies in the Hanover area. Again the Luftwaffe rose in force, and suffered accordingly. Among the successful pilots was Lieutenant Jack Daniels of the 339th who, perhaps inspired by the brand of liquor carrying his name, despatched five Fw 190s. The group's total for the day was 29, and the mission was particularly notable for Daniels, as his ace status had been achieved on his first mission.

The 356th Group added to its score when 26 aircraft fell to its guns — although it was said that the total might have been higher if the gun-freezing problem had been cured. Pilots of the 361st experienced 31 of these annoying stoppages during their various dogfights, but Don 'Doc' Baccus, one of the 359th's leading aces, got two Bf 109s.

It appeared that at that stage of the war, the greater

the effort by the *Jagdverbände* to intercept American bomber formations, the greater their losses would invariably be, particularly if only conventional fighters were employed. So it went on 27 November when the 357th from Leiston accounted for thirty. Leonard 'Kit' Carson nailed five, Chuck Yeager and John England four each, and Clarence Anderson, three.

The Americans noted another manifestation of green pilots flying the German machines when they persisted in staying in formation even while the Mustangs were hacking them down. Equally the sheer eagerness of the Americans to hunt down the enemy fighters brought about some amazing incidents of sheer, perhaps bloody-minded, bravery. Ray Wetmore, skilful exponent of air combat that he was, found a whole *Geschwader* of German fighters. He and his wingmen tried without success to call other fighters to their position. Having followed the Germans for hundreds of miles the two Mustang pilots became increasingly frustrated. Finally, they bounced them — 120 against two. And they got away with it...

Sporadic fighter activity continued through the end of November and into the early part of December. In actions on the 5th of the month, 8th AF fighters came home triumphant having shot down 91 of the enemy. Top scorers for the day were the pilots of the 357th (22) and 479th (14), the Luftwaffe vainly trying to protect the Munster railyards and Berlin's munitions and tank works that were the target for the bombs of 586 Liberators and Fortresses.

For about two weeks the enemy was conspicious by his absence in any numbers — and the early hours of 17 December showed why. Even though the Luftwaffe had abandoned the mass destruction of a single bomb wing, a similar idea had appealed to higher authority. Hitler chose his time carefully. Under a cloak of atrocious weather the Wehrmacht grouped its tanks and troops and waited.

15 Anything that moves

When news of the German Ardennes offensive was digested there was little that Allied air commanders could do. The continent was completely 'socked in' under a solid overcast and it would have been pointless to despatch heavy bombers and thereby risk needless casualties among friendly troops if their targets could not be located. For only a short time the Germans had things their own way; confronted by green American troops who were spread very thinly in the Ardennes sector, the German counter-offensive gained ground. It was a desperate gamble that was virtually bound to be at least blunted once the skies cleared and brought the full weight of Allied airpower to bear on the threat. And when the scope of the Germans' ambitions was realized, friendly ground troops soon rallied to make the enemy's progress difficult.

The 8th AF went out against strategic and tactical targets on 18 December and on the 19th attacked points in Luxembourg, Ehrang and Koblenz with the direct purpose of impeding the advance. The weather remained bad until the 23rd when more than 300 B-17s and B-24s from all three divisions bombed marshalling yards, communications centres and choke points behind the battle area. Still the weather hampered any really significant contribution being made.

Then indications showed that the skies would clear by the 24th. The 8th Air Force signalled to all groups: *every* available B-17 and B-24 will fly. The result was that 2,046 heavy bombers, the largest force ever despatched, made ready, as did 853 fighters from all but two groups. Duxford and Fowlmere were fogged in, preventing the 78th and 339th from participating in what turned out to be, with RAF and 9th Air Force contributions, the largest air strike of the Second World War.

Against this mighty force the Luftwaffe interceptions were puny, a dozen bombers going down during the operations. Freezing conditions claimed others in accidents, and the abnormally cold weather was to cause further fatalies in succeeding days. The fighter force lost ten machines, and claimed 74 shot down. As the bombers returned, any festivities planned for the following day were thrown awry by ground mist and frost which cloaked virtually all the 1st Division bases and there were many diversions. Also, the war situation was such that there was little time for celebration.

The tactical 9th Air Force appealed for help from the 8th's fighter force to protect its bases while the 'battle of the bulge' raged and accordingly the 352nd and 361st Groups moved to the continent. On 23

Robert Delhamer was assigned P-51D 44-11194, Super Gal II, *coded OS-B of the 357th FS* (via G. Hunsberger).

December the air echelon of the Bodney group moved to Asche in Belgium and the 361st bade temporary farewell to Little Walden and occupied St Dizier, being ready for action from there by the 25th.

Christmas Day 1944 was tragic for the 8th's fighter force, as it lost one of its top pilots. Back from leave in September, George Preddy was the leading 8th AF ace with at least 27 kills by the time the 352nd moved to Belgium. There the pilots found conditions primitive. The accommodation was in tents, each one containing six cots, a stove and a bucket of coal. A steel helmet served to give a man a receptacle for shaving and washing water. It was a sign of those unusual days that the group pilots were issued sidearms, which they had not previously carried, the sound theory running that a man could hardly expect to shoot his way out of enemy territory if he came down far behind the lines.

Now, though, the front line was on the 352nd's doorstep so each man tucked away a .45 automatic just in case he came down among unfriendlies. The pilot's tents boasted slit trenches which were initially utilized when the Germans sent over a 'bed-check Charlie' at about 21:30 hr the first night they arrived. Everyone raced for his trench and as there were not enough to hold them all, the braver souls ventured out to dig foxholes.

As the nights wore on, the pilots gave up these sleep deprivation activities (which was the sole purpose of the raids) and stayed in their tents. The helmets provided any protection they might need in the event that 'Charlie' dropped anything lethal right on their particular patch of territory.

The 352nd was tasked to provide continuous front line area patrol, with one squadron airborne, one ready to take off and replace the first, and the third on hold. On the 24th the group maintained the patrol but the weather was terrible and garbled radio messages did not help. No enemy sightings were made.

On Christmas Day, Preddy was scheduled to fly, along with other pilots of the 328th Squadron. Although the weather was still bad, Preddy joked that he knew it would be a good day as he had his fighting socks on, bright red ones at that. The squadron duly took off and climbed to 15,000 ft. A radar check revealed no enemy activity but after nearly three hours in the air a vector came through. Preddy led the 328th to a dogfight.

Attacking one of the Bf 109s, Preddy scored hits on a Messerschmitt that cut in front of him as he was turning with the first aircraft he selected. The enemy pilot baled out as the American's fire scored numerous strikes on his machine. George Preddy resumed the attack on his first victim and again, the German pilot baled out.

Having become separated from the rest of the squadron, Preddy and his wingman, James Cartee, continued the patrol. The two Mustangs were joined by a third, that flown by Lieutenant Jim Bouchier of the 479th, which had meanwhile mixed it with the Luftwaffe in the vicinity of Kassel. In its largest air battle of the war, the 479th destroyed seventeen enemy aircraft. Jim Bouchier had become lost in the ensuing combat and now the trio headed back to friendly territory following a route which took them over the Hurtgan forest. Under the trees, men of the 12th AA Group stamped their feet to keep some of the biting cold at bay. When their radio warned of the approach of 'two enemy' 109s from the south-west, at low altitude, strafing', all 40 mm and .50-cal machine-gun units stood by to fire. There was never very much time to identify enemy from friendly aircraft, particularly at low level — seconds at most. The sound of machine-gun fire reached the men. Suddenly, there they were, over the trees bordering the field where the quad .50-cal AA machine-gun was situated. They fired. Some sixty rounds left the barrels before the gunner realised they were Mustangs.

George Preddy's aircraft belly-landed in the same field as the guns which shot him down. Cartee veered off and circled the field several times before flying back to base. The 40 mm had also fired on the P-51 trio and Bouchier found his cockpit filling with smoke. He rolled over, having jettisoned the canopy, and jumped. He landed just as the AA gun crew approached. The horrified men soon realized their error. George Preddy, victor of so many combats in which his potential enemy was far more lethal, had been shot down by his own side. The subsequent reports said that he had been hit by at least two .50 rounds, causing fatal injuries.

More action came for the 8th on the days following that fateful Christmas, with enemy aircraft being shot down on the 27th, 29th and 30th. On the 27th, Ernest E. Bankey of the 364th became an ace in a day when, flying his P-51D *Lucky Lady VII,* he met a formation of enemy aircraft over Bonn. As well as his own kills, he shared another to finish the war with 11½ in the air and five on the ground.

★   ★   ★

In the early hours of 1 January 1945 the Luftwaffe launched Operation *Bodenplatte* against Allied airfields in Belgium and northern France. This ill-considered last-ditch strike was aimed at destroying aircraft that could be an immediate threat to the spearheads of the Army divisions heading west. But even at that time von Rundstedt's gamble was faltering and the operation carefully nurtured by the air force achieved little — indeed, *Bodenplatte* cost the Germans more aircraft than they destroyed. Initially surprised, Allied air forces recovered quickly and it was not long before their superiority was re-established.

At Asch the 352nd prepared for the morning patrol and escort missions, as had become the pattern of the previous weeks. At 09:10 hr Lieutenant Colonel Meyer had twelve P-51Ds of the 487th Squadron actually rolling out to take off when suddenly some fifty enemy fighters appeared over the airfield. Luckily the low flying Messerschmitts and Focke-Wulfs were distracted by some P-47s airborne in the vicinity and the Mustangs were not attacked while they were at their most vulnerable. It was a fatal mistake on the part of the Luftwaffe.

The AAF fighters were immediately in combat and in 45 minutes the squadron accounted for thirteen Fw 190s and ten Bf 109s — the only significant damage to a Mustang coming from American AA fire. This outstanding feat of arms earned the 487th Squadron a DUC — the only occasion when the award went to a fighter squadron rather than the group as a whole during hostilities. Meyer himself shot down two and only one of the twelve pilots failed to score. Captains Sanford Moats and William Whisner knocked down four each and Whisner and Meyer subsequently received Bars to their DFCs. For Meyer this was the second Bar to the medal and one not given to any other 8th AF pilot.

Other pilots in the 352nd were making a name for themselves, not always by destroying the enemy's aircraft. Lieutenant Bruno Grabovski's speciality was trains. Out on his personal 'war of the rails' during January, he managed to raise his score to 47 locomotives destroyed.

January also recorded the arrival of a new P-47 variant for the 56th Group at Boxted. Externally little changed from late-model P-47Ds, the P-47M was an interim model pending shipment of the substantially different P-47N. The first P-47M arrived on 3 January and while it staved off the alternative of the group having to convert to the Mustang, it did not give the Wolfpack very much advantage, particularly in all-important range. Fitted with a P&W R-2800-57 engine which was rated at 2,100 hp — 100 hp more than the R-2800-59 fitted to the P-47D-30 — the M model could attain 2,800 hp using water injection, whereas this 'war emergency' boost gave the earlier engine 2,300 hp. Known to the manufacturers as the 'C' series engine (the earlier ones being identified as 'B' series), the P-47M was potentially an excellent aircraft. But as seemed inevitable, it showed up serious teething troubles under operational conditions.

These proved to be similar to those experienced during the earliest days of 8th AF Thunderbolt service and fortunately a similar process of trouble-shooting eliminated most of the problems in a very short time. The entire production run of 130 P-47Ms was allocated to the 56th and the aircraft was flown in action before the end of the war. First recorded operational use of the new Thunderbolt sub-type was on 14 January, when the 8th sent the bulk of the fighter force on escort to 911 bombers attacking various German targets. The 56th drew a sweep on northern Germany — and had a memorable day. The Luftwaffe reacted to the strike and the Wolfpack was able to knock down nineteen enemy aircraft. But top honours went to the Leiston group — the 357th came home with the remarkable total of 56½ aerial victories for the day, a figure that was never surpassed.

Participating pilots reckoned the Luftwaffe had about 300 fighters in the air that day, its main target being the 3rd Division B-17s and 2nd Division B-24s bound for refineries and other oil-related targets in the Magdeburg-Brunswick area.

It is interesting to note a detail about this mission that shows how the Allied air forces were assisted in their operational planning by intelligence data drawn from various sources. Primary among them was the information gleaned from interception of German radio signals transmitted on Enigma machines, the codes for which had long since been broken by the British. Thus the Ultra system provided US air commanders with a continuous flow of information, backed by interrogation reports from the increasing number of German prisoners. Advance warning for 14 January indicated that the *Jagverbände* would employ 'company front' tactics using heavily armoured and armed Fw 190s making line abreast, head-on attacks at the bombers' own flight level. And as predicted, the German fighters did just that.

Field Order No 1515A was responded to by the 357th in the shape of 66 Mustangs. Of these, 56 met the bombers, the first three combat groups of the 3rd Division off the North Frisian Islands, and crossed inland at Cuxhaven at noon.

Group Commander Colonel Irwin H. Dregne spotted large formations of single-engined fighters approaching the bomber boxes from the south-east, flying at 28,000 ft. There were seventy-plus Fw 190s and above, at 32,000 ft, sixty-plus Bf 109s. The Focke-Wulfs were in company front formation, in waves of eight aircraft each. Dregne immediately sent the 364th and 362nd Squadrons down while the 363rd climbed to intercept the '109s. Such was the reaction speed of the Mustangs that few bombers were actually attacked. A wild mêlée of fighters ensued during which the skill of the Americans and inexperience of the Germans contrasted sharply. The

Above left *Top ace of the 357th was Leonard 'Kit' Carson with 18.5 victories in the air. His* Nooky Booky IV *is seen here with his ground kills added to the scoreboard, being run up by the crew chief prior to another mission in 1945. Carson's squadron was the 362nd.*

Left *Also flying with the 362nd was Captain Charles E. Weaver who was credited with eight air-to-air victories, plus ground kills. His stylish form of scoreboard is shown here on what is believed to be the only Mustang flown by him, 44-72199/A.*

Above *Remaining with the Thunderbolt throughout the war, the 56th Group was unique in using the P-47M, one of the most powerful models of the entire line. This one, 44-21112, was the mount of George Bostwick of the 63rd FS, who ended the war with nine air-to-air kills, plus ground-attack credits, as recorded under the cockpit.*

364th Squadron accounted for eighteen Fw 190s in the first few minutes of combat and finished up with 21½, the half being a '109 shared by Bob Winks with a pilot from the 20th Group. Captain John England's 362nd Squadron added another 21 kills while the 363rd scored twelve. The scoreboard included the kills of Lieutenants Weaver and Sublett, Lieutenant Colonel Evans and Captain Maxwell, all of whom with the exception of Weaver — who notched up his sixth victim — attained ace status. The 357th now boasted 38 aces, a remarkable record in less than one year of combat.

The 357th's feat was duly recognized by the award of a DUC. General Doolittle's message to the Group CO included these words: 'You gave the Hun the most humiliating beating he has ever taken in the air. Extend my personal admiration and congratulations to each member of your command, both ground and air, for a superb victory.'

While the Mustangs continued to find what action there was, the 56th took something of a back seat during the closing phases of the air war, at least as far as aerial victories went. The limiting factor was the range of its P-47Ms. The group remained in the UK for the duration and was not moved to a continental base, primarily because its support facilities could not be exactly duplicated anywhere else when it changed over to the P-47M. The only answer was to employ the Wolfpack to the limit of its range — but the aircraft had to carry maximum fuel in drop tanks to reach those areas of the shrinking Third Reich still in German hands. This meant in effect that the M model, which was thirstier on fuel than the P-47D, would need to carry underwing fuel tanks to cover the same distance as the D model could without tanks.

The occurrence of abnormally low cylinder head temperatures, breakdowns in the ignition system at high altitudes and ruptured carburettor diaphragms were only some of the technical defects that conspired to keep the new aircraft on the ground far more often

than they flew during their first weeks of service with the 56th. In the event, it was not to be until April that the group could pronounce the P-47M fully operational and be sure that the aircraft's teething troubles were over. In the meantime, the group's engineering personnel undertook the task of changing every engine when a second round of troubles occurred. This time the cause was traced to incorrect 'pickling' of moving parts prior to the R-2800s being shipped out from the USA: engines with less than fifty hours were exhibiting burned pistons and scuffed cylinder barrels. Once the fifty-hour mark was reached the engine seemed to settle down — it was in effect 'run in'. When all suspect low-time engines were changed, the P-47M gained a new lease of life and was in time to see action before the final collapse of Germany. This was a great boost to the morale of the 56th's pilots, who had high regard for the aircraft, which was the most powerful of all the Thunderbolt models that equipped the 8th Air Force.

The winter weather curtailed operations to a significant degree and although losses to ground fire were reduced, fighters faced the grim prospect of trying to

The prancing Mustang appropriately adorning Lady Val *the P-51D flown by Lieutenant Gordon of the 343rd FS, 55th FG.*

make home base in freezing mist, cloud and fog. Most groups had to record the occasional total loss of both aircraft and pilot, without a trace of either ever being found. On occasion returning fighters did not even attempt to reach England; there were a great many airfields in France, Holland, Belgium and Germany where they could put down safely to sit out the worst of the weather. Accidents continued to take their toll, though.

Along with a new model Thunderbolt, 8th AF squadrons began to receive the last wartime version of the Mustang in the guise of the P-51K. Fitted with an electrically feathering Aeroproducts propeller rather than the Hamilton Standard hydraulically operated unit, the P-51K was otherwise little changed from the D model. Both featured the late-war improvements incorporated into the Mustang airframe, including the K-14 gunsight and AN/APS-13 tail-warning radar.

16   Jet nemesis

As the bitter winter weather improved the coming spring of 1945 saw the German cause all but lost; in the west its last fling had failed and despite having three jet aircraft types operational, each of which had the measure of the best the Allies could muster, it was a classic case of 'too little, too late'. The Russian armies were shrinking the borders of the Third Reich from the east and the Allied effort in the west had regained momentum after the ill-fated attempt to cross the Rhine at Arnhem. Barring miracles all Germany would soon be overrun. No miracle, no eleventh hour saviour, was to manifest itself. For Germany, Hitler's lightning war of 1939-40 had turned into a nightmare of defeat after defeat. Nearly six years of blood-letting were almost at an end.

In the air the supreme reign of the Allied air forces was nowhere more obvious than in the mighty armadas of 8th Air Force bombers and fighters winging their way from England to shatter the last vestiges of enemy resistance. Now, even solid cloud cover offered little respite from the rain of high explosive delivered almost daily from the skies. Radar bombing was now backed by a range of devices to help the bombardiers put down their loads accurately on virtually any target. Assisting this effort were the fighters which, while maintaining the shield against German interceptors, also carried out other tasks vital to the 'big picture'. The latter included the mission of radio relay whereby Mustangs would orbit the target area and boost the signals transmitted from bomber and other fighter formations to ground stations. One pilot who drew such duty in January 1945 was Don Kocker of the 357th. His recollection of one flight showed that there was occasionally a light-hearted tinge to a basically grim business:

'One day I was assigned to a radio relay mission with another fellow having only a few missions to his credit. We spent a quiet three hours on top of the overcast north-west of Munich 'till we were released. A couple of calls to the RDF brought us out of the overcast in sight of the runway. As we rode back to the squadron ready room in the Jeep, my wingman asked ''how the hell did you bring us back here without see-ing the ground since we took off?''. I let him think I was that good for a while, then reminded him of the RDF and how to use it. We all had a lot of respect for those RDF operators

'Another day, in November 1944 as I recall, my flying skill was demonstrated for a different reason. I was flying element wingman when someone yelled, ''Blue Flight, break right''. The flight exploded apart... except for me, who took a gentle turn with a wary eye on the flak that had caused the excitement. I had forgotten to burn the gas out of the fuselage tank — and P-51 pilots will recall how the aircraft reacted to violent manoeuvres in that condition. My element leader admired my 'iron nerve', as he called it until I told him of my error... those days had their humour.'

With a current kill ratio over the Luftwaffe averaging seven to one, the AAF could, after the massacre of 14 January, look forward to a relatively easy time as the bomber force prepared to finish off the job it had started on 17 August 1942. Escort fighters began to meet the latest conventional German fighters as well as the more revolutionary types, in the final round of combats. Late-model Bf 109Gs and 'Ks exhibited the ultimate stretch of the airframe which could trace its origins back to 1934. Outclassed on nearly all counts by the P-51, the '109 only occasionally gave the American fighters any trouble, when the enemy pilot turned out to be an experienced man perhaps returning to combat after a period of convalescence, or an individual who had thus far avoided disastrous contact with Allied fighters.

German aeronautical expertise had also led to significant improvements to the Focke-Wulf Fw 190, always a more potent aircraft than the older Bf 109. Under Kurt Tank, the Focke-Wulf concern had substituted the air-cooled BMW radial engine of the early '190 series for the liquid-cooled Jumo-engine in Fw 190D models and the ultimate example in the shape of the Ta 152. Both were potentially a match for the P-51D — provided, as with most air combats involving equally matched opponents, there was a capable man at the controls, imbued with the will to

win the engagement and get the best out of his machine. Many German pilots no longer had that will, and the majority of the now-modest formations the *Jagdverbände* could put into the air were flown by young men sadly lacking the service time and flying experience of their comrades in arms who had previously made the fighter arm one of the most efficient in the world. These green young men often paid with their lives when the 8th AF went out to hunt them.

Such was the domination of the 8th's fighter force that it was possible to 'open a book' on which of the groups would reach the incredible total of 1,000 enemy aircraft destroyed. It was not a case of 'if' but 'when'. Way out in front of the others were naturally enough the 56th and 4th, the pilots of which groups had been at the game longest. But the majority of pilots in all fifteen groups wanted to increase their scores and everyone felt frustration when their

Left *Putting down at Eye, home of the B-17s of the 490th BG, pilots of the 352nd Squadron, 353rd Group, re-run a recent combat in front of (and on) Lieutenant Arthur C. Cundy's aircraft,* 44-15092/SX-B. *Cundy, fourth from left in the standing group, was tragically drowned in the North Sea when his engine caught fire on 11 March 1945 (via Paul Coggan).*

Below left Slender, Tender & Tall *was the name carried by two 487th FS Mustangs. This is the second* 44-14812/HO-T, *pictured in Belgium in 1945 (via Paul Coggan).*

Below *Kirke Everson's* Tar Heel *parked at Bassingbourn in 1945. The aircraft shows a scoreboard 3.5 short of his final total of 14.5 victories, thirteen of which were strafing claims. The rear-view mirrors were not atypical (USAF).*

particular flight failed to find much enemy activity either in the air or on the ground. It was galling to hear that another group, probably one flying not too far from their own patrol area, had come across an airfield or two crammed with aircraft and had duly worked it over to boost their score again.

While the 4th just pipped the 56th to the post for the honours for 1,000 destroyed when air and ground claims were added together, the 56th ended the war way out in front of the Eagles as far as air-to-air victories went with 647½. Taking this yardstick alone the Eagles actually came third in the listings, the 357th beating it by a margin of 26 (609 against 583½). Such successes were without question the result of the excellent leader-wingman system, followed by the AAF confidence and training. These advantages were reflected not only in the scores themselves, but in the fact that very few of the top 8th AF aces were killed in air-to-air combat.

By February 1945 the decimation of the conventional fighter units forced the Luftwaffe to make Herculean efforts to organize jet units with sufficient aircraft, primarily for bomber destruction. Consequently the month's increased activity was reflected in AAF pilots' combat reports which, together with an unprecedented level of encounters between bombers and jets, totalled 163, 118 being reported by fighter pilots. For the 8th the month of jet activity started on the 9th when about a dozen Me 262s went after bombers in the Fulda area north of Frankfurt. Five pilots, Captain Edwin H. Miller and Lieutenant William E. Hydorn of the 78th; Captain Don

Bochkay and Lieutenant Johnnie L. Carter of the 357th; and Stephen C. Ananian of the 359th, claimed kills. Captain Miller's was subsequently downgraded to 'probably destroyed', as his encounter report noted:

'On 9 February 1945 an Me 262 was approaching the box of bombers which we were escorting. I called the bounce from approximately 22,000 ft, diving on the '262 which was flying 14,000 ft below. I began firing at an extreme range, knowing that he would out-distance me the moment that my wingman and I were spotted. So on the first long burst the right engine began to smoke and the jet rolled over, falling through a cloud bank, and we were unable to follow and confirm the victory. This was considered a 'probable' which appears on my record.'

In the following weeks the 8th sent out its heavies against a variety of targets including vulnerable and vital oil production centres, the Luftwaffe offering very little defence compared to the effort it would have mounted to defend such areas in the previous years. It had, of course, been the pounding of oil and petroleum supplies that had been one of the very causes of this German inability. At that time, careful planning was necessary if an American raid was to be challenged with the number of fighters needed for even small success. Such a challenge was offered to a massive strike on 22 February when the heavies flew Operation 'Clarion'. This, a 41-target assault on marshalling yards (which also encompassed the 9th

and 15th Air Forces, the US 1st Tactical Air Force and the RAF's 2nd Tactical Air Force) was intercepted by comparatively small numbers of jets which were widely scattered, although there were upwards of forty over the various target areas. On a day when the 8th AF fighters scored only four definite aerial kills and 24 on the ground, the 352nd, 353rd and 355th claimed one Me 262 kill apiece.

More action came on the 25th, which was a red letter day for the 55th, then enjoying a new lease of life under the energetic command of Elwyn Righetti. Combat between the group's P-51s and the Me 262s resulted in a record seven German jet aircraft destroyed, a feat that was not to be equalled by any other 8th AF unit. Captain Donald Cummings' double made him the second AAF fighter to achieve two jet victories on one mission, and single '262s fell to Captain Penn and Lieutenants Anderson, Clemmons and Menegay. Lieutenant O'Neil and Captain Birtciel shared the seventh between them.

Another first for the day was the destruction of the only Arado Ar 234 the 8th had been able to claim up to that time, this falling to the 364th. The ninth victim of the day was another Me 262 shot down by Lieutenant Carl Payne of the 4th Group.

The 55th's victories were primarily in the vicinity of Giebelstadt aerodrome, with one of Captain Cummings' victims falling at Leipheim aerodrome. Sweeping the Giebelstadt area, the group's 38th Squadron spotted jets taking off at 10:00 hr, and

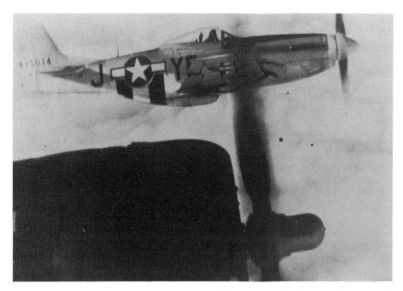

bounced them. Captain Cummings' combat report included the following details of this spectacular clash:

'I was leading Hellcat Yellow Flight on a fighter sweep at 10,000 ft in the vicinity of Giebelstadt A/D when several Me 262s were called in at 9 o'clock, taking off from the field. Captain Penn, the squadron leader, ordered us to drop our tanks and engage the enemy.

'I peeled off from 11,000 ft, making a 180 degree turn to the left in a seventy degree dive after a jet which was then approaching the airdrome. I commenced firing from approximately 1,000 yd in a steep, diving pass and after about three seconds observed many strikes. Since I was closing fast and approaching the airfield, which was beginning to throw up intense and accurate flak, I broke left and up, taking evasive action when about one-third of the way across the field. My wingman, who was behind me, saw the E/A touch ground, cartwheel and burn.

'During the above engagement my number three and four men had become separated from the Flight, so my wingman and I set out on a course of 180 degrees at 5,000 ft in search of ground targets. Near Leipheim A/D we spotted an unidentified aircraft crossing the SW corner of the field at 4,000 ft; 150 degrees. We increased our speed and closed on the E/A which we identified as an Me 262 with dark camouflage and large crosses on its wings. As I came in range, the jet made a sharp turn to the left, losing altitude. When I followed him, closing slowly, he started to let down his nosewheel, apparently attempting to land. Closing further to 400 yd, I commenced firing. The first burst missed, but when the jet attempted to turn to the right I gave it to him

again at about ten degrees deflection and observed many strikes. Large pieces of the E/A began to fly off and the fuselage exploded behind the cockpit. The '262 then rolled to the right and went straight in from 800 ft, exploding as it went.'

Lieutenant Carl Payne's section of the 334th Squadron was near Naunburg when an Me 262 was seen:

'I was flying Cobweb Blue Three on a strafing show. We were ten minutes SW of Leipzig at 8,000 ft when I spotted an Me 262 at about 4,000 ft and at 1 o'clock. I peeled off on him, calling in at the same time. I closed to about 400 yd and opened fire, holding it until about 100 yd. I hit him and knocked out his left jet. I overshot and pulled up to the right and made another pass.

'I was not hitting him as I should, so I moved up to ten to thirty feet behind him and started firing. He exploded and covered me completely with flames. After I hit him the first time, he went to the deck and stayed there until he exploded.'

Elsewhere that day the 4th Group bounced a section of Fw 190s which had been identified as friendlies while en route to the Dessau area for a freelance sweep. Aerodromes at Rohrensee and Kothen were strafed, the attack on the latter resulting in Captain 'Swede' Carlson losing flying speed and bellying-in. Carlson calmly got on the R/T and directed his fellow pilots on to worthwhile targets before the Germans captured him. Returning home, Blue Section was bounced by seven '190s and '109s which made no aggressive moves. Neither did the Mustangs. Both Americans and Germans were out of ammunition and the former were amazed to see their would-be attackers form up with them and fly together before breaking off and going on their way...

March and April 1945 were to see the highpoint of Me 262 action and a corresponding leap in the number destroyed by AAF fighters. Bombers were again the primary target for the German attacks which were widely reported; fighters alone recorded 438 encounters, 280 combats and claims of 43(destroyed)-3(probable)-45(damaged) in the air alone. On the ground 21 jets were destroyed plus eleven damaged.

Realizing that their closing speed gave too little time to aim if they approached a bomber formation head-on, the German pilots had developed a technique of a high-angle diving approach from behind which invariably took them through the ranks of B-17s or B-24s at a speed which left them immune from interception by the Mustangs, whereupon they would climb and repeat the process. This 'roller coaster' technique made maximum use of available cloud cover and the dense contrails made by the bombers. Formation attacks using flight positions similar to those of the Mustangs fooled bomber crews long enough for the jet pilots to get within range. Attacks were usually made at altitudes between 25,000 and 29,000 ft, a primary consideration being to mask the tell-tale smoke trail for as long as possible. But the German pilots were fully aware that prior warning of attack availed the bombers little — all the US fighter pilots could do was to place fighters between the bombers and the interceptors and try as best they could to break up a mass attack before it developed. Many pilots had seen what the 30mm cannon of the Me 262 could do to a Fortress or Liberator.

Fortunately for the 8th's bombers, the Germans had by that time one big disadvantage. Almost daily their territory shrank between the pincers of the Allied armies and previous encounters with jets had given all fighter groups an accurate picture of most of the airfields from which they operated. VIII FC consequently instigated 'capping' patrols to catch them taking off and landing. Each squadron or group was given an area to patrol in which was situated one or more such airfields — when the Me 262s were sighted, the Mustangs pounced.

By 14 March such tactics had netted three more Me 262s for the 8th, others having fallen to aircraft of the 9th AF. More were to follow for the 15th AF whose area of operations was by then overlapping that of the strategic 8th and tactical 9th, plus the RAF. On the 24th, the 56th Group encountered jets for the first time, the Wolfpack having just managed a reprieve for its P-47Ms The malfunctions experienced with these Thunderbolts had led to VIII FC starting conversion training on the P-51. It was, for the oldest and most successful Thunderbolt exponent in Europe, a lean time. But with the P-47M operational, the 56th showed it had lost none of its edge over the best the enemy could put up.

Lieutenant John Keeler shot down one Me 262 that day, with Lieutenant Norman Gould accounting for the first of two Ar 234s, the second jet bomber going down under the combined attack of Lieutenants Lear and Ball. In a bad period for the Luftwaffe's valuable jet reconnaissance capability, the 352nd's Captain Bryan despatched a third and Captain Barnhart of the 356th a fourth.

Sweeping ahead of bombers in the Berlin area, Lieutenant Keeler's 63rd Squadron element mixed it with two Me 262s:

'...It occurred near the Muritz Lake area north of Berlin. I was flying number three position in a flight led by Lieutenant Paul Dawson. It was a fighter sweep mission (to Holzzwickede) ahead of the B-17s and B-24s.

'An Me 262 passed less than 100 ft beneath our flight while we were orbiting at about 22,000 ft. I called the bounce and led the flight after the German jet. The Jerry spotted us coming in and began to pull away. We were ready to break off the chase when he started a turn. He continued in the turn until I had closed the distance between us to less than 200 yd. I fired a long burst and saw the right wing of the Me 262 explode. The jet snapped and plunged downward in flames.

'Our flight had become strung out in the chase and had dropped down between the leading '262 and one flying some 1,000 yd in trail. This second German jet scored a hit in the wing of Lieutenant Dawson's P-47 before breaking away from the flight.'

Captain Ray Wetmore claimed another Me 163 on 15 March, and three days later the Me 262s showed what they could do when conditions were favourable for them. In bad weather they largely avoided the escorts and shot down thirteen bombers, losing two of their own, probably to bomber gunners. On 19 March AAF fighters were more effective, with the 78th and 357th getting two each, and the 359th one. The 339th did well on 20 March with three Me 262s confirmed.

No less than six Me 262s fell to the guns of the 78th's P-51s on 21 March, a feat that was to be added to by the Duxford group before the month was out. Two pilots of the 361st also claimed Me 262s and one fell to the 339th Group. Captain Edwin Miller of the 78th followed up his 'probable' of 9 February with more positive results. His encounter report described his one victory:

'We were flying escort when an Me 262 approached the rear box of bombers and began leapfrogging through the entire group, scoring several

Not for nothing were they known as the 'Steeple Morden Strafers'. The 355th goes to work on a German dispersal (IWM).

hits. He then veered off, returned, and started attacking the rear box again. By this time we were on his tail. I tried a long shot and could see strikes all over his left wing which immediately caused him to lose speed. My wingman and I were then able to close on him, and I scored several strikes on both wings and the fuselage. The Jerry then peeled out and proceeded to head for the deck, and I was following him all the time, firing as we went. We broke through a scattered undercast and I was sitting right on his tail until my guns were completely empty. By that time I knew he was a ''dead duck'' and veered off to the left, pulling up just as he crashed into the ground.'

On 22 March the 78th shot down another three '262s, with the 55th claiming a single. The 56th was in action with the jets on the 25th, the result being another two downed. The 479th and 352nd shot down one Me 262 apiece on the same day. More action followed on 30 March when the 8th clashed with Me 262s in the Hamburg area. This time the

339th scored two and the 364th, 352nd and 361st one each. Colonel John D. Landers, then CO of the 78th after duty with the 55th and 357th, teamed up with another pilot to emerge victorious over one more '262. The last day of March brought a single 8th AF jet victory when one Me 262 fell to the 353rd's Lieutenant Tordoff after the jet had shot down a B-24.

Although German jet activity was the cause of great concern in Army Air Force higher echelons, the response by the fighter groups in Europe appeared to be holding the line. If the conventional fighters could manage by their makeshift tactics, to ward off the widespread decimation of the bomber formations that the Germans were aiming for, it would only be a matter of time before the jet airfields and production centres would be in the hands of Allied troops.

The gradual increase in the number of jet interceptions during March reached a crescendo in April — and showed that for all their potential superiority the German jets could not prevent high losses by overwhelming numbers of 'inferior' fighters. Combats began on 3 April, with three Me 262s falling to the 339th Group. The following day the 8th went after six

Left *Mustang of the 503rd FS, 339th FG, 44-13324.*

Below left *Lieutenant Colonel John Landers prepares to saddle up* Big Beautiful Doll *at Duxford and lead the 78th Group on another sweep. The aircraft is believed to be 44-72258, one of at least three Mustangs with this name flown by Landers (USAF).*

Right *George Vanden Heuval flew* Mary Mine, *44-64005/E9-L, of the 376th FS, 361st Group, stationed at Chievres, Belgium, in March 1945.*

jet airfields and Luftwaffe control stations in north central Germany. Rising to attack bombers were some fifty jets. These claimed five AAF bombers and a Mosquito, a type which had been used by the Americans for some time in various roles including, as on this day, to check the formation keeping of the four-engined main force.

Eight Me 262s and an Ar 234 were shot down, the 4th Group getting three and one each being credited to the 56th, 339th, 364th, 361st and 355th. A single Me 262 was shot down by the 56th on the following day. On 7 April the Germans lost three Me 262s to the 479th, one each to the 339th and the 355th; the 8th AF scored one more on the 9th, this falling to the 55th. Then came a black day for the Luftwaffe jet fighter force. Widespread destruction was wrought on the ground, the 8th's fighters accounting for no less than 309 positively destroyed plus 235 damaged — but it was in the air that the Germans suffered most. The total of twenty Me 262s downed seemed nothing in comparison with the losses on the ground, but by that time airfields were becoming crowded with aircraft that would not have constituted a very great threat to American bomber formations, even if there had been adequate stocks of fuel to fly them. The enemy had staked all on the jets and each one lost, particularly if the pilot was also killed or incapacitated, was little short of disastrous.

The action which came to be known as the 'Great Jet Massacre' resulted in a top score of five for the 20th Group on its 303rd mission. Well positioned over Oranienburg, the King's Cliffe flyers led the 8th AF groups on the best day's results against the jets. The 55th, 352nd and 353rd tied in second place with three Me 262s each, the 359th claimed two and singles fell to the 4th, 56th, 364th and 356th. The latter victory was chalked up by Lieutenant Wayne Gatlin of the 360th FS, who subsequently reported:

'I was leading Vortex White Flight escorting the 384th Bomb Group bombing Oranienburg. Just after bombing the target, jets were seen attacking the Group ahead of ours. I was on the right-hand side of the bombers going towards the tail end of our box when I saw an Me 262 making a pass from 6 o'clock high to the bombers. He appeared to be hitting two stragglers and then continued in a dive right on down through the box. I made a 180-degree diving turn (Split-S) to the right and was able to cut him off very easily. I slid in on his tail as he continued his dive and opened fire at zero degrees deflection and 200 yd range. I observed hits all over the jet and continued firing as he started smoking. I kept on him until his dive became almost vertical and I had to break off in order to pull out. After levelling off a bit, I cocked my wing and saw where he hit and burned.'

Further actions in April 1945 did not reach the level of the 10th but Me 262s were claimed on the 16th, 17th, 18th and 19th to finish the 8th Air Force's action against this most deadly of the jet types the Germans had committed to battle. Over this four-day period the score was fifteen to the 8th AF fighters, six jets falling to the 357th and one to the 55th.

17 Curtain

As well as the significant aerial victories, April 1945 was for the 8th Air Force the time of incredibly high scores from strafing attacks. The enormity of the Luftwaffe's demise was reflected in the fact that the 339th Group put in claims for 100 destroyed on two days, the 4th and 10th, feats of arms that were never surpassed. But the German flak which, as someone said with due emphasis, fired until the last day of the war, remained highly dangerous to low-flying fighters and this factor could never be ignored — indeed, great care was taken to ensure that needless losses were not incurred at this late stage of the game. Few pilots wanted the distinction of being the last to be shot down.

An illustration of the additional hazards faced if a pilot did have the misfortune to put down on what remained of Reich territory happened on 10 April. The 55th Group drew escort to B-17s attacking Dresden and duly accompanied them into the target area. Handing over escort to another group, the 55th went looking for likely targets on the ground. Leading the group was Lieutenant Colonel Elwyn Righetti, a gifted pilot who excelled in the art of strafing. Having steered the 55th through a bad patch, 'Eager Al' was held in high esteem by his willingness to undertake any mission at the head of his Mustangs.

Flying low north of the city, Righetti and his wingman, Lieutenant Carroll Henry, chanced upon an Fw 190 which Henry despatched while his leader made an exploratory pass over an airfield. Although he hit parked aircraft, Righetti's P-51 was hit by flak. He made three passes and claimed nine destroyed before having to put down, the Mustang's coolant having leaked away. Henry failed to see his leader's aircraft on the ground due to haze, and flew home to report Righetti's victories. These totalled 27, more than any other 8th AF pilot.

Confident that their leader would turn up, pilots of the 55th waited for news of his whereabouts. None came. Even after the end of the war, the fate of the 55th's CO was not discovered — and to this day no

Heavily landed on a muddy English field, 44-19726 appears beyond economical repair — at least as late in the war as 25 April 1945 when the incident occurred. Note the Mustang's prop some yards behind the rest of the airframe and the armourers carefully removing live ammunition. The aircraft was part of the 383rd FS, 364th Group (USAF).

confirmation of what happened to him has come to light.

★   ★   ★

On 16 April, part of the 8th's fighter element out over Germany was half the 505th Squadron of the 339th Group. Eight Mustangs led by Major Joe Thury were looking for trouble in the sector between Munich and Chiem Lake, their escort duty completed. With the bombers en route for home, the P-51s embarked on their strafing operations, as per SOP. Descending to 10,000 ft each pilot scanned the ground for signs of worthwhile targets.

One of the formation called in movement on the autobahn. Down went all eight fighters to orbit the spot for a closer look. What looked like a tractor was towing something along the road — something with wings. . . Thury's curiosity was aroused and a glance at the surrounding area indicated an open space adjacent to the autobahn. Camouflaged area — airfield. The flight dropped lower, every man concentrating on picking out details. Another look at the tractor showed it had an Me 262 in tow and from 4,000 ft the airfield was clearly visible.

On the edges of the airfield tall trees obviously concealed more aircraft. Movement and shadows indicated a jet fighter base in operation. 'We'll go down and hit the field,' called Thury. At 3,000 ft the American pilots picked out other enemy aircraft on the airfield, both Bf 109s and Fw 190s. They estimated there were over 200 of them.

The airfield was already pock-marked with bomb craters but the Germans had obviously patched the runways enough to fly some sorties from it — making it a prime target. At 1,000 ft the formation split, each flight widening out to make a long approach at 400 mph IAS. Gunsights on. Still no flak.

A Bf 109 filled his sights. Thury fired. The machine-gun bullets walked up to the enemy aircraft. Pieces began to fly off and almost immediately fire broke out. Thury's Mustang *Pauline* flashed over the pall of black smoke as the other Mustangs plastered other targets dispersed around the airfield. Several fires had been started. Thury selected one of the jets and lined up for a second pass. This was the dangerous part. There was still no flak but the second pass was the one the gunners waited for. They would have the range now. Thury and three other P-51s were committed to their firing passes.

Suddenly, there it was, the familiar orange golf balls arcing towards him and the others. Thury yelled, 'Get the guns first'. It was all over in a matter of minutes: as the gun locations were identified so the Mustangs systematically silenced them with a five-to-one ratio in firepower. Six flak guns against 48 air-craft machine-guns were not very hopeful odds.

Slight damage had been inflicted on the fighters, but nothing serious. They went back to work. Thury destroyed a second aircraft, some pieces of the Me 262 striking the Mustang as its guns chewed it up. Finally it began to burn. Two. The other pilots were working over their own sections and before the Mustangs turned for home smoke columns marked the extent of the day's attack. The pilots would claim twenty destroyed on the ground.

Back at Fowlmere and debriefing Joe Thury was surprised to be asked his opinion on whether the group should make a return visit to the same target the following day. Thury was understandably apprehensive. If a second pass over an airfield was dangerous a return attack could be suicidal. It did not take the Germans long to move in more flak. . . Thury weighed the odds: At that stage of the war there were plenty of worthwhile targets left — but they had to be found. The airfields already located had been well worked over. And this one belonged to the 339th. The pilots were eager for kills. The squadron would go.

The plan for the 17 April strafing attack was that the 505th Squadron would accompany the bombers as if they were on a normal escort mission. Then at the last moment all sixteen Mustangs would turn south towards Munich 200 miles south by south-east. Thury had forebodings that the Germans might be anticipating just the kind of repeat attack that the squadron CO, Colonel John Henry, had planned. But at that stage of the war everyone knew it was just a matter of time before the enemy threw in the towel; the young pilots were eager and there was every liklihood of a unit citation if the attack was successful. Morale was high.

But strafing enemy airfields was an unpredictable business. Sometimes if the defences were meagre or non-existent, victories were easy. But if the defences were on the ball, the risk to pilots became very high. The great majority of the top 8th AF aces had been lost on ground strafing operations rather than in air-to-air combat, and losses were proportionately higher in both pilots and aircraft than they had been in meeting the Luftwaffe in the air.

These thoughts occupied Thury as he and his fellow pilots planned the morning mission. There was perfect flying weather on the 17th and at 05:15 hr the pilots were heading for group operations, either on foot or the ubiquitous bicycle, a very common mode of USAAF transport in the ETO. Briefing was in the familiar Nissen hut. Thury, who would lead the 505th, had already studied the weather, maps of the target area and teletype reports. Attending the briefing were eighteen pilots, two spares being 'on the board' just in case.

Left *Lieutenant Colonel William C. Clark who led the 339th through the last weeks of the war, taking over on 14 April 1945. Adding ground strafing victories to a single aerial kill, he finished with a tally of nine, six of his ground victories being scored on 16 April* (USAF).

Below left Baby Max *lifts off from Fowlmere, probably for a local non-operational flight, judging by the lack of drop tanks. This Mustang was part of the 504th FS, 339th FG.*

Right *Lieutenant Colonel Carl Goldenburg was acting CO of the 339th Group for five days in December 1944, filling in, with Lieutenant Colonel Scruggs, for regular CO Colonel John B. Henry, Jr. Goldenburg's aircraft was named* Honey Child (USAF).

The weather officer did nothing to dispel earlier predictions that conditions would stay good, offering a high overcast all the way to the target area. Scattered clouds below this would easily be avoided by the formation. The assistant Group Operations Officer gave the compass course, coded distress calls, times and check points. Each man copied this information on to a clear plastic knee pad in red grease pencil that was easily wiped off in the event of a forced landing in enemy territory.

Thury chalked the outlines of the airfield and indicated the method of attack for the benefit of those pilots who had not been on the previous day's mission. There were variations today. Twelve Mustangs would be assigned as top cover patrol during the initial pass. They would circle the field and spot any AA fire, while four aircraft attacked. If, as Thury expected, the attackers drew flak, the high level fighters could gauge its strength. If the defences were too heavy, the attack would be called off. No point in needlessly risking pilots and aircraft. If enemy fire was light, the top cover would come down to strafe the guns as soon as their positions were pinpointed. With the guns silenced, the entire squadron would work the field over.

In order to achieve as much surprise as possible, radio silence would be maintained as far as Kassel, at which point the 505th would turn right following a 170 degree heading to Munich. Take off would be 11:49 hr. Watches were synchronized.

Pilots filed out of the briefing hut to find breakfast at squadron HQ — canned orange juice, coffee, fried Spam and toast. Eggs were available for the flyers, a privilege reserved for them. Thury gathered his pilots and went over a few last points. He advised kicking the P-51's rudder when strafing, so that the .50-cal bullets would spread over as wide an area as possible. He designated Major Archie Towers, squadron Operations Officer, as leader in the event that he himself was hit. Thury chose to make the first pass himself to draw fire. If he was knocked down, Towers would take over, decide on the strength of the defences and press home the attack as he saw fit. But the first decision was to gauge if the Mustangs could deal with the guns.

If Thury's initial pass was successful, three flights would attack with him, one off his right wing and two off his left. All aircraft would make left-turning gunnery passes to avoid any risk of collision which might happen if right and left circles were made. Pilots checked their position in the attack by coloured discs affixed to the wall, each with a name and flight colour. Red Flight would be led by Thury, with White, Green and Black following. One spare would

tag along at the end.

With a late take-off without need to rendezvous with the bombers, time dragged. Pilots drew helmets and oxygen masks, G-suits, Mae Wests and parachutes. Still more time to kill. Thury walked to his aircraft and talked to his Crew Chief. The ground crew had worked through the night, giving *Pauline* a wax job estimated to boost her speed by 10 mph. Thury would be grateful for that.

As the bomber stream had passed over at 10:00 hr the fighter pilots knew that they had nearly two hours to wait. Finally, it was time. Thury strapped himself in and ran through the take-off checks. Flight Surgeon Fred Scroggins had a word of warning. 'Be careful, Joe. It isn't that important.' Thury acknowledged. 'Clear,' he yelled. 'Clear,' the Crew Chief replied. The Merlin spit and caught, turned over smoothly. It was 11:45. The chocks were whipped away and *Pauline* moved slowly out, dust being churned by her propeller.

Thury paused at the end of the Fowlmere runway, letting the rest of the squadron taxi in behind him. He closed the canopy and spun his right hand round and round, his left hand easing the throttle open. On his right his wingman's Mustang stood ready to take off in line abreast. Seventeen Mustangs ran their engines to maximum revs. Thury's hand chopped forward and down. Roll.

At precisely 11:49 *Pauline* lifted off Fowlmere's pre-fabricated runway. In minutes the two-abreast squadron take-off was completed and all aircraft executed a wide left turn to enable everyone to form up. At 160 mph indicated each Mustang climbed into the haze and headed south-east. Out over the Channel and making landfall at the Dutch coast they were up with the rear of the bomber stream, still climbing. At the designated altitude of 27,000 ft, they levelled off. Speed was increased as Thury checked geographical features below. Holland passed under the wings. Germany ahead. The Rhine.

The Mustangs moved out into combat formation. Bombers were overhead, now virtually immune from attack. Kassel was ahead when Thury signalled for a turn to the south. It was 13:45. Gun switches were checked and the aircraft began a slow descent, increasing speed. Munich became visible 25 miles ahead. The target was near.

Thury called the squadron, 'This is Upper Leader. Drop tanks.' Thirty-four tanks tumbled down onto German soil as Thury ordered the top cover flights to increase speed. His own speed increased as the rate of descent steepened.

Munich passed to their right as the 505th got lower

Left Lieutenant Farmer of the 339th Group with 44-13987, Dibbo (USAF).

and Thury picked out the target airfield about fifteen miles distant. He turned left to follow the east-west autobahn at 4,000 ft altitude. The airfield loomed ahead. Thirteen Mustangs took up position at 10,000 ft while their four fellow pilots raced in at 400 mph. The top cover went to full throttle to stay above the action.

Thury made a 45 degree left turn, aiming for the left side of the airfield. To fly down its centre would have been unnecessarily risky. Over the trees bordering the edge of the field, he selected an Fw 190 parked in the far left corner. He opened fire. Thury's aim was spot on. The '190 blew up as the Mustang flashed through the smoke, staying low. There was no flak.

Watching Thury's safe pass, the top cover came down, peeling off to set up for their own firing passes. Thury circled left, wondering. Any German gunners would be waiting for their targets to come closer...

Thury maintained his turn to line up again. Nine Mustangs were about to fire, four of them having joined their leader. High closure speeds meant that the top cover aircraft overtook Thury, who had slowed after the firing pass. They were line abreast as they burst on the airfield.

A flare arced up from the centre of the airfield. On the signal, the German gunners opened fire simultaneously. Aircraft were hit. The air was filled with smoke and dust as the orange golf balls sought out the silver fighters. Thury's wingman took hits but flew on. Shells found their mark on his own aircraft as he pressed the mike button. 'Hit nothing but guns.'

Thury cleared the field and looked back, staying low. His mind was racing. Something about the angles of fire... it didn't start at the ground. He looked again at the smoke puffs. They came from the trees. Thury called this to the others. The Germans had erected platforms, hoping to put the guns and crews out of the reach of the fighters' fire, which scythed through everything at ground level.

Now the pilots could see them. They came down and fired into the trees. Thury estimated twenty guns. His formation carried 102 and despite their ammunition being of smaller calibre, the aircraft did not have to reload. There were some seconds' respite as the aircraft came in. Three and four passes were made on the flak. It lessened as the weapons and crews were destroyed or disabled. By the fourth pass the opposition was noticeably weaker and as Thury brought *Pauline* in for a fifth time, he had time to select another aircraft target without much danger.

Thury's target was an Me 262. He set it on fire and lined up on a Bf 109. Pass number six. Mustangs were all over the airfield and fires were breaking out everywhere. Having recovered somewhat, the Germans opened up with small arms and rifles.

Thury left the '109 in flames as the golf balls and rifle fire started again. Thury got two Fw 190s parked close together. That made five.

He pulled up and watched his squadron at work. There were many fires now and his own ammunition was running low. The Mustangs had also lost their speed, most of them down to 300 mph or so, easier targets for the 20mm flak. Last pass.

Thury had an aircraft in his sights when the Mustang staggered. A hole appeared in the right wing leading edge. His speed dropped. Thury kicked the rudder to bring the P-51 out of its right-hand slew and climbed over the trees. 'I'm hit. Can't get any speed.'

Lieutenant James Starnes pulled alongside Thury's Mustang and looked it over. He reported the damage to his leader, who yelled to Archie Towers to take over. He had to head for home. The Mustang was staggering along at 130 mph as Thury turned her nose north-west towards England, telling the deputy leader to break off the attack if the flak got any heavier. With Starnes' aircraft close to his own, Joe Thury gave his Mustang full power to get above any flak that might be in the area. S-turning to keep station, Starnes climbed alongside the damaged *Pauline*. A glance back showed that that particular target wouldn't require another visit.

At 3,000 ft Thury recognised Augsburg, sixty miles north-west of Munich. He was at 5,000 ft with the left rudder pedal hard over and the stick held to the left to keep the aircraft from banking into the damaged right wing. Skirting the Ruhr guns the pair of Mustangs reached Belgium. *Pauline* was running hot. Thury opened mixture to full rich to help cool the Merlin. The aircraft flew on. The North Sea, the cliffs of Dover, Cambridgeshire. He would make home base.

Lieutenant Starnes radioed Fowlmere to alert the base for Thury's emergency landing. Crash crews and ambulances took up their position adjacent to the main runway. Many eyes scanned the sky for first sight of the two Mustangs heading in from the south-east. Two specks changed into the checker-nosed fighters.

Thury elected a straight in approach. A slight left turn to line up. It would be a fast landing, at 130 mph. Steady. The mainwheels touched and stayed locked down. *Pauline* rolled along the prefab, slowing now. The pilot finally eased his left leg away from the rudder pedal. It was 17:25 hr.

The faithful Mustang completed the mission by allowing the pilot to taxy right into its allocated revetment. People scrambled on to her wings, including Flight Surgeon Scroggins and IO Charles Hammond. Joe Thury, who normally didn't drink, took two slugs of post-mission whisky. He had seven ground kills to his credit out of a grand total of 59 for the 505th Squadron.

In the fullness of time, Joe Thury received the Silver Star for the 17 April mission, and the 339th Group a Distinguished Unit Citation. Thury was to end the war the second highest scorer of ground kills

Above left *Wreaking havoc on enemy dispersal points was almost an everyday occurrence for the 8th's fighter groups. As the German bomber force was eclipsed by the need for ever more fighters, types such as the He 111 were parked idly on many aerodromes — easy meat for American 'Jabos' (IWM).*

Left *Joe Thury's* Pauline *rests between missions on the Fowlmere PSP. Coded 6N-C, the aircraft was 44-14656 of the 339th's 504th Squadron.*

Right *Mixed echelon formation of a P-51B, two Ds and a D-5 without dorsal fin by pilots of the 339th's 503rd Squadron.*

Above *The 364th Group was one of the few which flew Mustangs fitted with 'zero length' launchers for high velocity aircraft rockets, as seen on* Babs in Arms *of the 383rd FS. Targets for such weapons were, however, few in the closing weeks of the war, this photo being taken at Honington on 21 May 1945, after the last missions had been flown.*

Left The Onley Genevieve IV *leads* The Yakima Chief *and a third 434th Squadron Mustang. Bob Kline flew the former aircraft and Harold Stott the latter.*

Left *Close-up of the insignia on Stott's aircraft.*

Above right *When Don Gentile went home, they decorated a P-51D (a Mustang variant he did not fly in combat) like* Shangri-La, *the P-51B he had wrecked just before going home on leave. An immaculate Gentile is seen with the D model used to promote AAF recruiting and the war effort.*

in the 8th Air Force, with 25.5 — just behind Elwyn Righetti. Although he did not reach ace status in terms of aerial kills, the man who had escorted the crippled *Pauline* on 17 April did. James Starnes finished the war with six confirmed in the air and 6.5 destroyed on the ground, being one of twelve 339th pilots who became aces.

A sad end to the 17 April mission for Joe Thury was that *Pauline* had to be junked, the numerous holes from small arms and shrapnel putting her beyond economical repair. Thury had flown *44-14656* for some months and had got to know the aircraft's idiosyncrasies well — and nobody should imagine that even mass-produced fighters were all the same.

Elsewhere, 17 April recorded no less than 752 aircraft destroyed on the ground, including 68 by the 352nd; 110 by the 353rd; 125 by the 78th and over 100 by the 4th, bringing the Eagles' total to more than 1,000 destroyed. Succeeding days would see the final missions by the 8th AF fighter groups and the last of the kills made against the Luftwaffe. The 4th flew its last mission on 20 April, as did the 361st and the following day it was the turn of the 55th, 56th and 339th Groups. A slight change of emphasis was noted on some of these final sorties in that the American fighters did not shepherd their own bombers but those of the RAF, then flying in daylight on a regular basis.

On 25 April RAF Lancasters dropped more high explosive on the ruins of Hitler's retreat in the Bavarian Alps at Bertchesgarten, accompanied by Mustangs of the 78th Group, flying their last sorties over enemy territory. That same day was also the final operational entry for the group records of the 353rd, 355th, 357th and 364th.

The last fighter group to become operational with the 8th AF, the 479th went out with a bang by claiming the last aerial kill credited to the force. Lieutenant Hilton Thompson downed an Ar 234 in the vicinity of Salzburg and thus became the fifth 8th AF fighter pilot to shoot down two jets in air-to-air combat. A few more air actions involving the German jets were to come but 25 April (also the last day on which the 8th Air Force flew its final bomber sorties of World War 2) marked the end of a ten-month struggle against aircraft which technically at least completely outclassed piston-engined fighters.

The USAAF fighters had racked up an impressive record during the period, claiming 146(destroyed)-11(probable)-150(damaged) in the air and 121 on the ground. Records indicated that jets had been encountered on 1,233 occasions, resulting in 705 combats. The 8th AF had led the victory claims against the jets, but the 15th and 9th AAF and the RAF had also scored jet kills, primarily by fighters.

As the war moved towards its inevitable end, more bomber pilots who had requested a transfer to fighters realized that unless their documents were processed very quickly, hostilities would be at an end before they had any chance to fly operationally. One who just missed was Dick Quinton:

'I finished my 35 missions in a B-17 with the 452nd Bomb Group's 731st Squadron when I decided I hadn't had enough and wanted to fly the P-51. Colonel Phil Tukey had me in the process of being transferred to his 356th Group. I visited him twice in April and ate there with him while waiting for the papers to go through. The war finished before they

Left *The news everyone wanted to hear. A quartet of 355th Group pilots which includes Costa Patrinely and Robert Finnesey pose for the cameraman to make a historic picture in front of* The Buckeye Flash, *a Mustang which in common with many others in the 355th, carries other names, including* Sally *and* Pauline.

Below *Even with the war over, accidents occurred and pilots were, tragically, killed through no fault of the enemy. One landing that did not end badly was this ground loop by a 'war weary' P-51B-15 on 19 July 1945, at the 364th's base, Honington (USAF).*

Bottom *At first glance this photograph might have been taken during the war but it actually shows the Swedish Air Force base at Salenas on 1 February 1947. Ex-8th AF Mustangs forced to divert to Sweden during hostilities were retained by the Swedes, who pressed them into service with their own air arm. Various groups are represented, including the 339th, 352nd and 78th. The nearest aircraft is 44-72072 which became 26126 in Swedish service.*

could get the paperwork through.'

Others were destined to sit out those frustrating last weeks of the war as PoWs. Bert McDowell, Jr, had flown 55 missions with the 55th Group's 338th Squadron in his P-51D *Betty Mae* when on 6 February he was shot down. McDowell's was the only combat loss to the group that day, although four other Mustangs were forced to crash-land on the continent. He said of his subsequent adventures:

'I evaded successfully for two days and nights before being captured by the Germans only ten miles from our lines and was a 'guest' for the remainder of the war.'

By late April the fighter groups of the 8th Air Force had all but completed their wartime missions and the month saw the majority record their last forays into enemy territory. In numerical order these last missions for each group were as follows:

4th — 25 April; 20th — 25 April; 55th — 21 April; 56th — 21 April; 78th — 21 April; 339th — 21 April; 352nd — 3 May; 353rd — 25 April; 355th — 25 April; 356th — 7 May; 357th — 25 April; 359th — 20 April; 361st — 20 April; 364th — 25 April; 479th — 25 April.

Escort to the last 8th Air Force heavy bombing mission of the war was provided by all groups except the 55th, 56th, 339th and 359th. The others put up 584 P-51s to cover 589 B-17s despatched to the Pilsen armaments factory in Czechoslovakia. The only air combat victory was the 479th's Arado Ar 234, and William B. Hoelscher of the 4th bounced an Me 262 near Prague/Ruzyne aerodrome. He obtained several strikes before his Mustang was hit by flak and he was forced to bale out. With the dubious distinction of being the last 8th AF fighter to be listed as missing in action, Hoelscher evaded capture and eventually made it back to England — by which time Debden, like many of the other wartime stations, was relatively quiet.

★   ★   ★

So ended the millenium of the Third Reich, 988 years short; its demise was in no small way due to the diminutive fighter aeroplanes flown with raw courage by the men of the 8th. Having grown very rapidly from malnourished infancy, this young air arm had matured into a giant-killer of unprecedented power in a remarkably short space of time. Within the nature of the war it was obliged to fight, the force was perhaps one of the most economical instruments of democracy, its achievements being out of all proportion to its size. Both in terms of aircraft lost — and particularly lives sacrificed — in the cause of final victory, single-seat fighters were perhaps vastly under-rated weapons, certainly at the start of the 8th Air Force's offensive. In an era which still clung to the myth that 'the bomber will always get through'

(implying no assistance) it came to be realized that the bomber needed all the help it could get. Fortunately that help was forthcoming.

★   ★   ★

On 26 February 1946 a parade at Honington marked the end of the 8th Air Force's sojourn in the United Kingdom. Brigadier General Emil Kiel was present, as was Air Marshal Sir James Robb, AOC-in-C RAF Fighter Command, Air Vice Marshal S.D. McDonald and other senior RAF officers. Personnel representing both air forces heard an RAF band give a respectable rendition of the *Star-Spangled Banner* and as the American flag was hauled down Air Marshal Robb accepted the keys to the station from Brigadier General Kiel.

In his address the USAAF general referred to the fine teamwork displayed by the Royal Air Force during the 8th's stay, saying that this assistance had enabled every mission to be completed without ever suffering from a single instance of any lack of co-operation. He hoped that the same spirit would prevail between the two countries in settling the problems of the future, and reminded his audience that at its peak the 8th had numbered over 200,000 personnel and was able to put 1,400 heavy bombers and 800 fighters into the air at one time.

'A year ago today the official communique stated that three Berlin railway stations, their sidings and traffic handling facilities were attacked by the largest force of US heavy bombers ever to be sent over the Reich capital.'

Air Marshal Robb thanked the general for the magnificent part played by the 8th during its four years on operations from British soil and asked him to convey to General Carl Spaatz his conviction that although the last physical tie between the two services had been severed, the link of comradeship forged in the skies over Europe would remain. In speaking these words the Air Marshal could not ignore the conditions prevailing that day and he apologized for them, saying that they were unfortunately typical of Honington — seemingly in true 8th AF tradition, the farewells were made in heavy rain turning to snow. Even more familiar to the men of the 8th was the fact that Brigadier General Kiel was unable to leave the ceremony in one of the last remaining B-17Gs in England.

Not even the winding up of the mightiest Army Air Force to have seen action in World War 2 could be completed without due regard to England's weather. Many men would have called that 'SNAFU'; for the fighter force which had been raised at Debden in the rain it was perhaps fitting that the enemy which no human effort could really overcome, had the last word.

Appendix: The aces

The term 'ace' was first applied by the French in World War 1 to fighter pilots who shot down five enemy aircraft. Publicizing their exploits gave the general public a welcome chance to read about individuals rather than the largely anonymous masses of troops engaged in the huge and often confusing land battles. Air fighting caught the popular imagination and helped boost morale, a fact quickly recognized by other nations.

In World War 2 most of the combatants used the prowess of their fighter pilots as a propaganda tool, none more so than the Americans and Germans. To reach ace status in the USAAF a man had also to have knocked down five enemy aircraft in aerial combat. For the Germans ten victories was reckoned as the minimum to make a pilot an *Experte*.

The 'five down' rule did not change until US air forces in Europe undertook wholesale strafing of enemy aerodromes. So dangerous was this work that it was decided that ground kills should be added to an individual pilot's score. There were those who put far more store by aerial victories and some pilots did not even count their ground claims; most post-war ace lists do make a distinction between air and ground kills.

In the air, partial victories were initially reckoned in fractions and later, decimals, so that a pilot who claimed a quarter share of a kill with others on multiple occasions, would eventually claim 'whole' victories. It has been established that US pilot victories were generally very accurate, backed as they were by visual confirmation by fellow pilots and, most important, gun camera film. The German claims are also estimated to have been accurate in most cases.

In this book reference is made to 8th AF pilots aiming to better the score of Eddie Rickenbacker in World War 1 and Dick Bong in the Pacific Theatre. It is not perhaps without significance that both these pilots scored all their kills in the air, leading to an impression, at least in the eyes of group PROs, that aerial victories counted that little bit more. Often the pilots felt so too but it was inevitable that the 'colourful' dogfighting ethos of the past was still adhered to, even though this had largely passed into history by 1944/45.

Glossary

AA	Anti-Aircraft		FS	Fighter Squadron
AAF	Army Air Force		IAS	Indicated Air Speed
A/D	Aerodrome		ILS	Instrument Landing System
ASC	Air Service Command		IO	Intelligence Officer
ASR	Air-Sea Rescue		MIA	Missing In Action
BG	Bomb Group		MTO	Mediterranean Theatre of Operations
CAS	Chief of the Air Staff		PFF	Pathfinder Force
CBO	Combined Bomber Offensive		PSP	Pierced Steel Planking/Plating
DUC	Distinguished Unit Citation		RAF	Royal Air Force
E/A	Enemy Aircraft		RDF	Radio Direction Finding
ERS	Emergency Rescue Squadron		R/T	Radio Telephone
ETA	Estimated Time of Arrival		SF	Scouting Force
ETO	European Theatre of Operations		SNAFU	'Situation Normal, All Fouled Up'
FG	Fighter Group		SOP	Standard Operating Procedure
FO	Field Order			

Index

People